DR. BENJAMIN RUSH

DR. BENJAMIN
RUSH

THE FOUNDING FATHER
WHO HEALED A WOUNDED NATION

———

HARLOW GILES UNGER

DA CAPO PRESS

Hachette Book Group supports the right to free expression and the value of copyright. The purpose of copyright is to encourage writers and artists to produce the creative works that enrich our culture.

The scanning, uploading, and distribution of this book without permission is a theft of the author's intellectual property. If you would like permission to use material from the book (other than for review purposes), please contact permissions@hbgusa.com. Thank you for your support of the author's rights.

Da Capo Press
Hachette Book Group
1290 Avenue of the Americas, New York, NY 10104
dacapopress.com
@DaCapoPress, @DaCapoPR

Printed in the United States of America

First Da Capo Press edition 2018

Published by Da Capo Press, an imprint of Perseus Books, LLC, a subsidiary of Hachette Book Group, Inc. The Da Capo Press name and logo is a trademark of the Hachette Book Group.

The Hachette Speakers Bureau provides a wide range of authors for speaking events. To find out more, go to www.hachettespeakersbureau.com or call (866) 376 6591.

The publisher is not responsible for websites (or their content) that are not owned by the publisher.

Print book interior design by Trish Wilkinson.

Library of Congress Cataloging-in-Publication Data
Names: Unger, Harlow G., 1931–
Title: Dr. Benjamin Rush : the founding father who healed a wounded nation / Harlow Giles
     Unger.
Other titles: Founding father who healed a wounded nation
Description: First Da Capo press edition. | New York, NY: Da Capo Press, [2018] | Includes
     bibliographical references and index.
Identifiers: LCCN 2018012566 (print) | LCCN 2018012680 (ebook) | ISBN 9780306824333
     (e-book) | ISBN 9780306824326 (hardcover)
Subjects: LCSH: Rush, Benjamin, 1746-1813. | Statesmen—United States—Biography. |
     United States. Declaration of Independence—Signers—Biography. | Revolutionaries—
     United States—Biography. | Physicians—Pennsylvania—Philadelphia—Biography. | College
     teachers—Pennsylvania—Philadelphia—Biography. | University of Pennsylvania—Faculty—
     Biography. | United States—Politics and government—1775–1783. | Social reformers—
     United States—Biography. | Philadelphia (Pa.)—Biography.
Classification: LCC E302.6.R85 (ebook) | LCC E302.6.R85 U55 2018 (print) |
     DDC 973.3092 [B]—dc23
LC record available at https://lccn.loc.gov/2018012566

ISBNs: 978-0-306-82432-6 (hardcover), 978-0-306-82433-3 (ebook)

LSC-C

10 9 8 7 6 5 4 3 2 1

Frontispiece: Portrait of Benjamin Rush, M.D., by Charles Willson Peale, 1783. (WINTERTHUR MUSEUM)

To my father, Lester J. Unger, M.D.,
and five generations of physicians and surgeons in my family
who, like Benjamin Rush, M.D., devoted their lives to
the care and healing of humanity and advancement of science.

Herman Jarecky, M.D. (1863–1937)

Arthur S. Unger, M.D. (1883–1967)
Lester J. Unger, M.D. (1888–1974)
Jonas J. Unger, M.D. (1891–1967)

Roger H. Unger, M.D.
Harold M. Unger, M.D. (1926–2015)

James Edwin Unger, M.D.
Stephen Wise Unger, M.D.

Joshua Mostkoff Unger, M.D.

CONTENTS

Post Mortem 247

LIST OF ILLUSTRATIONS

ACKNOWLEDGMENTS

M Y SINCERE THANKS to the physicians who were gracious enough to vet this manuscript and its many sections dealing with technical and scientific aspects of eighteenth- and early-nineteenth-century medicine and psychiatry. John A. Fracchia, M.D., was especially kind in sharing his knowledge of medicine, science, and American history. In addition, vascular surgeon Joshua Mostkoff Unger, M.D. was most helpful in checking the accuracy of the sections on blood, while psychiatrist Theodore J. Jacobs, M.D.—an author himself—was kind enough to examine the critical materials on psychiatry.

I am also grateful to Valerie-Anne Lutz, head of Manuscripts Processing at the American Philosophical Society Library in Philadelphia, for finding the Julia Rush letters cited in this book—and, to my knowledge, never before published. To that end, my thanks also go to Joseph DiLullo at APS for converting the delicate, difficult-to-read Julia Rush letters into legible documents. Ms. Lutz, Mr. DiLullo, and the staff at the American Philosophical Society Library made my research a rewarding and joyful experience.

Finally, I owe an enormous debt of thanks to Robert Pigeon, a great friend and mentor as well as executive editor at Da Capo Press of the Perseus Books Group and my editor for eight books over ten years. And although their names never appear on this or any other book covers, the members of the wonderful publishing and editorial team at Da Capo Press deserve recognition along with my personal thanks for the great skills they demonstrated in producing this book—and for their friendship. In addition to Robert Pigeon, they include John Radziewicz, Publisher; Lissa Warren, Vice-President, Director of Publicity; Kevin Hanover, Vice-President, Director of Marketing; Matthew Weston, Marketing Manager; Cisca Schreefel, Manager, Editorial Production; Justin Lovell, Assistant Editor; Trish Wilkinson, Designer; and Martha Whitt, Copy Editor. I'm grateful to you all. My deepest thanks as well to website designer/developer Tom Bowler for his magnificent work on my website.

CHRONOLOGY

January 4, 1746 Benjamin Rush born in Byberry Township, on Delaware River near Philadelphia.

1754–1759 Attends uncle's academy; prepares for College of New Jersey at Princeton.

1759–1760 Attends Princeton; graduates with B.A.

1761–1766 Medical apprentice to Dr. John Redman, Philadelphia.

1766–1768 Attends University of Edinburgh (Scotland) Medical School; graduates with M.D.; advance medical studies in London; befriended by Benjamin Franklin, other London luminaries; visits Paris.

1769 Begins practicing medicine in Philadelphia; named Professor of Chemistry, College of Philadelphia.

1770 Publishes first American chemistry text.

1772 Founds American temperance movement; publishes works on dangers of drink, tobacco.

1773 Joins abolition movement.

1774 Joins American Philosophical Society; publishes landmark work on native Americans; hosts Continental Congress leaders; helps Thomas Paine write *Common Sense*.

1776 Marries Julia Stockton; elected to Continental Congress; signs Declaration of Independence.

1777 Goes to war; appointed Surgeon General, Middle Department; serves in field and military hospitals.

1778 Resigns over mistreatment of wounded troops; publishes historic proposals for saving soldiers' lives.

1780 Testifies in court martial of director of military hospitals; resumes practicing medicine.

1783 Joins staff of Pennsylvania Hospital; founds Dickinson College.

1786 Helps found Philadelphia Dispensary, the first free clinic in America for the poor.

1787 Joins College of Physicians of Philadelphia; helps found Franklin College in Lancaster; elected to Pennsylvania Constitution-ratification convention; emerges as leading American humanitarian: calls for free public schools and universal education, women's rights, penal reform, an end to capital punishment, humane care for the mentally ill, other social reforms.

1789 Named professor of medicine at College of Philadelphia; publishes first volume of epic four-volume *Medical Inquiries and Observations*. (See Appendix A, page 251).

1791 Helps found Philadelphia's first church for African Americans.

1792 Appointed professor of medicine at University of Pennsylvania Medical School.

1793 Calamitous yellow fever epidemic; government flees Philadelphia; thousands die; heroic Rush efforts; critics assail Rush treatment techniques.

1794 Publishes account of 1793 epidemic; new epidemic strikes; press attacks intensify.

1795 Chairs national convention of abolition societies.

1796 Named chairman, Theory and Practice of Medicine, University of Pennsylvania Medical School; completes and publishes landmark four-volume *Medical Inquiries and Observations*.

1797 President John Adams appoints Rush treasurer of the US Mint; new yellow fever epidemic; Rush buys farm to escape city; sues press critic.

1800 Rush wins precedent-setting libel suit; editor Cobbett flees to England.

1803 Elected president of abolition society.

1805 Resumes friendship, correspondence with John Adams.

1807 Introduces veterinary medicine to the United States; helps found American Bible Society.

1811 Effects reconciliation between former presidents Adams and Jefferson; they begin historic correspondence.

1812 Publishes first American psychiatry text, *Medical Inquiries and Observations upon the Diseases of the Mind.*

April 19, 1813 Dies in Philadelphia; buried in Christ Church Burial Ground, near Benjamin Franklin.

Children of Benjamin (1746–1813) and Julia Rush (1759–1848)

John Rush (1777–1837)
Anne Emily Rush (1779–1850)
Richard Rush (1780–1859)
Susanna Rush (1782–d. at 4½ months)
Elizabeth Graeme Rush (1783–d. at 4½ months)
Mary Rush (1784–1849)
James Rush (1786–1869)
William Rush (1787–d. at two months)
Benjamin Rush (1789–d. at two weeks)
Benjamin Rush (1791–1824)
Julia Rush (1792–1860)
Samuel Rush (1795–1859)
William Rush (1801–1864)

Note: Without knowingly altering the intent of the original writers, the author has modernized spellings, punctuation, grammar, and syntax in some eighteenth- and nineteenth-century letters, manuscripts, and publications cited in this book. Readers may find the original language, spellings, and punctuation in the works cited in the notes. Unless otherwise noted, illustrations were obtained from the Library of Congress or sources in the public domain.

Prologue

B ENJAMIN RUSH, M.D., was the Founding Father of an America that other Founding Fathers forgot—an America of women, slaves, indentured workers, laborers, prisoners, the poor, the indigent sick, and mentally ill. Ninety percent of the population in the United States lived in that other America—without money, uneducated, often illiterate, barred from voting, without rights to life, liberty, or the pursuit of happiness, either before or after American independence from Britain.

Alone among fifty-six signers of the Declaration of Independence, Rush heard the cries from that other America, renewed his pledge to sacrifice his life, fortune, and sacred honor, and set out to heal the nation's wounds and eliminate injustice.

Aroused by Patrick Henry's call to war, Rush recruited troops, lobbied Congress to fund the war, and wrote fiery pamphlets that raged against British oppression and won him election to the Continental Congress of 1776. The only "M.D." to sign the Declaration of Independence, Rush rode off to war, charging onto the field of battle at Trenton—not to kill, but to heal. Later, he barely escaped capture at the Battle of Brandywine as he treated the wounded in the face of gunfire from advancing British troops. After watching troops die unattended, he set off a bitter conflict with General Washington and Congress by demanding up-to-date medical care and field hospitals and spurring establishment of the Army Medical Corps.

Although he lacked the wealth and property of other Founding Fathers, Rush emerged from war as the nation's first great humanitarian—a champion of abolition, equal rights for women, universal public education, universal health care, and public sanitation. He fought to ban child labor and badgered the Pennsylvania state legislature to build free public schools and hospitals, end the slave trade, reform state prisons, and end cruel punishment of prisoners, including forced labor and capital punishment for noncapital crimes.

Fighting cruelty and injustice wherever he found it, he demanded that hospitals and state authorities treat mental illness as a disease instead of imprisoning "the maniacal" as devil's disciples or perpetrators of willful misbehavior. A pioneer in treatment of the mentally ill, he developed an early form of psychotherapy, occupational therapy, and medical treatment for mental illness a century before Freud, earning the American Psychiatric Association designation as "Father of American Psychiatry."

And when the worst yellow fever epidemic in American history swept through Philadelphia in 1793, he worked heroically, day and night for months, risking his life to treat as many as one hundred fifty patients a day—sustained on the one hand by his passion for healing the sick and, on the other, by the love of his beautiful, devoted wife, Julia.

Named professor of medicine at the University of Pennsylvania Medical School, Rush changed the world of science and medicine in America, teaching and training more than 3,000 students and publishing hundreds of papers and books. Many of his works formed the foundation of American medical education, medical practice, and medical ethics for more than a century after his death.

Rush admittedly meddled in "everything under the sun" and constantly alienated entrenched interests across the nation. He advocated temperance, opposed tobacco use, scolded newspaper editors for biased reporting, and criticized fellow physicians for carelessness, incompetence, and greed.

"A better man than Rush could not have left us," Thomas Jefferson grieved in a letter to John Adams after learning that their mutual friend Rush had died. Jefferson told Adams he knew no one among the Founding Fathers "more benevolent, more learned, of finer genius, or more honest."[1]

John Adams agreed. Calling Rush his closest friend, Adams lamented, "As a man of Science, Letters, Taste, Sense, Philosophy, Patriotism, Religion, Morality, Merit, Usefulness, taken all together, Rush has not left his equal in America, nor that I know in the world."[2]

CHAPTER 1

——◆——

The Making of a Physician

F REEDOM'S FIRES HAD lit the souls of his ancestors for five generations, beginning with Captain John Rush, Oxfordshire's legendary "Old Trooper," who led a troop of horse in Oliver Cromwell's army against King Charles I.

"He was once ordered out with command of a reconnoitering party," Philadelphia physician Benjamin Rush recounted the family history to his children. "Soon afterward his mare came into camp without him.

"'Poor Rush is no more,' Cromwell sighed. 'He has not left a better officer in my army.' But then the Old Trooper came in covered with mud and was received with joy. His mare had fallen into a ditch and thrown him off. The enemy thought him dead and pursued his mare . . . [while] he rose from the dead and returned to camp."

After exposure of a Protestant plot to kill Charles III, John Rush, his wife, six sons, and a daughter climbed aboard a boat crowded with fellow Quakers fleeing the king's wrath and followed William Penn to America in 1683, settling by the Delaware River near Philadelphia.

"I know nothing of his family in the part of England from which he came," Benjamin Rush continued his tale to his children, who sat at his feet enraptured by their father's warm, rich voice. "It is sufficient gratification to me to know that he fought for liberty and migrated to a remote wilderness in the evening of his life to enjoy the privilege of worshiping God according to the dictates of his own conscience."[1]

Although one of the Old Trooper's relations in England had begged him to leave at least one grandchild behind before leaving, he refused. "'No! No! I won't,'" the Old Trooper responded, according to Rush. "'I won't leave even a *hoof* of my family behind me.' He had been persecuted for his religious principles and left his native country in a fit of indignation at its then intolerant government. . . . He and his whole family were Quakers. . . .

"I am the eldest son of the fifth generation descended from him," Rush smiled at the sixth generation seated on the floor before him.[2]

Benjamin Rush greeted life on January 4, 1746, in a comfortable stone house on his Quaker father's prosperous, ninety-acre farm in Byberry, Pennsylvania, twelve miles from Philadelphia on the Delaware River. "Before the house flowed a small, but deep creek abounding in pan-fish," Rush recalled. "Behind the house . . . an orchard planted by my father . . . bore fruit. My family were pious people," he said, "chiefly Quakers and Baptists whose conversations centered on wolves and bears and snakes in the first settlement of the farm . . . [later] cows and calves and colts and lambs . . . [then] reapers and mowers and threshers . . . and at all times, prayers."[3]

Benjamin Rush was only five when his father died. Four years later, when he turned nine, his mother, Susanna, also of English ancestry, sent Benjamin and his younger brother Jacob to West Nottingham Academy, an academically demanding preparatory school for the College of New Jersey (later Princeton University). Founded and run by Susanna's brother-in-law, the renowned Presbyterian minister Samuel Finley, Nottingham Academy offered what was then a traditional classroom curriculum—writing, mathematics, geometry, algebra, astronomy, physics, history, logic, rhetoric, Latin, Greek, English, French, and German. In addition, Finley prepared his boys for frontier life with instruction in "hunting and gunning." Although Rush disapproved of both as "a risk to morals and health,"[4] he embraced the rest of Finley's curriculum, as well as the man himself.

"Few men," Rush said of Finley, "have ever possessed or displayed greater talents as a minister of the Gospel and scholar . . . as a teacher of

Benjamin Rush's birthplace on a farm along the Delaware River near Philadelphia. (LIBRARY OF CONGRESS)

an academy and as a master of a family. His government over his boys was strict but never severe nor arbitrary. . . . The instrument with which he corrected was a small switch . . . he struck the palm of the hand . . . never more than three times. . . . He took pains to promote good manners among his scholars. . . . Many of my schoolmates filled important stations and discharged the duties of useful professors with honor to themselves and benefit to their country."[5]

In 1759, Rush turned fifteen and enrolled at Finley's alma mater, the College of New Jersey at Princeton. Although he was admittedly "idle, playful, and mischievous" at times, he discovered "some talents for poetry, composition, and public speaking . . . [and] a love of knowledge."[6]

Rush earned his bachelor of arts after two years, and his degree earned him an apprenticeship in medicine under Princeton alumnus Dr. John Redman, Philadelphia's leading physician. "In addition to preparing and

Nassau Hall, the central structure of the College of New Jersey (now Princeton) as it looked in 1760, when Benjamin Rush earned his B.A. To the right is the college president's house, which British troops burned to the ground with Nassau Hall during the Revolutionary War. (PRINCETON UNIVERSITY ARCHIVES)

compounding medicines,* visiting the sick and performing many little offices of a nurse to them," Rush explained, "I took charge of his [Redman's] books and accounts. . . . I read all the books in medicine that were put into my hands by my master or that I could borrow. . . . I kept a commonplace book [journal] in which I recorded everything that I thought curious or valuable. . . . I studied Dr. [Herman] Boerhaave's† lectures upon physiology and pathology with the closest attention."[7]

---

*At the time, American doctors ran their own apothecary shops, compounding and selling medicines they prescribed to patients and assigning apprentices to run the shops and fill prescriptions. Most drugs were either herbal medicines such as rattlesnake root or chemical compounds, often with a base of mercury—to induce vomiting or explosive bowel movements thought to rid the body of disease.

†Herman Boerhaave (1668–1738) was a Dutch scientist who pioneered clinical medical education and development of the academic hospital. His theory of medicine described the human body as a "hydraulic machine," in which the flow rates of its various fluids determined the degree of each individual's health. Thus, simple

Rush passionately embraced the British school of medical thought of Dr. Thomas Sydenham and the Dutch school of Boerhaave. The thinking of both was eminently logical; both believed they had solved the mysteries of disease and sickness. Sydenham said that all diseases were simply "fevers"—in effect, they were all one and the same—transmitted by airborne pollutants, or "miasma," which invaded the body through the respiratory system and worked its way into the bloodstream. Normally, the vascular system automatically responded by trying to expel infected matter through the stool, sweat, or sputum, but if the disease remained in the blood, a doctor needed to extract it by cutting into a vein with a lancet.

Boerhaave broadened the scope of Sydenham's thinking, systematizing clinical observation and expanding bloodletting and purging into what he called "depletion therapy"—adding emetics and purgatives to supplement bloodletting as a means of reducing inflammation caused by disease. In an era more than a century before cellular microscopy, Rush found the logic self-evident. Embracing Sydenham's work with passion, Rush spent all but two weeks of the next five years learning and practicing his new craft.

In the midst of Rush's apprenticeship, Philadelphia's Dr. William Shippen, Jr., announced plans to teach the first anatomy course in America—to medical students, of course, but also to entertain "any gentlemen who may have the curiosity to understand the anatomy of the Human Frame."[8] To demonstrate human anatomy in his course, Shippen paid professional grave robbers to steal cadavers from graves of slaves or paupers. Like Redman, Shippen boasted impeccable credentials, having graduated from both the College of New Jersey at Princeton and Scotland's University of Edinburgh Medical School. Rush joined ten other medical students who enrolled in Shippen's course—only to have an angry mob block the alleyway and smash the windows of Shippen's lab to protest his mutilation and desecration of human cadavers. Whenever the mobs appeared, Shippen and his students fled and hid, but he continued buying bodies and teaching his lucrative course for much of his life.

---

physics—controlling the flow of bodily fluids—lay at the heart of all of Boerhaave's treatments. Physicians continued citing Boerhaave theories into the early twentieth century, and his name still appears in medical literature in conjunction with "Boerhaave's syndrome," a form of esophageal rupture resulting from forceful vomiting.

In 1765, the penultimate year of Rush's apprenticeship, Britain's Parliament outraged him and many other American colonists by passing the first direct tax ever imposed in America—a stamp tax to help pay costs of military protection against continuing Indian attacks along the frontiers. In effect for decades in England, the stamp tax required consumers, producers, or merchants to purchase one or more revenue stamps to affix on each of fifty-five articles, including legal documents, periodicals and such student essentials as textbooks, diplomas, and college degrees. Parliament's tax on usually penniless students incensed Rush, who raged at having to buy a £5 stamp from the government to get a degree he had earned and paid for during years of hard work. With other students, Rush leaped into the "public commotions" against the tax and embraced the growing political movement for American sovereignty.

"An effigy of our stamp officer has been . . . affixed to a gallows," Rush effused to a friend. "Our merchants have . . . entered into an association to import no more goods from London . . . which in my opinion promises more for us than anything hitherto attempted."[9] The Stamp Act not only frayed Rush's political loyalty to England, it inspired a newfound allegiance to individual liberty.

As Rush was completing his apprenticeship, Dr. Redman urged him to complement his bachelor of medicine degree with a doctorate—preferably at the University of Edinburgh medical school, then considered the finest in the English-speaking world. Rush agreed and, in September 1766, he put American political troubles behind him and set sail for England to begin two years of study in Edinburgh. He arrived on October 22, took a coach to Edinburgh, and following the custom of Pennsylvania travelers to Britain, he wrote to Benjamin Franklin, Pennsylvania's agent in London, in case he needed official help during his stay.

"As I have the happiness of being born in the province where you have resided many years," the twenty-year-old wrote to Franklin, "I was anxious to come under your patronage, as I well know your great love and partiality to the Province of Pennsylvania would readily induce you to favor any one of its natives even though unknown to you."[10] Franklin, who enjoyed befriending visiting Americans, sent Rush a gracious reply, wrote letters of introduction to prominent friends in the arts and sciences, and,

Eighteenth-century Edinburgh, dominated by its castle, when Rush attended University of Edinburgh medical school.

because of his interest in science, began what would become a lifelong correspondence and friendship with young Rush.

After Rush found lodgings in Edinburgh, he toured a city that was unlike any he had ever seen or imagined.

"Edinburgh is built upon a third less ground than Philadelphia," he wrote to a friend in America, "but contains double the number of inhabitants . . . eighty thousand souls.

> The reason they occupy so much less room is owing to the height of their houses, in each of which seven or eight families reside. This way of living subjects the inhabitants to many inconveniences, for as they have no yards, they have no necessary houses [outhouses], and all their filth of every kind is thrown out of their windows . . . in the night generally. Unhappy are they who are obliged to walk out after ten or eleven o'clock at night. . . . This is called being *naturalized*.[11]

The University of Edinburgh had been founded in 1583 and the medical school a century later under a charter from King Charles II. Famed for its anatomy courses, the university suffered chronic shortages of cadavers, forcing students to compete with professional grave-robbers at night—extracting the dead from their graves and calling it "resurrection."

Unfortunate passerby being "naturalized" in Edinburgh,
when Benjamin Rush attended medical school

In addition to anatomy, Rush studied chemistry, natural philosophy (physics), medicine, and "the practice of the infirmary." In summer he studied higher mathematics and restudied Latin, which was the language of medical textbooks then. Repelled by the drunken orgies that marked Edinburgh night life, he used his evenings to "make myself master of the French language and acquire so much knowledge of the Italian and Spanish languages as to be able to read them."[12] During his second year, he took advanced courses of first-year subjects and, on June 19, 1768, received his M.D., following a battery of examinations and publicly defending his thesis on "the digestion of food in the stomach"—a startlingly original study of his own vomitus.*[13]

---

*Rush titled his 1765 dissertation *De Coctione Ciborum in Ventriculo* [Latin: "Digestion of Food in the Stomach"]. See also *Autobiography*, 43.

Rush then joined the Royal Medical Society, where recent graduates met with professors at informal weekly gatherings to discuss medical matters and cement social and professional ties. In addition, Benjamin Franklin's friends invited Rush to salons and dinners where the newly minted physician's modest ways and pleasing personality won the embrace of Britain's intelligentsia.

"I had the pleasure of being domesticated in [visiting overnight] several very amiable private families in Edinburgh," Rush recalled. "Some of them were persons of rank, but they were all distinguished more or less for learning, taste, or piety."[14]

Some, such as Scottish historian/philosopher David Hume, Rush said, "distinguished themselves" with a quick wit and biting tongue. Indeed, Rush was dining with Hume when another guest asked Hume to recall a fact from his renowned six-volume *History of England.** Hume seemed puzzled, and his questioner persisted argumentatively, "But you mentioned it in your history!"

"That may be," Hume snapped back, "but there are many things which I have forgotten—including you."[15]

Rush met three other people in Edinburgh who made deep impressions. John Bostock, a Scottish medical student, claimed a forebear who, like Rush's own ancestor, had commanded a company in Cromwell's army.

"He declared himself an advocate for the republican principles for which our ancestors had fought," Rush recalled. "Never before had I heard the authority of kings called in question. I had been taught to consider them nearly as essential to political order as the sun is to the order of the Solar System. For the first moment in my life, I renounced . . . the absurdity of hereditary power."

After meeting Bostock, Rush concluded that "no form of government can be rational but that which is derived from the suffrages of the people who are the subjects of it."[16]

---

*David Hume, *The History of England* [certain volumes carry title of *The History of Great Britain*], 6 vols. (London: The London Printing and Publishing Company, 1754).

Bostock gave Rush one of Cromwell's swords and a leaf from Cromwell's family Bible with a record of his marriage and the names and birth dates of his children "by his own hand."[17]

Another meaningful encounter Rush experienced in Edinburgh was with Richard Stockton, an American lawyer from Princeton, New Jersey, and, like Rush, a graduate of both Samuel Finley's Academy and the college at Princeton. By then a Princeton trustee, Stockton had come to invite Scotland's renowned Presbyterian divine, Dr. John Witherspoon, to assume the college presidency. To Stockton's deep disappointment, Witherspoon refused, citing his wife's fear of ocean travel and distress at prospects of separating from friends and relations. With Stockton's reluctant approval, Rush went to Witherspoon's home in Paisley to plead with the divine.

"All America waits . . . for your answer," Rush petitioned the Scottish priest. "Must poor Nassau Hall indeed be ruined? . . . Must that school of the prophets, that nursery of learning become a party to faction, bigotry, and party spirit?"

Predicting the college's demise if Witherspoon did not assume its leadership. Rush tried flattering the clergyman, citing the widespread popularity of his sermons. "Recollect the pain you will give the friends of the college and the lovers of religion in America. . . . I tremble to think of the consequences of your refusal. Will you suffer your sun to set so soon?"

Rush turned to Mrs. Witherspoon and displayed what would develop into a gift for calming frantic patients by charming her with the tale of his own, joy-filled sea voyage from America. In fact, he had been seasick most of the way, but he now "obviated such of the objections as she had formerly made to crossing the ocean" and the great priest embarked for America with his family soon afterward.[18]

Although he could not know it at the time, coaxing Witherspoon to assume Princeton's presidency would prove an enormous contribution to the college and to his country's future. Beginning in 1768, Witherspoon transformed the College of New Jersey from a small religious school into one of America's leading universities, on a par with Harvard and Yale. As president of Princeton, the Scottish cleric would influence the shape of the early US government more than any other single educator in

The great Scottish divine, Rev. John Witherspoon, whom Benjamin Rush convinced to sail to America and assume the presidency of the College of New Jersey (later Princeton University). (PRINCETON UNIVERSITY ART MUSEUM)

American history. A proponent of the Scottish "common sense" school of philosophy, Witherspoon would teach James Madison, the father of the Bill of Rights and future President; future vice president Aaron Burr, Jr.; ten of the nation's first cabinet officers; seventy-seven of the first US senators and congressmen; twelve future state governors; and three future US Supreme Court justices. And in 1776, he would be one of only eight foreign-born signers of the Declaration of Independence.

In September 1768, Rush left Edinburgh for London where he attended "lectures and dissection" by a famed Scottish surgeon, "saw an immense variety of diseases and practices," and attended informal medical discussions with London's most prominent physicians, including Sir John

Benjamin Franklin as agent for Pennsylvania in London
patronized visiting Americans such as Benjamin Rush.
(WHITE HOUSE)

Pringle, the court physician. With the new year, Rush put his studies aside
and presented himself at Benjamin Franklin's London home. It proved an
exhilarating step for the Pennsylvania farm boy.

"The doctor [Franklin] had acquired knowledge, reputation, and powerful connections," Rush explained. "It was my peculiar happiness to be
domesticated in his family. He introduced me to a number of his literary
friends. He once took me to Court with him and pointed out to me many
of the most distinguished public characters of the nation. I never visited
him without learning something." One by one, the "public characters" he
saw and met filled Rush with a range of intellectual and political ideas that
would convert him into one of America's most brilliant thinkers.

I spent many agreeable evenings with [American artist] Mr. [Benjamin] West*, who introduced me to . . . the most celebrated . . . artists in London and in particular to Sir Joshua Reynolds,† by whom I was soon invited to dine with Dr. [Samuel] Johnson, Dr. [Oliver] Goldsmith, and several other distinguished literary characters.

Rush found Johnson's conversation "offensive" at times, filled with ecclesiastical and political bigotry. He belittled others for "asking questions . . . not always of the most interesting nature." Rush grew incensed as Johnson turned on the aging Irish novelist/playwright/poet Oliver Goldsmith, whom Rush called "a man of gentle and unoffending manners."[19]

"Dr. Goldsmith asked me several questions relative to the manners and customs of North American Indians," Rush explained. "Dr. Johnson, who heard one of them suddenly interrupted him and said, 'There is not an Indian in North America who would have asked such a foolish question.'

"'I am sure,' Dr. Goldsmith replied, 'there is not a savage in North America that would have made so rude a remark to a gentleman.'"[20]

Rush said Johnson seemed to seek controversy. Rush later dined with Goldsmith, the author of the popular novel *The Vicar of Wakefield* and the equally popular play, *She Stoops to Conquer.* "He was entertaining," Rush said of Goldsmith, "but he wanted the usual marks of great and original genius."[21] Goldsmith would die six years later.

Rush won over famed historian Catherine Macaulay, who invited him to her weekly evening coterie. "I met there some of the first literary and political characters in the British nation," Rush recalled. "The subjects of conversation, which were literary and political, were discussed with elegance and good breeding."[22]

---

*Born in Pennsylvania, Benjamin West had established himself as an outstanding portrait painter when he went to visit England in 1763. A close friend of Benjamin Franklin, West was so taken by the British and European art world, he never returned to America.

†England's leading portraitist at the time, Reynolds was a gifted conversationalist and close friend of such London luminaries as Dr. Samuel Johnson, playwright Oliver Goldsmith, actor David Garrick, and political leader Edmund Burke.

The celebrated historian Catherine Macaulay took a great liking to the brilliant young American medical student Benjamin Rush and corresponded with him for years after his return to America. (NATIONAL PORTRAIT GALLERY)

Rush described Mrs. Macaulay as "sensible and eloquent, but visionary in some of her ideas of government [and] . . . among the brightest of . . . those illustrious souls who have employed their pens and sacrificed their lives in defense of liberty."[23] Taken by the young American's passionate acceptance of women as intellectual equals of men, Macaulay confessed that she had been "a thoughtless girl till she was twenty" before reading a volume of history in her father's house and developing a love of books and writing. After marrying a Scottish physician in 1760, she set to work on her epic eight-volume *The History of England from the Accession of James I to the Revolution*—a work that transformed her into "the

Celebrated Mrs. Macaulay" by espousing the right of citizens to depose their monarch. A harsh critic of British government policies in America, she immediately won both the heart and mind of the young Dr. Rush.

When Rush told her the printer had made a number of grammatical errors in her masterwork, Macaulay smiled: "No, they are my errors and not the printer's. I have constantly refused to have them corrected lest it be suspected that my history was not altogether my own."[24]

Macaulay told Rush that England's history represented the constant struggle of a people fighting to secure individual rights—much like the struggle of Americans at the time. A few days after visiting her, Rush wrote like a love-stricken adolescent to acknowledge that "the exalted opinion I had always entertained of your character and principles has been much increased by the interview I had with you.

> The objects you have in view are the noblest that ever animated a human breast. . . . All the pleasures of riches, science, virtue, and even religion itself derive their value from liberty alone. No wonder . . . those illustrious souls who have employed their pens and sacrificed their lives in defense of liberty have met with such universal applause. Their reputations . . . shall . . . outlive the ruins of the world itself. You, Madam, will shine among the brightest . . . inasmuch as you are the only individual of your sex who has hitherto been distinguished in this noble cause.[25]

While in London, Rush also met Virginia's Arthur Lee, who, like most of the sons of Virginia's wealthiest landowners, had sailed to the English "motherland" for their education. As one of the younger of six Lee sons, he inherited none of the thousands of acres in Virginia that his father had accumulated, but he did receive a generous bequest of £1,000 (arguably equivalent to £1,800,000 today) to provide for his education and a comfortable start in life. After traveling to England and graduating from Eton, he decided to study medicine. Like Rush, he obtained his M.D. at Edinburgh, but grew bored and abandoned medical practice and was studying law at London's Middle Temple when Rush arrived in London. Like four of his brothers, Lee rebelled at the British government's efforts to tax the American colonies, and he soon became the eyes and ears in

London's political world for his older brother Richard Henry Lee and other American opponents of British efforts to restrict American liberties. Developing close ties to British republicans, Lee became an intimate of John Wilkes, a republican politician and journalist who had won election as the Member of Parliament from Middlesex—only to have the king veto his election and send him to King's Bench Prison for insulting the king. Supporters flocked to London and rioted outside Wilkes's prison, shouting "No liberty, no King," only to have troops fire into the crowd, killing seven and wounding fifteen.

"Mr. Wilkes was the object of universal attention," Rush remarked. "The nation was divided into his friends and his enemies, according as they espoused or opposed the measures of the government." Wilkes's wealthiest supporters saw to his transfer to luxurious quarters in the prison, and Arthur Lee invited Rush to a dinner Wilkes prepared for a few friends.

British radical journalist/politician John Wilkes invited the young Benjamin Rush, M.D., to dine in Wilkes's prison cell. Rush called him "an enthusiast for American liberty." (NATIONAL PORTRAIT GALLERY)

"Mr. Wilkes abounded in anecdotes and sallies of wit," Rush enthused. "He was perfectly well bred. Not an unchaste word or oath escaped his lips. I was the more surprised at this, as he had been represented a monster of immorality."[26]

Rush wrote his brother Jacob that Wilkes was "one of the most entertaining men in the world. He is an enthusiast for American liberty."[27]

Rush visited the Houses of Parliament, sitting for a few seconds, like a mischievous schoolboy, on the throne in the House of Lords, then going to the House of Commons and thinking to himself, "This is the place where the infernal scheme for enslaving America was first broached."[28]

Before leaving England, Rush met William Cromwell, Oliver Cromwell's great grandson. Ten years old when Oliver Cromwell died, he was seventy when Rush met him. "He showed me his [great] grandfather's commission appointing him Lord Lieutenant of Ireland. It began with the words, 'To our Trusty and well beloved son.'" Cromwell showed Rush his forebear's watch and letters and gave Rush wax impressions of two seals Cromwell carried on the watch.

After meeting with Cromwell, Rush watched King George III and his family at a chapel service, then attended a session of the House of Commons to hear speeches by the Irish political leaders Colonel Isaac Barre and Edmund Burke—both of them outspoken advocates of American autonomy. He spent a few evenings at the theater and saw performances by the heralded actor David Garrick before leaving for Paris on February 16, 1769. Franklin gave the young man letters of introduction and a letter of credit that Rush accepted reluctantly. "You may be exposed to unexpected expenses," Franklin insisted.[29]

Rush did, in fact, run into unexpected expenses and had no choice but to draw on the letter of credit. Years later, he would repay the loan to Mrs. Franklin in America.

"Nothing worth relating occurred in my journey to Paris," Rush reported in a blasé comment that reflected, perhaps, a growing nonchalance in the presence of celebrated figures.* "There appeared to me to be but

---

*Rush reported his comments in a never-published manuscript he called "French Journal: Account of a Trip to Paris," which remains today in the J. Pierpont Morgan Library, New York, NY.

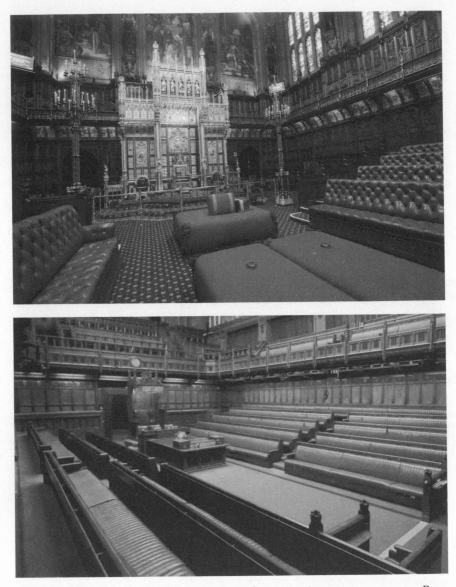

The British House of Lords (above), where the young American commoner Benjamin Rush could not resist sitting on the throne, and the House of Commons (below). (PARLIAMENT OF THE UNITED KINGDOM)

one Frenchman in Paris. There was no variety in their manners. The same taste in dress pervaded all classes. . . . The same phraseology was heard in their language." Curiosity, Rush said, drew him to Versailles to explore the palace and gardens, which he conceded were magnificent.

> I saw the king, Louis XV, pass through a large hall to . . . his chapel, where he went to mass. I stood within a few feet of him. . . . Let such as maintain divine right of kings come and behold this monarch, sitting with a common prostitute, picked up . . . from the streets of Paris* . . . and let them declare, if they can, that they believe him to be the Lord's Anointed. . . . I heard Mr. Wilkes say on the day I dined with him . . . that he had once dined with twelve gentlemen in Paris, eleven of whom declared it their duty to surrender their wives to the king if desired."[30]

---

*After the king's former mistress Madame de Pompadour died in 1764, Louis XV spent four years experimenting with a procession of women until his keen eye spotted the beautiful twenty-two-year-old Jeanne Bécu, who, according to one account, was dining with his valet. Said to be the illegitimate daughter of a seamstress, Bécu had gone to work in a Paris brothel at fifteen. Taken by her beauty, the brothel owner took her as his own before using her and other young girls to win favors at court by taking them to the king's country palace in Compiègne, north of Paris, for the pleasure of the king's servants. When the fifty-eight-year-old king saw her, the legend goes, she so aroused his lust that he snatched her up and took her to his royal chamber, despite his valet's warning that she had slept on the streets and might transmit venereal disease. To minimize scandal, the king ennobled her by ordering her to marry Count Guillaume du Barry, who barely finished uttering his marriage vow before the king seized Madame's arm and, exercising his *droit du seigneur*—the right of the king to sleep with his vassal's bride on the wedding night—led her to the royal bed to consummate the Count's marriage. Prime Minister Étienne-François duc de Choiseul described du Barry as "contemptible scum," but the king ignored his prime minister and, in April 1769, he held "a formal presentation at court of a whore from the streets of Paris and her elevation to the rank of Royal Mistress." Harlow Giles Unger, *Improbable Patriot: The Secret History of Monsieur de Beaumarchais, the French Playwright Who Saved the American Revolution* (Hanover, NH: University Press of New England, 2011), citing Charles Théveneau de Morande, *Le Gazetier cuirassé ou Anecdotes scandaleuses de la Cour de France* and *Mémoires secrets d'une femme publique* (Paris: *Publiés à cent lieues de la Bastille sous l'enseigne de la liberté*, 1772).

Rush toured all the noted Paris churches and public buildings, which he described as "splendid." At a concert one evening, he discovered formal European "court" music—what twenty-first-century music lovers call "classical." Rush embraced the works of Arcangelo Corelli (1653–1713), the Italian composer and violinist who had introduced a new virtuoso style on the violin in orchestral composition.

He visited the medical school, of course, and the world's first school of veterinary medicine. He visited all the public hospitals, finding the Hôtel de la Charité "remarkably neat and clean," but the huge, central Hôtel Dieu "crowded and offensive. I saw four persons in one bed." In talking with physicians, he deemed them fifty years behind those in England and Scotland.

Treatment of the insane stunned the young American, witnessing for the first time half-starved, naked, and unkempt humans in heavily barred prison areas, chained to floors and walls, soiled by their own excreta, subject to whip-snaps at the whim of attendants.

The Foundling Hospital won his heart, however: "Eighteen or twenty children were admitted the night before I saw it," he wrote in his journal.

> The door of the hospital is always open, and a basket, made like a cradle, is placed near it into which the infant is placed. A bell is then rung to give notice to the keepers of the hospital. . . . It is supposed that one-eighth of all children born in Paris are brought up by means of this institution. The motto over the door is very appropriate: "*Mon père et ma mère m'ont abandonné. Mais Le Seigneur a pris soin de moi.*" ["My father and my mother have abandoned me, but the Lord hath taken care of me."][31]

Before leaving Paris, Rush used letters from Franklin to meet two men of consequence. The first was Jacques Barbeu-Dubourg, a physician friend of Franklin and translator of Franklin's writings into French. Unbeknownst to Rush, he was also a secret intermediary for the French court in its dealings with Franklin and other independence-minded American leaders. The other contact of great consequence was the celebrated Denis Diderot, author of the monumental *L'Encyclopédie*. A great admirer of Benjamin Franklin, Diderot invited Rush to his astounding library, where he showed the young American a portrait of Jean-Jacques Rousseau. Diderot introduced Rush to Rousseau's *Social Contract, or Principles of Political Rights,* * a tract that had stunned the world in 1762—and now stunned Rush—with a revolutionary socio-political concept: *L'homme est né libre, et partout il est dans les fers.* ["Man was born free, and everywhere he is in chains."][32]

Scoffing at the myth of divine right of kings, Rousseau pronounced men born in "a state of nature"—like other species. But unlike other species, man had joined others of his kind in forming governments to provide mutual protection. Government was therefore an instrument of people rather than the reverse, making slavery of any kind an abomination. Rousseau's pronouncements represented heresies that would help spark the French Revolution decades later. For the moment, it set off a revolution in Benjamin Rush's thinking, turning him into a dedicated humanitarian, an implacable foe of slavery and other injustices.

With his curiosity about France satisfied, Rush left Paris, crossed the Channel to Dover, and boarded the coach for London—only to have the driver stop by a wood midway, saying he had heard a voice calling for help.

"I ran to inquire the cause of it," Rush related, "and discovered a poor woman lying upon a blanket upon the ground who told me she was in labor. I told her I was a physician and offered to relieve her." With the help of a lady from the coach, "I delivered her of a fine boy. She was speechless . . . but in this state she took my hand and pressed it to her lips in the most affecting manner." A few minutes later, her husband arrived with help, and Rush ordered his coachman to take them all back to the nearest village where "we left her in a comfortable house with as much money as was sufficient to support her for several days. I was informed two years afterwards . . . that she had called her little boy by my name."[33]

Rush spent his last days in Britain with Franklin, whose "paternal friendship," as Rush put it, "attached me to him during the remainder of his life"—and further inspired Rush to devote his life to improving the

---

Du contrat social ou Principes du droit politique (Amsterdam: Marc-Michel Rey, 1762).

human condition.[34] Before leaving London, Rush delivered a letter from Diderot to David Hume, "which gave me an opportunity of spending part of a forenoon in his company."[35] Hume tried explaining his empirical approach to science and medicine, insisting that every disease was tied to its cause not only by proximity in time and place but by a "necessary connection" not always evident to the human observer.

Hume cited the case of a billiard ball striking and propelling a second ball. With both balls present at the same time and place, the connection of their collision makes the cause of the second ball's movement inescapable. If, in addition, the light of a candle in the room went out at the same moment, an observer would lack any evident connection between the impact

British philosopher David Hume, like Catherine Macaulay, was fascinated by and liked the young American student Benjamin Rush, inviting him to inspect the extensive Hume library. (SCOTTISH NATIONAL PORTRAIT GALLERY)

of the two billiard balls and the sudden darkness. But, Hume said, the fallibility of the human mind would nonetheless provoke some observers to call the extinguished candle a "miracle"—or, perhaps, God's punishment for gambling and a clear sign for banning billiards.[36]

Of his visit, Rush could only say, "I now saw that men do not become wise by the experience of other people."[37]

Rush did not play billiards.

In June 1769, Rush sailed for America and reached New York on July 14, equipped now with the finest formal education available in the English-speaking world. He had earned a B.A. from the College of New Jersey at Princeton and an M.D. from the University of Edinburgh. He had trained for years under the finest physicians in Philadelphia, Edinburgh, and London, and he had accumulated an endless array of knowledge in history, political science, and the arts from such intellectual giants as Benjamin Franklin, Samuel Johnson, David Hume, Catherine Macaulay, John Wilkes, Benjamin West, Sir Joshua Reynolds, and Denis Diderot—and even Jean-Jacques Rousseau, albeit indirectly.

A week after landing in New York, he reached Philadelphia intent on healing the sick. He settled in a house with his only surviving brother, Jacob, who was setting up a law practice, and his sister Rachel, who had just divorced her husband and, without a home of her own, willingly assumed housekeeping chores for her two brothers.

Despite his wealth of education and training, however, Benjamin Rush had no patron in the medical community to help him begin practicing. Making matters worse, he had spent his last funds returning to America and arrived without a penny. Rush was bankrupt, and, without family wealth, influence, or connections, he had no money of his own to open an office or buy into an established practice. He faced poverty and an abrupt end to his medical career before it had started.

CHAPTER 2

The Making of a Patriot

Twenty-two-year-old Benjamin Rush returned to Philadelphia from Europe pulsating with what he called "a natural sympathy with distress of every kind." Without funds to open an office or buy into an established medical practice, he nonetheless walked the streets of Philadelphia determined to cure the ills of the world—or at least those of Philadelphia's slums—by practicing "street medicine." Reciting the entreaties of eighteenth-century Dutch physician Herman Boerhaave to "attend the poor because God is their paymaster," Rush began to practice medicine among the city's poor, whom God, it seemed, had endowed with the worst ills.

"My natural disposition made this mode of getting into business agreeable to me," Rush enthused, as he worked his way among the unbathed, lice-infested, malnourished men, women, and children who peopled what seemed a special hell that God—or perhaps the devil—had devised for them alone. Rush slogged through streams of sewerage and other detritus in one alleyway after another, entering each open door to shout, "Doctor calling! Anyone need the doctor?"

Within seconds they responded, like ants marching from their hills to feast on prey. One woman, then another, and another—some with babies in their arms, all with clots of grey-faced children, mucous dripping from their noses and ears, their dirty little hands glued to their mothers' filthy skirts. No physician ever set foot in the city's squalid alleys. Yet here he was—a Founding Father *and* physician—embracing them, cooing to each mother, each child, that all would be well, that he would make hurts stop hurting and give them medicine to make them feel better. And he did—and they did.

Visiting one household after another, Rush treated them all, boasting proudly as he staggered home exhausted at night, his clothes and hands immersed in filth, that he was "fully employed." Years later, he would look back on his early days in the slums and ascribe "the innumerable blessings of my life [to] my services to His [God's] poor children."

Although he could not know it, Rush toiled in what was still a dark age of medicine, with only the most primitive medical knowledge, instruments, and medicines at his or any other doctor's disposal. Ironically, the century-long Age of Enlightenment that had cast some light on so many other sciences had left medicine in darkness. Newton, Boyle, Watt, Priestly, and others had illuminated and expanded knowledge of physics, chemistry, zoology, minerology, mathematics . . . every corner of science but medicine. Only doctors still embraced teachings more than 2,000 years old, described in dead languages from extinct civilizations. Few who called themselves doctors had attended medical schools; those who had usually reserved their ministrations for the very rich. The rest were mostly "empirics"—quacks, who concocted alcohol-based syrups they patented as "medicines" to sell to the sick and desperate, as well as the healthy who could not afford conventional liquor. Guaranteed to plunge sick and healthy alike into drunken stupors, patent medicines saved no one, although they let some of the dying slip away painlessly while inflicting such severe "morning-after" pains on the healthy they forgot what had ailed them in the first place.

Rush, on the other hand, seemed to work miracles—without patent medicines. His passion to heal imbued his patients with passion to heal. Those that did hailed him as a saint—not only for his gift of healing but for his kindness and understanding—his evident love in treating the penniless and deprived, whom other physicians refused to visit, let alone touch or treat.

His "miracles," of course, were often nothing more than suggestions for improved hygiene and diet. The buildings he entered lacked water;

the patients seldom bathed. Many believed bathing in water—especially warm water—allowed disease to enter the body. The few patients who did wash themselves filled a pail or tub at a nearby well and reused the same water to wash the entire family, with father bathing first, mother next, and the children last. Chamber pots sat in the corners of some rooms until their odors grew so oppressive that residents dumped the contents out the windows, turning alleyways below into sewers, as well as playgrounds for children and walkways for all. Streets and dwellings alike reeked of excreta, while the absence of toilet paper only added to the foul body odors of slum dwellers. Everyone lived with body lice and bedbugs, and most patients Rush saw bore festering bacterial and fungal sores and infections.

Philadelphia was a city of 55,000, America's capital city of sorts, its greatest port and center of trade, its seat of learning. Its gleaming squares, churches, stores, markets, and public gardens made the city center an urban jewel on a continent best known for vast forests and isolated log cabins. Hidden near Philadelphia's docks, however, an area of frightful slums stood in stark contrast to the elegant Georgian houses of brick and bright white wooden trim that lined the streets and squares where bankers, merchants, and other gentlemen lived. Strolling about as if in London's moneyed West End, Philadelphia's elite wore the latest fashions they'd seen in Reynolds or Gainsborough portraits. They cloaked any cranial or facial blemishes with wigs and powder and disguised their distaste for bathing with costly French perfumes. Slaves in showy livery followed at respectful distances with the purchases of their masters or mistresses. Unconcerned with—even unaware of—the slums, Philadelphia's ruling elite believed God had predetermined the lot of the advantaged and disadvantaged, or, as Calvin had put it, some had been "predestined to salvation and others to destruction." The members of Philadelphia's moneyed class believed themselves among the former.[1]

Benjamin Rush, M.D., however, thought differently. He believed Man himself determined the lot of the advantaged and disadvantaged and that the former had an obligation to improve the lot of the latter.

Like most doctors then, Rush carried few instruments other than lancets for bleeding or removing pus and cloth strips for cleaning and bandaging wounds and sores. The stethoscope lay more than a half-century in the future, as did the simple medical thermometer. He carried pain killers—opium, rum, and "white lightening" (whiskey) were common—and he offered patients emetics and laxatives to rid the stomach and intestines of what he and they believed were diseased foods and prevent them from entering the blood stream. Like other doctors—and every quack—Rush also carried herbal "remedies" that combined with prayer to heal enough of his patients to add to his reputation as a miracle healer.

With most patients unable to pay him, however, Rush remained almost as poor as they during his first days, weeks, and months of practice.

"From the time of my settlement in Philadelphia in 1769 'till 1775," Rush later told his children, "I led a life of constant labor and self-denial. My shop was crowded with the poor in the morning and at meal times, and nearly every street and alley in the city was visited by me every day.

> Often have I ascended the upper story of huts by a ladder and . . . been obliged to rest . . . upon the bedside of the sick (there being no chairs) where . . . I risked not only taking their disease but being infected by vermin. . . . When my days were thus employed in business, my evenings were devoted to study. I seldom went to bed before 12 o'clock."[2]

While most Founding Fathers simply shrugged their shoulders as they passed the slums that abutted Philadelphia's elegant core, Rush reacted with outrage at what he saw as an urban cancer infecting the heart of American society. All but destitute himself, however, he could do little to treat it.

It was fortunate indeed that he had anticipated his financial plight before leaving Europe and had applied for a post as chemistry professor at the new medical department of the College of Philadelphia (later the University of Pennsylvania). Founded in 1765, it formed the core of America's first medical school, with the eminent Philadelphia physician Dr. John Morgan as professor of theory and practice of "physic," as medicine was then called. A decade older than Rush, Morgan, like Rush, was a graduate of Finley's academy and the College of New Jersey at Princeton, and the two had met when Rush was still a medical apprentice attending Morgan's lectures.

Morgan's appointment was followed by the appointment of four other multitalented professors: a professor of anatomy, surgery, and midwifery;

a professor of *materia medica* (therapeutic medicines or, more recently, pharmacology); a professor of clinical lectures at the hospital; and a professor of chemistry. Dr. William Shippen, Jr., who had taught Rush anatomy, took the chair of anatomy, surgery, and midwifery.

By the time the college prepared to fill its chemistry chair, Rush had gained considerable renown for curing or improving the health of almost all those under his care. In 1774, he acquired his first private patients by introducing a new, all-but-painless method of treating smallpox he had seen in London. "The method of infecting the arm with a small puncture instead of a long incision proved very popular and brought me many patients," Rush said.

In the first application of preventive medicine in America, Rush organized a group of like-minded physicians to use the new method to wipe out the disease in their city by founding the Society for Inoculating the Poor Gratis. Members of the society used a needle-like instrument* to stick the poor with pox-infected serum free of charge every Tuesday morning in a room in the State House (now Independence Hall). Within weeks, the rate of smallpox in the city had dropped dramatically.

Rush's application for the chair in chemistry had come with extravagant recommendations by several renowned British chemists, but it was Thomas Penn, one of the "proprietors" of Pennsylvania, who ensured Rush the chair. Penn promised the college a gift of a "chymical apparatus"—a completely equipped chemistry laboratory—if Rush won the appointment. The trustees agreed, making Rush America's first professor of chemistry. He proved a gifted lecturer and instructor, attracting large numbers of students who endowed his financial stability by paying six pounds each (about $15 then) to hear his lectures.

"I was enrapt," said Charles D. Meigs, who would later become one of America's most prominent obstetricians.† "His voice, sweeter than any flute, fell on my ears like droppings from a sanctuary . . . his earnest, most

---

*The hollow needle used for injections today was not invented until the mid-nineteenth century.

†Meigs revolutionized obstetrics by opposing obstetrical anesthesia and asserting that obstetricians transmitted diseases to their patients by failing to wash their hands before delivering babies. Most washed their hands after deliveries.

sincere, most persuasive accents sunk so deep into my heart that neither time nor change could eradicate them."[3]

Rush's wide-ranging interests beyond medicine drew him to the American Philosophical Society, which Benjamin Franklin had founded twenty-five years earlier with some friends with common interests. Winning election to the group in 1769,[*] Rush became an enthusiastic and active participant for the next forty years, filling a number of offices, delivering many important learned papers, and becoming intimate friends with its members. He delivered his first paper in 1774—a startling landmark study he called "An Inquiry into the Natural History of Medicine among the Indians of North America and a Comparative View of Their Diseases and Remedies with Those of Civilized Nations." Despite its ungainly title, it revealed for the first time the European role in spreading new diseases among American aborigines.

"The small pox and the venereal disease were communicated to the Indians of North America by the Europeans," Rush charged. "Nor can I find that they were ever subject to the scurvy [before the Europeans arrived]. . . . Their peculiar customs and manners seem to have exempted them from this, as well as from the common diseases of the skin." He said he had heard of only two or three cases of the gout among the Indians, but "only among those who had learned the use of rum from white people."[4]

In 1770, Rush enhanced his growing reputation by publishing a paper with an imaginative theory (and no foundation in fact[†]) linking *cynanche trachialis,* a common illness later called croup, to tracheal spasms. Without

---

*From the time of its founding, the American Philosophical Society attracted the finest minds and most influential figures in America—George Washington, John Adams, Thomas Jefferson, Alexander Hamilton, James Madison, and John Marshall, among others. Its foreign members included Alexander von Humboldt, the Marquis de Lafayette, Baron von Steuben, and Tadeusz Kościuszko. The nineteenth century saw Charles Darwin, Louis Pasteur, John James Audubon, and Thomas Edison add their names to its membership, while Robert Frost, Linus Pauling, and Margaret Mead became members during the twentieth century. The society has about 1,000 members today.

†An inflammation and obstruction of the trachea and bronchial tubes, croup is caused by a virus.

modern instruments for tissue research, physicians at the time often concluded that symptoms of a disease were its causes rather than the reverse.
Indeed, physicians into the mid-twentieth century routinely used medicines to suppress coughing or sneezing, believing that by eliminating
symptoms of a cold they would eliminate the cold itself—a dangerous
assumption in many cases. With his paper on croup, Rush proved he was
no exception.

To Rush's distress, his daily forays into Philadelphia's slums often took
him past the popular London Coffee House, where public officials and
merchants met to do business over cups of coffee—and to trade slaves.
Outraged by the spectacle, Rush translated Rousseau's *Social Contract*
into action by joining the nation's first abolition society: the Pennsylvania
Society for Promoting the Abolition of Slavery and the Relief of Free Negroes Unlawfully Held in Bondage. Only just founded by Quakers, the
society boasted leaders that included the charismatic Anthony Benezet, a
French-born Quaker schoolteacher and passionate champion of the poor,

Disgust at the slave auction (right) at the London Coffee House in Philadelphia
provoked Benjamin Rush to embrace the abolition movement. (Library Company of Philadelphia)

the oppressed, and, particularly, the enslaved. At Benezet's urging, Rush wrote an inflammatory pamphlet *Address to the Inhabitants of the British Settlements in America on Slavekeeping.*[5] Among other demands, he called for raising tariffs to levels so high as to make importation of slaves unprofitable.

"The first step to be taken to put a stop to slavery in this country," Rush growled, "is to leave off importing slaves." He then described the cruelties inflicted on slaves, with one "losing a foot as punishment for running away . . . another led to the gallows for eating a morsel of bread . . . another in a flame of fire—his shrieks pierce the heavens—O! humanity—justice—liberty—religion!—Where are ye fled?"

Far from being a utopian chimera, he said, abolition was already a fact in many European countries. "Let such of our countrymen as engage in the slave trade be shunned as the greatest enemies of our country."

Rush and Benezet were elated when the Rush pamphlet spurred the Pennsylvania state legislature to impose a tax of seven to fourteen pounds sterling on the sale of every slave. In effect, the tax proved "an almost total prohibition of the slave trade," Rush rejoiced.[6]

As Rush's pamphlet reached New York and Boston, it worked against him, however, "exciting the resentment of many slaveholders against me . . . giving rise to an opinion that I had meddled with a controversy that was foreign to my business."[7] At the time, slave-keeping was legal everywhere in the British-North American colonies.

By then, however, Rush had become addicted to public service, a one-man army ready to war against any and every social evil he encountered. Appalled by widespread poverty, violence, drunkenness, and human degradation in Philadelphia slums, he emerged as the first American physician to call for temperance. In what he called *Sermons to Gentlemen upon Temperance and Exercise*, Rush termed chronic alcoholism a disease rather than the result of willful behavior, and he intuitively divided the population into those who could and could not consume spirits without succumbing to addictive drinking, or alcoholism. He later expanded his "sermons" into a larger work he called *An Enquiry into the Effects of Spirituous Liquors upon the Human Body and Their Influence upon the Happiness of Society* (see Appendix A).

Calling "spirituous liquors . . . the foundation of fevers, fluxes [diarrhea, dysentery], jaundices, as well as dropsy, palsy, epilepsy, insanity, and other diseases," he presaged research findings of the twentieth century, warning that "spirituous liquors destroy more lives than the sword.

> War has its intervals of destruction—but spirits operate at all times and seasons upon human life. . . . Spirits . . . impair the memory, debilitate the understanding, and pervert the moral faculties. . . . They produce not only falsehood, but fraud, theft, uncleanliness, and murder . . . poverty and misery, crimes and infamy, diseases and death.

Instead of spirits, Rush suggested consuming "water, cider, malt liquor and wines which," he said, "inspired cheerfulness and good humor."[8]

Rush's work sparked the founding of the American temperance movement. A century later, in 1885, representatives of the Women's Christian Temperance Union would gather at Rush's gravesite to pray and then plant an oak tree "in token of their reverence for . . . the instaurator of American temperance reform."[9]

His *Sermons to Gentlemen upon Temperance and Exercise* also included the first printed reference to golf in the Americas. A sport he learned and enjoyed as a medical student in Edinburgh, it was all but unknown in the New World.* "Golf," he explained, "is an exercise which is much used by the gentlemen in Scotland.

> A large common in which there are several little holes is chosen for the purpose. It is played with little leather balls stuffed with feathers, and sticks. . . . He who puts a ball into a given number of holes, with the fewest strokes gets the game.[10]

Exhilarated by the public health controversies he had provoked, Rush—like Don Quixote of La Mancha[11]—set out to undo all the wrongs of British American society and bring justice to the downtrodden. In addition to spirits, Rush targeted tobacco as a threat to personal and public

---

*The first golf course in America would not be built until 1851, in Chicago.

health—more than two centuries ahead of his time. Although off the mark in calling tobacco the cause of tuberculosis, he was not as far off target claiming that he had "lately discovered that the use of that vile weed, especially in chewing and smoking, predisposes very much to the intemperate use of strong drinks.

"The use of tobacco in any way is uncleanly," he declared. "Now uncleanliness has been proved to be unfriendly to morals. Many diseases are produced by it, some of which become fatal." Tobacco did much harm indirectly, he added, by producing burns and stains in clothing and furniture.[12] Again, his pronouncements stirred up opposition to his meddling in an industry that was not only foreign to his profession but a source of pleasure to tens of thousands of Englishmen and a source of income to thousands of Americans who grew, processed, shipped, and sold tobacco in southern and mid-Atlantic states—and Connecticut in the North.

Just as the Rush campaigns against slavery, alcohol, and tobacco were gaining momentum, however, protests in Boston against British taxes sparked a political storm that drew his and everyone else's attention from social reform to political reform. In the eight years that had followed repeal of the 1765 Stamp Act, Parliament had tried to pay costs of maintaining British troops in North America by imposing a number of "back-door" taxes on colonists. Although American protests forced the British to repeal most of them, Parliament left a tax on tea in place, and, in 1773, tea merchants incited Boston mobs to rage through the streets in protest.

In Philadelphia, Rush responded with a polemic in the *Pennsylvania Journal*: "To His Fellow Countrymen: On Patriotism." He warned that "vessels were freighted to bring over a quantity of tea taxed with a duty to raise a revenue from America.

> Should it be landed . . . farewell American Liberty! We are undone forever. . . . Let us with one heart and hand oppose the landing of it. The baneful chests contain in them a slow poison in a political as well as a physical sense. They contain something worse than death—the seeds of SLAVERY.[13]

Two months later, a Boston mob dumped 340 chests of East India Company tea worth £10,000 into Boston harbor. Although prominent Americans such as Virginia planter George Washington condemned the "tea party" as vandalism, anti-tax activists in other major cities called for a colony-wide embargo on British tea. In Philadelphia, printer-activist William Bradford urged local merchants to stop buying British tea, and when a ship carrying British tea put into the harbor, protesters—Rush among them—streamed to the waterfront to host a "tea party" similar to Boston's. Protesters in New York, Charleston, and other ports followed suit, after which a second Boston Tea Party provoked British troops to march into Boston and declare martial law. They sealed off the city and threatened to starve inhabitants until they submitted to parliamentary rule and reimbursed the East India Company for its tea-party losses.

Outraged by what they called the overreaction of British authorities in Boston, newspapers along the Atlantic coast charged Parliament with declaring "war against the town of Boston."[14] Colonial leaders who had condemned the original Boston tea party agreed to meet in Philadelphia, initially hoping to effect a rapprochement with British authorities.

"I was not idle at this time with my pen," Rush boasted in his autobiography, written decades later. "I wrote under a variety of signatures, by which means an impression . . . in favor of liberty was made upon the minds of its friends and enemies."[15]

On September 5, 1774, fifty-five leading figures from every colony but Georgia converged on Philadelphia for America's First Continental Congress. Among them were George Washington and Patrick Henry of Virginia; John and Samuel Adams of Massachusetts; John Jay of New York; and Joseph Galloway and John Dickinson of Pennsylvania. A throng of independence-minded Philadelphians, including Benjamin Rush, streamed from the city to cheer the arrivals as they approached.

The irrepressible Rush jumped into one carriage to welcome its passengers, who turned out to be America's most celebrated lawyer, John Adams, with his cousin Samuel Adams and their friend, Robert Treat Paine, also a Boston lawyer. Awed by their presence, Rush introduced himself as a friend and protégé of Benjamin Franklin and proffered an invitation to stay at the Rush home. Facing the alternative of sharing pallets in a tavern attic with a dozen or more strangers and sots, the Adamses accepted.

As they continued into town, John Adams questioned Rush about the local political scene. Rush responded with passionate slogans and quotations from Franklin, Hume, Johnson, and Macaulay.

Tired and sore after more than five days of bone-jarring coach travel from New England, Adams wanted nothing more than a bed in which to sleep. To his diary he later complained of Rush being "too much of a talker," but conceded he was "elegant, ingenious . . . has been much in London . . . acquainted with Macaulay . . . and others of that stamp."[16]

Once rested, Adams gradually took to the young physician, almost a dozen years his junior, but, like Adams, a passionate humanitarian. Both favored sweeping social reforms as well as independence, and few Founding Fathers were more passionate about abolition than Adams and Rush. Before the first session of Congress had adjourned, the two had formed the basis of what would be a close lifelong and historic friendship. Marked by reams of correspondence, their profound emotional and intellectual ties displayed what Plato had described as two "princes" in whom "the spirit and power of philosophy, political greatness, and wisdom" met in one and gave the new American state "a possibility of life."[17] Two of the only Founding Fathers whose motives for revolution contained no hint of lust for personal power, gain, or glory, they sought only to better the condition of man—politically, physically, and spiritually. Periodically, Thomas Jefferson joined in the interchange, completing a triumvirate of three of the most learned and most worldly Founding Fathers.

"I shall always recollect with pleasure the many hours we have spent together, from the day we first met on the banks of the Schuylkill in the year 1775," Rush would write to Jefferson years later, recalling the start of their friendship. "If the innocent and interesting subjects of our occasional conversations should be a delusive one, the delusion is enchanting. But I will not believe we have been deceived in our early and long affection for republican forms of government. They are, I believe, not only rational but practicable."[18]

In the history of the western world, only the conversations of Plato, Montesquieu, Locke, Voltaire, and Rousseau may have matched the "enchanting delusion" of words and thoughts exchanged between John Adams, Thomas Jefferson, and Benjamin Rush in Philadelphia in 1775 and 1776.

"I waited upon nearly all the members of this first Congress and entertained them at my table," Rush recalled.

John and Samuel Adams domesticated themselves in my family. Their conversation was at all times animating and decided in favor of liberty and republicanism. . . . Patrick Henry from Virginia was my patient under the inoculation for the small pox. . . . I spent a long evening . . . with General Washington, the two Adamses, General [Charles] Lee and several other gentlemen who acted a conspicuous part in the American Revolution.[19]

By the time the fifty-five delegates met in convention in early September, most agreed that Britain's military action in Boston was "intolerable" and warranted colonial opposition, but they disagreed on the form and degree of opposition. Conservatives called for negotiations and reconciliation, but radicals prevailed with resolutions for a ban on British imports, consumption of British-made goods, and exports to Britain, Ireland, and the British West Indies. After agreeing to unite their colonies in a "Continental Association," the delegates adjourned on October 26. The following day, delegates staged a gala dinner for Philadelphians who had hosted and entertained them—including Benjamin Rush. Rush, in turn, used the occasion to cement friendships that would draw him into the inner circle of American patriots hailed later as the nation's "Founding Fathers."

A few days after the dinner, Rush noted in his diary, "a certain Thomas Paine arrived in Philadelphia from England with a letter of recommendation from Dr. Franklin." Rush met Paine quite accidentally in a bookstore, where they started chatting about the prospects of "the independence of the American colonies from Great Britain."

Before they met again, Rush had "put some thoughts on paper" about American independence and asked Paine to "write a pamphlet on it.

I suggested he had nothing to fear from the popular odium to which such a publication might expose him. For he could live anywhere, but that my profession and connections tied me to Philadelphia, where a great majority of the citizens and some of my friends were hostile to a separation of our country from Great Britain. He readily assented . . . and, from time to time, called at my house and read to me every proposed chapter as he composed it. . . . I gave it—at his request—the title of "Common Sense."[20]

Thomas Paine used some notes of Benjamin Rush to help write his inflammatory pamphlet *Common Sense*—even using the title Rush said he had suggested. (NATIONAL PORTRAIT GALLERY)

In Massachusetts, the State House reorganized itself as a Provincial Congress—in effect, declaring independence from England. It named Boston merchant-king John Hancock head of a Committee of Safety, with power to call up a militia. On February 1, 1775, he did just that and the state prepared to war against Britain. After British troops responded by landing in Salem, Massachusetts, Patrick Henry called Virginians to war in his famous address to the House of Delegates in Richmond: "Our brethren are already in the field!" he thundered. "Why stand we here idle? . . . I know not what course others may take, but as for me, give me liberty, or give me death."[21]

Henry's words echoed across the colonies, inspiring Benjamin Rush to write to the Philadelphia press, demanding that Congress respond to the British "with the sword in their hand."[22]

The original pamphlet *Common Sense*, which George Washington characterized as having worked "a powerful change in the minds of men." (Colonial Williamsburg Foundation)

On April 19, 1775, open warfare erupted in Massachusetts: British troops marched from Boston to Lexington to arrest rebel leaders John Hancock and Samuel Adams; a brief encounter on Lexington Green left eight Americans dead and ten wounded—mostly farmers and their sons. The British continued marching to nearby Concord to seize stores of rebel gunpowder. By evening the next day, 4,000 farmers—so-called Minutemen—had swarmed in from the surrounding country, positioned themselves behind stone walls along the road, and set off a rain of musket fire that sent British troops racing back toward Boston in panic. By the end of the day, nearly 150 British troops lay dead or wounded, while the farmers suffered 49 dead and 42 wounded.

News of the massacre at Lexington so incensed Rush that he "resolved to bear my share of the duties and burdens of the approaching revolution."

Patrick Henry called on the colonies to unite in a
war of independence against Britain after British
troops declared martial law in Boston. (UNITED
STATES SENATE)

Calling Lexington "the signal for the commencement of our independence," Rush inundated the press with articles "calculated to prepare the
public mind"[23]

On April 23, the Massachusetts Provincial Congress voted to raise an
army to fight the British, and, within a month, Rhode Island, Connecti-
cut, and New Hampshire agreed to send 9,500 men to join the 4,000
Massachusetts Minutemen surrounding and laying siege to British-held
Boston. In May, when the Second Continental Congress convened in
Philadelphia, Massachusetts delegate John Adams proposed that it adopt
Patriot forces surrounding Boston as a Continental Army. In a stroke
of genius to unite North and South, he nominated Virginia's Colonel
George Washington commander in chief of the largely northern forces.
The states agreed and united in opposition to British rule.

At the urging of Massachusetts lawyer John Adams, the Continental Congress named Virginia planter George Washington commander in chief of the Continental Army. (Brooklyn Museum)

Already friendly with most delegates, Rush attended a party on the banks of the Schuylkill River in June to celebrate the Washington appointment. At twenty-nine, Rush was among the youngest of those present. Jefferson was thirty-two, John Adams forty, George Washington forty-three, and Franklin, who had returned from France, nearly seventy.

"The first toast that was given was, 'The Commander in Chief of the American Armies,'" Rush reported. "The whole company instantly rose and drank the toast standing. . . . A silence followed it, as if every heart was penetrated with the awful but great events which were to follow."[24]

After Washington rode off to Massachusetts to take command of the Continental Army, Benjamin Franklin, who headed Pennsylvania's Committee of Public Safety, ordered construction of gunboats to protect

A trustee of the College of New Jersey, Princeton lawyer Richard Stockton had met fellow-alumnus Benjamin Rush in Scotland and sent him to recruit Rev. John Witherspoon as the new college president.

Delaware River approaches to Philadelphia. With completion of the first dozen ships, the public safety committee named Rush physician and surgeon to the Pennsylvania "navy." Ever the social reformer, he immediately complained to the committee that "our recruits suffer much from the lack of blankets." He called on the committee to "request every family in the city to furnish one or more blankets from their beds according as they could spare them."[25]

In August 1775, Rush went to Princeton to visit Rev. John Witherspoon and college trustee Richard Stockton, who invited Rush to stay at "Morven,"* the 5,500-acre estate his grandfather—also Richard Stockton—had purchased from William Penn in 1701.

---

*Possibly named for Morven Mountain in Scotland.

A 1776 portrait by Charles Willson Peale of the beautiful and talented Julia Stockton Rush at the time of her marriage to Benjamin Rush.

Once settled in Morven, Rush met Stockton's eldest daughter, Julia, then a devout, docile Quaker between sixteen and seventeen. Although she was fourteen years younger than he, he fell deeply in love "from the moment I saw her" and "determined to offer her my hand."

Admired for her beauty, she was superbly well educated, Rush wrote to a friend in Scotland, and boasted "brown hair, dark eyes, a complexion composed of white and red, a countenance at the same time soft and animated, a voice mild and musical, and a pronunciation accompanied with a little lisp.

"Think only what the friend, companion, wife, in the full meaning of those words, should be and you will then have a just idea of my happiness."[26]

After returning to Philadelphia, he wrote to the Stocktons for permission to visit their daughter and, after several visits, "my suit was blessed with success and I was married on the 11th of January, 1776."[27]

Fortunately for Rush, the substance of his thoughts on marriage apparently coincided with those of the still-immature and thoroughly star-struck Julia. Almost as naïve in some ways as his child bride, he believed—and instructed his beloved—that marriage was "the subordination of your sex to ours [as] enforced by nature, by reason, and by revelation."[28]

Benjamin and Julia wed in Princeton, with the college president, Rev. John Witherspoon, performing the ceremony. With honeymoons yet to come into fashion, the newlyweds spent their first days of marriage at Morven, with Julia "subordinating" herself to her husband—for the moment.

Events far from Morven, however, ended their idyll, and, leaving Julia with her parents, Rush returned to Philadelphia, where the release of Paine's *Common Sense* had sent the debate over independence into the streets. Within months, the printer sold 120,000 copies. "Its effects were sudden and extensive," Rush beamed. "It was read by public men, repeated in clubs, spouted in schools, and, in one instance, delivered from the pulpit as a sermon by a clergyman in Connecticut."[29] George Washington agreed: "I find *Common Sense* is working a powerful change in the minds of men. [It] will not leave numbers at a loss to decide upon the propriety of a separation."[30]

In March 1776, the British army evacuated Boston, ceding the city and the rest of New England to the Americans. After Massachusetts formally declared independence from Britain, the Continental Congress in Philadelphia passed a resolution on May 15 urging each of the colonies to follow suit by formulating constitutions and establishing independent state governments. On June 18, Pennsylvania did just that, holding a Provincial Conference that replaced its delegates to the Continental Congress with a new pro-independence delegation that included Benjamin Rush, M.D. Rush exulted to his wife:

The spirit of my great ancestor, who more than once dyed the sword which hangs in our bedroom with the blood of the minions of arbitrary power, now moves me to declare—nay, I trust the spirit of God himself moves me to declare that I will never desert the cause I am embarked in till I see the monster tyranny gnash [his] impotent teeth in the dust in the Province of Pennsylvania.[31]

Even as Rush plunged deeper into Pennsylvania's political maelstrom, he continued treating Philadelphia's poor—trotting into the slums at dawn to battle disease, imagining Cromwell's sword in his hand, often not returning home until midnight to sleep a few hours before resuming the battle at sunrise. He missed Julia desperately but found a few moments to dash off a letter to her every other day.

"My Dearest," he wrote on May 27, 1776. "I did not know 'til we parted how much you were a part of myself, and I feel some abatement of my affection for my country when I reflect that even she has deprived me of an hour of my dear Julia's company."

Two days later he wrote,

> My Dearest Life,
> I wept over both your letters. I thank you for your tender regard for my welfare. . . . The hand of heaven is with us. Did I not think so, I would not have embarked in it. . . . I think, write, talk, work, love—all, all—only for you. Adieu.

And three days after, on June 1, 1776: "My dearest Julia," he began. "My heart dotes upon you. . . . I have a thousand things to say to you." But he had to end: "Adieu, my love."[32]

On June 29, Virginia declared independence, and three days later, Congress adopted Richard Henry Lee's resolution "that these united colonies are, and of right, ought to be free and independent states."[33] On July 4, 1776, President of Congress John Hancock appended his bold signature to a parchment document—the Declaration of Independence. On July 20, Rush took his seat in Congress, and, two weeks later, on August 2, added his name to a list of signatures that would grow to fifty-six. Like all signatories, he pledged his life, fortune, and sacred honor to his province's independence from Britain. In doing so, he and other signers committed treason and would hang without trial until dead if captured by British authorities.

The signing of the Declaration of Independence in the summer of 1776. Benjamin Rush, M.D., is seated in rear left center, directly in front of a top-hatted gentleman. (UNITED STATES CAPITOL)

Rush recalled "the awful silence which pervaded the house when we were called up, one after another, to the table . . . to subscribe to what was believed by many . . . to be our death warrants."[34] Benjamin Harrison, the fat and jolly Virginia delegate who had married Martha Washington's cousin, lightened the scene, quipping to rope-thin Elbridge Gerry from Massachusetts: "When the hanging scene comes, I shall have all the advantage over you. It will be over with me in a minute, but you will be kicking in the air half an hour after I'm gone."[35]

Rush described the signing in a letter to Jacques Barbeu-Dubourg, Benjamin Franklin's friend whom Rush had met on his visit to Paris in 1769 and who still served as an intermediary between the French Court and American agents in Paris. "My countrymen have done me the honor of making me a member of Congress," Rush announced.

I can therefore from authority assure you that a fixed determination still prevails in that body to establish the liberties of America or perish in their ruins. No difficulties discourage us, no losses depress us. We look only to heaven and France for succor.

Aware of congressional plans to send John Adams to seek aid from the French court, Rush assured Barbeu-Dubourg that "this illustrious patriot [Adams] has not his superior, scarcely his equal, for abilities and virtue on the whole continent of America."[36]

After signing the Declaration of Independence, Rush plunged into the congressional debate over uniting the states in a formal confederation. The majority of delegates favored creating some sort of central national government to which states would cede specific, albeit strictly limited, powers. The states divided, however, over voting in the new congress. Smaller states demanded equal representation, with each state casting one vote, while larger states demanded congressional voting power determined by the size of the population of each state.

"We have been too free with the word independence," Rush called out to Congress in his maiden speech. "We are dependent on each other, not totally independent states. . . . I would not have it understood that I am pleading the cause of Pennsylvania. When I entered that door, I considered myself a citizen of America."[37]

Fearing that three states with the largest populations—Virginia, Pennsylvania, and Massachusetts—would control Congress, the smaller states grouped together and overwhelmingly defeated popular representation, leaving each state with equal voting power in the new congress. Although Rush had opposed the small states, they nonetheless joined Pennsylvania in naming him to the Committee of Inspection charged with executing orders of Congress, and he left to inspect Pennsylvania's bare-bones military and naval facilities. He returned with a litany of complaints about the "want of suitable accommodation for a hospital" at Fisher's Island, south of Philadelphia at the mouth of the Schuylkill River where it joins the Delaware River.

As demands for troop supplies increased, suppliers took full advantage, hoarding supplies in greatest need and raising prices accordingly. Rush's committee responded by refusing to pay the higher prices and cancelling orders. The cancellations, however, produced shortages that threatened the health of troops and ignited Rush: "To show its impracticality, I read a passage from Hume's *History of England** with similar attempts to subject articles of trade to legislative prices that had not only failed but produced a scarcity that bordered on famine.

> I now saw that men do not become wise by the experience of other people. . . . With the best disposition to act properly, the people of America imitated the blunders of nations in situations similar to their own and scarcely succeeded in a single undertaking 'till they had exhausted all the errors that had been practiced in the same pursuit in other countries.[38]

Despite the impasse in Congress, the euphoria following the signing of the Declaration of Independence still reigned, augmented by news of remarkable triumphs in the field by George Washington and his Continental Army. In an unprecedented engineering feat, Washington's chief of artillery, Henry Knox, had supervised the transport of nearly four dozen cannons over more than 200 miles of deep snow to the heights overlooking Boston. With the mouths of rebel cannons staring down at them, British commanders ordered the vaunted British army to evacuate the city and, in effect, cede New England to the Americans.

Flush with victory, Washington moved his forces to New York to seize control of New York and its huge deepwater harbor and, in effect, the entire Northeast. What seemed like certain victory for Washington, however, turned into disaster and almost certain defeat. Instead of transporting his 10,000 troops from Boston to Halifax, Canada, British general William Howe shifted course and sailed to Staten Island, New York, and the entrance to New York harbor, where they landed unopposed and gained complete control of the harbor. Ten days later, 150 British transports sailed into New York Bay with 20,000 more troops, including 9,000 Hessian mercenaries. The huge expeditionary force stormed ashore in Brooklyn, overrunning 5,000 American defenders, killing 1,500 and capturing the American army's entire meat supply.

---

*David Hume, *The History of England*, 6 vols. [certain volumes carry title of *The History of Great Britain*] (London: The London Printing and Publishing Company, 1754).

Only a thick fog allowed American survivors to escape after dark across the East River to New York Island (Manhattan) on August 29. The British renewed their pursuit the next day, however, forcing Washington and his men to retreat to the northern tip of Manhattan on the Harlem River and cross to the Westchester County mainland. The British were waiting and launched a massive assault at White Plains that sent the Americans fleeing in disarray. Some moved northward along the Hudson River Highlands, while Washington led the rest—a contingent of about 5,000—westward to the Hudson River and across into New Jersey.

Wintry winds enveloped the Northeast earlier than usual in the fall of 1776, and, with the British in close pursuit, Washington and his men staggered westward through sheets of icy rains to the Delaware River, where they barely reached safety by swimming and wading to the opposite bank in Pennsylvania. By early December, desertions had reduced Washington's army to slightly more than 3,000 men and left New York and most of New Jersey in British hands.

In contrast, a second American force under British-born General Horatio Gates in Saratoga, New York, near Albany, had crushed British forces marching southward from Canada to try to isolate New England from the rest of the American colonies. Although Congress had considered naming the highly experienced Gates commander in chief of the Continental Army, it was loathe to place a British military leader in command of Americans and, at John Adams's behest, it chose the American-born, albeit less experienced, Washington. Now it had second thoughts.

After Washington's humiliating flight from New York, enemy troops swept southward and westward across New Jersey, coming within sight of the American capital at Philadelphia. Congress fled to Baltimore on December 12 to discuss the possibility of surrender. As British troops approached Princeton, New Jersey, Rush galloped to "Morven," his father-in-law's home, where Julia was pregnant with the first Rush child. Rush bundled his wife and members of the Stockton family into a comfortable carriage and led them to a safe retreat at a relative's house in Cecil County, Maryland. He embraced his wife for what he feared was the last time, then loped off to join Congress in Baltimore and await capture by British troops and summary execution on the gallows.

As the Continental Congress contemplated and debated surrender to the British, however, the young blood in Benjamin Rush rebelled against passive surrender. Determined to contribute what he could to help salvage victory, he sought out former German officers he had treated in the German community near Philadelphia and finally met a German baron who said he was "personally acquainted with many of the Hessian officers" in the British army.

Rush immediately wrote to Virginia's Richard Henry Lee, who had been the first delegate in Congress to propose American independence the previous June:

> As they serve for pay only, he [the baron] thinks the bounty, pay, and clothing offered by Congress, so much above what they now enjoy, that, if they were properly tendered, they would serve us with more cheerfulness than the king of Britain. He offers to go in person, into Howe's army, at the risk of his life, and is sanguine enough to think he could immediately bring off two hundred recruits with him. . . . I need not suggest to you the necessity of secrecy if the baron's scheme is adopted.[39]

Rush assured Lee that "all the [German] back counties near Philadelphia are in motion" and that "several hundred of the militia join George Washington daily." He urged Lee to reject defeatism and spur Congress to increase its support of the war effort. "Vigor, firmness, and decisive measures are more necessary than ever," he argued. "Dispute less and do more in Congress or we are undone."[40]

After writing to Lee, Rush raced off to importune Pennsylvania militia commanding officer Joseph Reed to send troops to reinforce Washington's depleted army. Reed agreed, saying he already had a plan to present to the commander in chief. Knowing the British were less likely to kill or imprison a physician, Reed asked Rush to join him and deliver the plan in the event Reed was killed or captured on the way north. The two men then set off on the harrowing ride past British encampments to Washington's camp on the Delaware River opposite Trenton, determined to help win the war or die along the way.

CHAPTER 3

Broken by a Cannon Ball

A PRINCETON GRADUATE like Rush, Pennsylvania militia colonel Joseph Reed had studied law with Richard Stockton, Julia Rush's father, at the Middle Temple in London. He told Rush he believed that by reinforcing Washington's force with Pennsylvania's powerful militia, he could reverse the fortunes of the Continental Army.

"We are all of the opinion . . . that something must be attempted to revive our expiring credit," Reed told Washington after he and Rush arrived. "Our affairs are hastening fast to ruin if we do not retrieve them by some happy event."[1]

Washington responded in hushed tones: "Christmas day—at night— one hour before day is the time fixed for our attempt on Trenton. For heaven's sake keep this to yourself, as the discovery of it may prove fatal to us."[2]

As the Continental Congress debated ending the Revolution, Washington staged a quick, dramatic strike to save it.

In the dead of night on December 25, he led some 2,400 troops onto a flotilla of small boats and rowed through a blinding snowstorm across the ice-choked Delaware River. At 8 the next morning, they reached the east bank, near Trenton, New Jersey, and found the 1,400-man Hessian garrison still abed, dissuaded by the storm from posting their usual patrol. Shocked awake by the reality of their plight, the terrified Germans raced into the snow in night clothes to fire at the approaching Americans. But they were too late. Washington's troops were fighting their way up King Street through the center of Trenton and forced the Hessians to surrender.

Cheers echoed across the American landscape as news of Washington's triumph spread from King Street in Trenton to Philadelphia; then to the congressional meeting house in Baltimore; northward to Boston; southward to Charleston. Washington's startling roundup of more than 1,000 Hessian troops—in their underwear no less—amazed the world. A small, undisciplined mob of ragtag farmers and hunters with muskets had overwhelmed two battalions of the western world's best-trained, best-equipped mercenaries. The triumph provoked laughter in the halls of Versailles, where King Louis XVI grew convinced an alliance with Washington's American rebels might help him defeat England and restore Canada to French rule.

On the edge of Trenton's battlefield, however, Benjamin Rush, M.D., was trying desperately to treat the ghastly wounds of war for the first time in his young career, and without realizing it, laying the foundation for what would become the Army Medical Corps. After months in Philadelphia's slums treating hideous sores on vermin-covered patients, he thought himself ready for battle, but, clearly, he was not.

"It was the first time war appeared to me in its awful plenitude of horrors," he retched. "I want words to describe the anguish of my soul, excited by the cries and groans and convulsions of the men."[3] He was not alone. America had but two medical schools—at New York's King's College (now Columbia University) and Philadelphia's College of Philadelphia (later, University of Pennsylvania). Each graduated only a handful of physicians each year, leaving most would-be American "doctors" to train as apprentices to older men. Few if any—regardless of training—had ever seen, let alone treated, battlefield trauma. Congress authorized only one physician/surgeon for every regiment of about 1,000 troops, leaving the army with too few health-care professionals and almost none able to care for men at war.

"The first wounded man that came off the field was a New England soldier," Rush recalled. "His right hand hung a little above his wrist by nothing but a piece of skin. It had been broken by a cannon ball."[4]

Although still an unpaid civilian, Rush ordered the soldier carried to a house by the river which the army had appropriated for use as a hospital. With only enough rum and brandy for wounded officers, Rush had no choice but to force a stick between the half-conscious soldier's jaws and order him to "bite hard," hoping he would not fracture his teeth. Two medical assistants pinned the soldier to the operating table, while Rush severed the hand. Already in shock from blood loss, the soldier only groaned.*

The cannonball had splintered most of the two bones of the lower arm—the radius and ulna—above the now-severed hand, and Rush let his fingers move up the arm above the elbow, palpating until he found whole, uninjured tissue that he marked and washed as best he could. Laying four fingers of one hand across the upper arm, he cut through the flesh with a lancet in his other hand, then inserted leather retractors to separate muscle and other tissue from the humerus, or upper arm bone, and created a loose cuff of flesh. He folded the arteries, buried them under the cuff to stem the bleeding, then seized a small bone saw and, in less than a minute, cut through the bone and severed the lower part of the arm. The soldier had passed out, and Rush carefully folded and sutured the cuff of flesh over the stump of bone, wrapped it with bandages torn from linen sheets, and placed a wool cap over the bandaged stump. Rush knew that only about one-third of such amputees survived the procedure. Sterilization of medical instruments and patient wounds was more than a century in the future.

By evening, twenty other injured soldiers—some of them British—lay on makeshift pallets or on the ground, with Rush dressing wounds of enemy and American soldiers as best he could, before collapsing on an empty pallet and plunging into a deep sleep for about three hours. An aide roused him with news that Washington's force had gone ahead to Princeton and defeated a British force.

---

*Use of anesthetics in surgery was still sixty-five years in the future. Boston surgeon Crawford W. Long is believed to have been first to use it in 1842, when removing a tumor from a patient's neck. Although the anesthetic effects of nitrous oxide had been discovered in 1800, there is no evidence of its use in surgery at the time.

"We set off immediately for Princeton," Rush related, "and near the town passed over a field of battle still red in many places with human blood. We found a number of wounded officers and soldiers belonging to both armies. Among the former . . . General [Hugh] Mercer . . . wounded by a bayonet in his belly in several places, but he received a stroke with a butt of a musket to the side of his head, which put an end to his life a week after the battle."[5]

A wounded British officer from Scotland, Captain John McPherson, seized Rush's hand and gave him a note from a fellow British officer who had attended Edinburgh University with Rush and fallen in action at Princeton. "He loved you like a brother," McPherson moaned to Rush, who then scoured the battle field to recover his friend's body and see to his proper burial. It was Washington who found the dead soldier, and, learning of his having been a friend of Rush, ordered his burial with military honors in a village churchyard. Rush later planted an appropriate tombstone on the Scotsman's grave.

Rush had no sooner finished caring for McPherson when, to his horror, he saw his father-in-law, Richard Stockton, staggering along the road. The British army had plundered his home—stolen every stick of furniture, his valuable manuscripts, and all his livestock—and taken Stockton to New York as a prisoner. As a signer of the Declaration of Independence, Stockton had faced death for treason, but Rush sent an urgent message to Richard Henry Lee in the Continental Congress for help. A signer of the Declaration with Stockton and Rush, Lee used his high-level British connections from his student days in England to arrange Stockton's parole and his return to Princeton to the ash heap that had been his home. Besides Morven, the British had plundered almost every home in Princeton and all but leveled Nassau Hall and Princeton's church.

"Princeton is indeed a deserted village," Rush wrote to Lee. "You would think it had been desolated with the plague and an earthquake as well as with the calamities of war. The college and church are heaps of ruin. All the inhabitants have been plundered."[6]

After overseeing the leg amputations of four British soldiers, Rush left camp to escort his father-in-law to Maryland, where Julia and the rest of the Stocktons had taken refuge, with Julia giving birth to hers and

Benjamin's first child, a boy. They named him John Rush, for Benjamin's father, but called him "Jack."

Although his absence from Philadelphia cost Rush reelection to Congress in February 1777, he was neither "offended nor mortified" because, in his words, he wanted "to be more useful to my country." Congress obliged by appointing him physician-general of the Middle Department of the Continental Army, an area stretching from the Hudson to the Potomac Rivers. Placed in charge of what Congress euphemistically called "military hospitals," Rush discovered as many horrors within the hospitals under his command as he had on the battlefield.

"A greater proportion of men have perished with sickness in our army than have fallen by the sword," Rush complained to every officer he could find—to no avail. The faults within the Medical Department reflected those of the army itself—a strange hybrid that combined a Continental Army under nominal control of Congress and eleven or more state militias, each under the control of a state governor. The governors, in turn, appointed relatives or cronies as colonels—most with little or no military training—to lead each state regiment, and they, in their turn, appointed equally unqualified relatives, friends, or family physicians as regimental surgeons.

As often as not, regimental surgeons demanded that the Continental Army Medical Department fill their requests for "medicines" with no questions asked. One regimental surgeon ordered more than one hundred gallons of rum and an equal amount of wine over six months—without substantiating the need for his order or ever describing its disposition. A few deeply committed physicians reported irregularities to higher authorities, who simply passed complaints to the very state governors who had appointed the miscreants.

A doctor at Fort George, by Lake George, New York, reported more than 1,000 sick soldiers jammed into sheds without clothing or bedding, "laboring under the various and cruel confluence of smallpox." Colonel Anthony Wayne declared the hospital "a house of carnage"—without effect. By February 1777, more than 5,000 men in the Northern Army had contracted smallpox, and almost one-fourth of Washington's army had been hospitalized. Washington ordered 1,000 of his men who had died of hunger and exposure to be buried in unmarked graves in Potters Field.[7]

Rush charged that "the evils of this system" extended beyond the battlefield. "If it be criminal in an officer to sacrifice the lives of thousands by his temerity in battle," Rush railed, "why should it be thought less so to sacrifice twice their number in a hospital by his negligence?"[8]

While waiting for action by Congress, Rush decided to seize Cromwell's sword—figuratively, of course—and act on his own. He wrote and published a stirring pamphlet—*Directions for Preserving the Health of Soldiers*—that gained the full and immediate attention of both civil and military authorities.[9] Published twice during the Revolutionary War— once in the widely circulated *Pennsylvania Packet* of April 22, 1777—it opened with the startling claim that "a greater proportion of men perished with sickness in our armies than have fallen by the sword.

> The gallant youth . . . who had plighted his life to his country in the field and . . . courted death from a musket or cannon ball was often forced from the scene of action and glory by the attack of fever and obliged to languish for days or weeks in a hospital and, at last to close his eyes, deprived of the sweet consolation of a dying soldier of ending his life in the arms of victory or in an act of just resentment against the enemies of the liberties of his country.

Rush went on to demand radical changes in five areas of army life: dress, diet, cleanliness, encampments, and exercise.[10]

Although obvious by twenty-first century standards, Rush's forward-looking prescription was a product of intuition rather than empirical data on either the causes of most diseases or how they spread. More than a century would pass, for example, before scientists discovered the ties between mosquitoes and transmission of the yellow fever virus to humans. Nonetheless, Rush demanded that the army dress its soldiers in thick flannel rather than linen. Although he could not know or understand the effects, flannel was, in fact, too thick for mosquitoes to penetrate with their snout-like biting apparatus. He called for soldiers to wash their hands and faces daily, their bodies three or more times a week. Even Roman soldiers bathed regularly, Rush scolded, "to preserve their health."

He urged soldiers to keep their hair cut short—shave closely around and above the ears to the crown of their heads—and to comb their hair regularly. He urged soldiers to change clothes frequently and to sleep in separate beds. He warned against setting up camp near swamps, marshes, mill ponds, or other damp environments, and he called for frequent disposal of human wastes. "A fatal hospital fever was generated in . . . May 1777 by our sick being too much crowded," Rush explained to anyone who would listen.

> Several of the attending surgeons and mates [medical assistants] died of it . . . I called upon the Director General [of the Army Medical Department] and asked for more rooms for the sick. This was denied. Here was the beginning of suffering and mortality in the American Army which nearly destroyed it. . . . No order was given or executed for food, medicines, liquors, or even apartments for the sick.[11]

Before Rush could appeal to Congress, a British force of 15,000 had landed at Head of Elk (now Elkton) on the northern shore of Chesapeake Bay and was marching northward unopposed toward Brandywine Creek, the last natural barrier on the way to the national capital at Philadelphia. Washington deployed a force of just over 10,000 along the opposite bank on the Philadelphia side.

On September 11, Benjamin Rush reached the edge of the battlefield at Chadd's Ford as the British and Americans opened fire. Throughout the day, the battle raged with ever-greater intensity. Washington had badly miscalculated the strength and intentions of his enemy, however, and, while he concentrated troops and fire power at the center of the British line, British General Lord Cornwallis quietly slipped away to the northwest with 8,000 British and Hessian troops. Cornwallis crossed the Brandywine at its narrowest point, far from the battle at Chadd's Ford, looped around and behind the American army's right flank and threatened to encircle Washington's entire force.

As paralyzing British fire swept across American lines, Washington's troops turned about and fled in panic, leaving Rush all but alone beneath a rain of unrelenting shellfire to minister to the fallen. About him lay dead and dying men and boys, screaming in pain, their tatters soaked in blood, sweat, and dirt. Some begged for help, others called to God; some cried out for their mothers, and others just muttered incomprehensibly and sobbed. British troops closed in from three sides—south, west, and north—with Rush almost falling into enemy hands as he staggered among the fallen, trying to help the wounded and gather names of the dying to inform their families.

"A few days later," Rush recalled, "I went with several surgeons into the British camp with a flag from General Washington to dress the wounded . . . who were left on the field of battle. Here, I was introduced to a number of British officers [who] . . . treated me with great politeness." One colonel thanked Rush for having treated fallen British troops as well as Americans at Trenton.

"I was much struck upon approaching General Howe's line with the vigilance of his sentries and picket," he wrote to John Adams, whom he now considered "my dear friend." As head of the Board of War and Ordinance, Adams had acquired considerable power in Congress.

"They spoke, they stood, they looked like the safeguards of the whole army," Rush told Adams of his visit behind British lines to treat the wounded. Citing the discipline, order, economy, and cleanliness of the enemy's troops, he expressed a sense of "mortification" as he passed through Washington's army "without being challenged by a single sentry.

> I saw soldiers straggling from our lines in every quarter without an officer, exposed every moment to be picked up by the enemy's light horse. I heard of 2,000 who sneaked off with the baggage of the army to Bethlehem [Pennsylvania]. . . . I was told by a captain that they would not be missed, for George Washington never knew within 3000 men what his real numbers were. I saw nothing but confidence about headquarters and languor in all the branches and extremities of the army.[12]

The differences between the discipline and order of the British and Americans infuriated Rush, but when he complained, "it gave offense and was ascribed . . . to lack of attachment to the cause of my country," he told Adams.

> The waste, the peculation . . . are enough to sink our country. It is now universally said that the system was formed for the Director General and not for the benefit of the sick and wounded. . . . The sick suffer, but no

redress can be had for them. Upwards of 100 of them were drunk last night. We have no guards to prevent this evil.[13]

Before Adams had even received Rush's first letter, Rush sent an even more shocking accusation: "The disorders of our army do not proceed from any natural faults in our men," he reported.

> Our country affords the finest materials for making soldiers as good as any upon the face of the globe. The same may be said of our officers. . . . The fashion of blaming our soldiers and officers for all the disorders of our army was introduced in order to shelter the ignorance, cowardice, the idleness, and the drunkenness of our major generals.[14]

His letter to Adams was the third of eight he would send between October 1777 and February 1778, none of which elicited a significant response. In all fairness to Adams, though, he served on nearly seven dozen committees—more than any other congressman—and even if he had wanted to reply, he simply had no time.

In February 1778, Congress voted to send Adams to Europe to seek financial and military support from the French government, and, before leaving, he found a moment to answer Rush.

"I have read so many of your letters within a few months containing such important matters," Adams replied, "that I am ashamed to confess I have answered but one of them. . . . I beg leave to assure that I hold your correspondence inestimable and will do everything to cultivate it.

> Your sentiment that we are but half taught in the great national arts of government and war are, I fear, too just. . . . The great fault of our officers is want of diligence and patience. They don't want bravery or knowledge. . . . I am very glad you have not laid down your commission, and I conjure you by all the ties of friendship to your country not to do it. Men who are sensible of the evils in the Hospital Department are the most likely to point them out to others and to suggest remedies.[15]

Although the letter calmed Rush somewhat, John Adams's departure left him discouraged. Without a close ally in the top echelons of Congress, he feared it would be impossible to reform the care of wounded troops. Meanwhile they were dying by droves in hospitals—faster than in battle, and despite his rank, he was helpless to save them. He grew ever more furious as each of his appeals went unanswered.

"In the autumn and winter," Rush wrote in his autobiography, "the mortality among the soldiers in the hospitals revived from want of room and air, and many other things necessary for sick people. Many hundreds of them were buried every week. . . .

> I remonstrated in vain with the Director General for more accommodations and comfort for the sick. At this time [he] had immense power supported by two brothers in law in Congress. . . . I should have retired from the public service . . . but I loved my country and the brave men who had offered their lives for its defense. . . . I was sure men not interested in the continuance of error and vice could not fail of yielding redress to the complaints I should lay before them.[16]

Rush was wrong.

The Director General blocking reform was the well-connected Dr. William Shippen, Jr., the same Shippen who had taught Rush anatomy when Rush was an apprentice learning medicine. Shippen's sister had married Brigadier General Benedict Arnold, and Shippen's wife, Virginia-born Alice Lee, was the sister of the two powerful Virginia congressmen— Richard Henry Lee and his brother Francis Lightfoot Lee. The former had proposed the congressional resolution for independence and had been elected president of Congress for a year. Both he and his brother had signed the Declaration of Independence and ensured the appointment of their younger brother—Dr. Arthur Lee—as a US envoy in Europe. All the Lees, moreover, were longtime intimates of Washington, who was born and raised near the Lee plantations in Westmoreland County and served with the Lees in Virginia's House of Burgesses. Adding to Shippen's influence in Congress, he and his wife, Richard Henry Lee's sister Alice, insisted that Richard Henry make their house his temporary home when he was in Philadelphia attending Congress. Thus Shippen's house became a center of entertainment for members of Congress and their influential friends.

Rush was well aware of Shippen's links to the Lees and to the commander in chief, but nonetheless decided to risk his career—and possible court martial—with a letter he sent to Washington the day after Christmas 1777. More patriot than politician, Rush detailed the atrocious conditions in military hospitals and charged Shippen with responsibility. In addition, he accused Shippen of fiscal malfeasance in the purchase of medicine and supplies.

"I have delayed troubling your Excellency with the state of our hospitals in hopes you would hear it from the Director General, whose business it is to correspond with your Excellency upon this subject," Rush wrote to Washington. He charged that American troops suffered a great disproportion of sickness over British troops, resulting from "the negligence and ignorance of officers in preserving the health of their men."

Rush charged that nine out of ten who died "under our hands" had died from "fevers *caught* [his italics] in our hospitals."[17]

Rush went on to accuse Shippen of crowding too many injured soldiers in each room and depriving them of essential supplies. "I have seen twenty sick men in one room . . . large enough to contain only six or eight well men without danger to their health," Rush charged. "The hospitals are but half provided with the stores necessary for sick people. . . . There is a want of hospital shirts, sheets, blankets to be worn by the sick. . . . There is a want of guards and an officer to command at every hospital." Patients, he charged, left the hospitals "when they pleased, catch colds, sell their arms, blankets, and clothes to buy rum . . . they plunder the inhabitants with impunity. . . ."

Rush concluded by asserting that "the medical establishment is a bad one. It places all power in the Director General and gives him the most incompetent officers . . . who are never obliged to go inside of a hospital. . . . If he provided only medicines and stores . . . it would be more than enough for him. But the Congress have made him supreme in the practice of physic [medicine] and surgery and have made him the sole judge of all wants [needs]. . . . The offices held by the Director General are held by *three* physicians in the British hospital who are all independent of each other."[18]

A week passed . . . two . . .

Imprudently impatient, Rush concluded that Washington had ignored his complaints. In fact, Washington could do little. He was struggling to retain his own post as commander in chief of the army. After his crushing loss at Brandywine, the British had marched into the American capital of Philadelphia unopposed, and, to try to prevent further British advances, Washington staged a suicidal counterattack near Germantown that almost sealed his ouster as commander in chief.

He sent two separate columns along what a schematic diagram showed as parallel roads to Germantown for a two-pronged pincer attack on the British. In fact, one road followed a longer serpentine course, allowing the column on the straighter, shorter road to reach Germantown before its twin column. Faced with an impenetrable wall of British fire and no support from the second column, the first column retreated. A dense fog suddenly enveloped the area, and the retreating column collided with second American column, which was still advancing and, mistaking them for enemy soldiers, fired. Caught between American and British fire, the trapped column lost 700 men, with 400 more taken prisoner.

As British commanders doubled over with laughter, the remnants of the American government fled for their lives to Lancaster, about eighty miles west of Philadelphia, while Washington led the remnants of his army into winter quarters atop an elevated plateau at Valley Forge, about twenty-five miles west of Philadelphia. Although Washington had forwarded Rush's letter to Congress, Congress was in such disarray it left it unopened in a pouch crammed with other unattended communications.

After settling briefly in Lancaster, most members of the Second Continental Congress scattered across the country to get home to their families and await inevitable defeat and arrest by British authorities for treason. Twenty-one of the more than fifty members stood firm, however, and reconvened about twenty-five miles farther west in York, Pennsylvania, across the Susquehanna River, still bent on winning independence from Britain.

Their hopes revived with the arrival of General Gates, the hero of Saratoga, site of the only significant army victory in the war other than Trenton. By then, even Richard Henry Lee, Washington's friend and neighbor from Virginia, had grown openly critical of Washington's military skills, and, with encouragement from Quartermaster General Thomas Mifflin, Lee coaxed the small group still sitting in Congress to create a Board of War with supreme powers over Washington and the military. Congress named General Gates board president and his aide, Colonel Thomas Conway, inspector general.

Bitter over Washington's earlier refusal to appoint him a major general, the Irish-born Conway used his newfound authority to plot Washington's ouster. While disparaging Washington and his generals in unsigned letters to Congress, he enlisted Gates into the plot by appealing to the Englishman's ambitions and heaping scorn on Washington.

"Heaven has been determined to save your country," Conway flattered Gates, "or a weak general and bad counselors would have ruined it."[19]

Facing dismissal as commander in chief, Washington was in no position to act on the Rush complaint about the Medical Department. "It is to be regretted," Washington answered Rush disingenuously in early January 1778, "that a department . . . on which so much depends should yet be inadequate," but he said "those Gentlemen" in charge of the Hospital Department—Shippen et al.—were "best able to point out the defects."[20]

Fired by indignation at what he felt was Washington's complacency, Rush threw political caution to the wind, all but galloping to York to confront Congress with his charges against Washington's administration of the Medical Department—and ready to resign if it failed to respond.

He arrived just as General Gates and Conway were presenting their criticisms of Washington's administration of the military. Demanding that Congress adopt his plan for reforming the Medical Department, Rush grew all-but-irrational:

"Let not this matter be debated and postponed in the usual way for two or three weeks," he railed at Richard Henry Lee. "The salvation of America, under God, depends upon its being done in an *instant* [his italics]." When Lee failed to respond "in an instant," Rush assailed Congress for its "absence of public advocates for the miserable and oppressed." He sent formal complaints to Pennsylvania delegate James Searle and New York delegate William Duer—with no tangible results. He then appealed to Generals Gates and Greene, accusing members of Congress of "a union in politics that is often fatal to liberty . . . [and] in my opinion, high treason." More than a gadfly, Rush seemed ready to incite a revolution within the revolution.

Unaware of Thomas Conway's intentions, but aggrieved by Washington's failure to act, Rush embraced arguments favoring replacement of Washington as commander in chief. Rush concluded that Washington's "talents are unequal to those degrees of discipline and decision which alone can render an army successful."[21] His notebook described Valley Forge:

> The troops dirty, undisciplined & ragged . . . bad bread; no order; universal disgust . . . encampment dirty & stinking . . . 1500 horses died for want of [forage]. . . . The commander-in-chief and all the major generals lived in houses out of the camp.[22]

Aboil in anger, frustration, and fears for the healthy as well as wounded soldiers, Rush wrote to the man he trusted most in government, John Adams, but Adams was facing impossible problems of his own trying to raise money from an absolute monarch in France to help commoners in America overthrow a fellow monarch in Britain.

"Patience! Patience! Patience!" Adams counseled his young friend—somewhat impatiently. "Patience," Adams declared, is "the first, the last, and the middle virtue of a politician."[23]

But Rush was no politician nor did he want to be one. He was a physician—a humanitarian—trying to heal the wounded, not govern them, and he found it impossible to remain patient in the face of the suffering he had witnessed.

"We lost a city, a victory, a campaign by that want of discipline and system which pervades every part of the army," Rush railed to Adams. He predicted that "if Howe should lie still, desertions, sickness, accidental deaths, and executions would waste our whole army in a year."[24]

Rush ignored Adams's advice and sent his complaints in an unsigned letter to Virginia Governor Patrick Henry, the powerful leader of America's most powerful state—a man Rush believed powerful enough to rectify matters with a single word.

"The common danger of our country first brought you and me together," Rush reminded the man he had inoculated against smallpox two years earlier at the Continental Congress. "We have nothing to fear from our enemies," Rush declared. "America can only be undone by herself.

> She looks to her councils . . . but alas! where are they? Her representation in Congress dwindled to only twenty-one members. Her Adams, her Wilson, her Henry are no more among them. . . . her army . . . *a mob*. Discipline unknown. . . . The quartermaster's and commissary departments filled with idleness and ignorance and peculation. Our hospitals crowded with 6,000, but [only] half provided with necessaries and accommodations, and more dying in them in one month than perished in the field during the whole of the last campaign.[25]

Instead of ending with an appeal to which Henry would almost certainly have responded favorably, Rush plunged into the controversy over Washington's military prowess. As he had before, he was "meddling in an industry . . . foreign to his profession"—an area about which he knew nothing and one which—for once—he should have avoided.

"The Northern Army," Rush wrote to Patrick Henry, "has shown us what Americans are capable of doing with a general at their head." Calling himself "one of your Philadelphia friends," he charged that "a Gates, a Lee, or a Conway would, in a few weeks, render them an irresistible body of men." He urged Henry to "awaken, enlighten, and alarm our country."[26]

While waiting for a reply, Rush again wrote to John Adams, whom Congress had now elevated to the new post of minister plenipotentiary (ambassador) to France.

"I know not whether to rejoice or condole with my country in your late appointment," Rush wrote to Adams. "I am aware that your abilities and firmness are much wanted at the Court of France, and after all that has been said of the advantages of *dressing, powdering,* and *bowing* well as necessary accomplishments for an ambassador, I maintain that knowledge and integrity with a common share of prudence will outweigh them all."

After telling Adams that Americans "pant" for French military intervention in the war with Britain, he told his friend he planned to resign as a medical officer, adding, "While you are . . . gazing at the folly and pageantry of animals in the shape of men cringing at the feet of an animal called a king, I shall be secluded from the noise and corruption of the times and spending my time in the innocent employments of husbandry on a farm in Jersey with an amiable wife and rosy boy."[27]

Adams thanked Rush for his congratulations "on my new and most honorable appointment. . . . Pray help me by corresponding constantly with me."[28]

Before Rush could answer Adams, however, he received an angry letter from his wife, Julia, who had evidently tired of her husband's prolonged failure to rejoin his family.

"When will the days of our calamity end?" she demanded to know. "Your letters of this week are more unfavorable than any I have received from you."

After making a show of feigned understanding, she reminded her husband that he had a family that lacked a father. "Our [sixteen-month-old] son John you know wants a little opus from you now and then. He does not read as much as I could wish, though he makes fair promises. A letter to him or a postscript to one of mine from you would not be amiss." Julia told her husband that John was rebelling against his mother and treating the servants badly, and Julia felt it "best for him to be reminded that he is not out of the reach of your authority."[29]

Before Rush could fulfill his promise to retire to his father-in-law's farm in Jersey, Patrick Henry made one of his most important and little-known decisions of the Revolutionary War: he sent the letter he received from Rush by express rider to Washington at Valley Forge.

"I am sorry there should be one man who counts himself my friend who is not yours," Henry wrote to Washington.

> The censures aimed at you are unjust. . . . But there may possibly be some scheme or party forming to your prejudice. . . . Believe me, sir, I have too high a sense of the obligations America has to you to abet or countenance so unworthy a proceeding. . . . But I will not conceal anything from you by which you may be affected; for I really think your personal welfare and the happiness of America are intimately connected.[30]

Washington was emotional in thanking Henry, explaining that the Rush letter "is not the only insidious attempt that has been made to wound my reputation.

> There have been others equally base, cruel, and ungenerous. . . . All I can say is that [America] has ever had, and I trust she will ever have, my honest exertions to promote her interest. I cannot hope that my services have been the best; but my heart tells me they have been the best I can render.[31]

Washington told Henry he was aware of "the intrigues of a faction . . . formed against me. . . . General Gates was to be exalted on the ruin of my reputation and influence. . . . and General Conway, I know, was a very active and malignant partisan, but I have reason to believe that their machinations have recoiled most sensibly upon themselves."[32]

Deeply touched by Henry's loyalty, Washington revealed his own, personal feelings for the first time, along with the true plight of his encampment on the bluff above Valley Forge—a site that represented another military blunder by the commander in chief. Although the cliff at its eastern end provided a natural defense against attack from Philadelphia and its gentle western slope provided an accessible escape route, it lacked one essential: water. The camp had no springs, streams, or wells. The water that fed the forge and gave the area its name flowed at the foot of the bluff below camp, all but inaccessible to the troops. Conditions at the camp, therefore, began deteriorating from the moment they arrived.

"I can only thank you again, in language of the most undissembled gratitude, for your friendship," the embarrassed commander in chief wrote to Henry.

> It is not easy to give you a just and accurate idea of the sufferings of the troops. I fear I shall wound your feelings by telling you that on the 23rd [of December], I had in camp not less than 2,898 men unfit for duty by reason of their being bare foot and otherwise naked. . . . I cannot but hope that every measure will be pursued . . . to keep them supplied from time to time. No pains, no efforts can be too great for this purpose. The articles of shoes, stockings, blankets demand the most particular attention.[33]

Henry responded immediately, confiscating nine privately owned wagon-loads of clothing and blankets to help meet the needs of troops at Valley Forge. He promised Washington more of the same and pledged that "nothing possible for me to effect will be left undone in getting whatever the troops are in want of."[34]

In the weeks that followed, however, several Virginia officers at Valley Forge informed Henry that the food and clothing he had sent to Quartermaster General Thomas Mifflin for delivery to camp were being sold in markets in nearby towns. Henry wrote to Congress demanding an explanation. While waiting, he received another letter from Washington, warning of famine in camp and possible mutiny.

As frustrated now by congressional inaction as Rush, Henry vented to Richard Henry Lee: "I am really shocked at the management of Congress," he declared. "Good God! Our fate committed to a man [Mifflin] utterly unable to perform the task assigned to him! . . . I grieve at it."[35]

A congressional investigation found that Mifflin, a Philadelphia merchant before the Revolution, had been diverting supplies bound for Valley Forge into his own warehouses, where he resold them to area merchants. When Washington confronted him, he confessed to participating in the Conway Cabal and resigned. With Mifflin's subsequent revelations, Conway resigned, Congress dissolved the Board of War and sent Gates back to the battlefield, and it gave Washington all-but-dictatorial powers to conduct the entire war as he saw fit. Washington persuaded Rhode Island Major General Nathanael Greene–also a merchant in private life—to accept the Quartermaster General's post, and, within days, Valley Forge had a surplus of clothing, food, and other supplies.

Although Rush had played no part in the Conway Cabal, his complaints about the commander in chief's administrative failures, coming as they did at the same time as the Conway group's complaints, led the press and Washington himself to assume that Rush had conspired with Conway.

Recognizing the enormity of his political errors, Rush feared arrest and charges of insubordination and treason before a court martial. "I foresaw my own destruction,"[36] he admitted, and envisioned the end of both his career in medicine and his goal of healing the nation's wounds. To avoid the spectacle of a court martial, he decided to resign from the army, but his decision came too late. A courier arrived with a summons for Benjamin Rush, M.D., Founding Father, to appear before an angry Congress in York, Pennsylvania. Still facing treason charges by the British government for signing the Declaration of Independence, he now faced treason charges by the American government he had helped create by signing it.

CHAPTER 4

"*The Revolution Is Not Over!*"

ALTHOUGH ON TARGET with his criticisms, Rush had picked the wrong time, the wrong place, and the wrong man to challenge and blame by citing George Washington for failing to provide medical care to wounded troops. But Rush was a scientist, and, unlike most Americans, he viewed Washington as a man—superior in many ways to most men, but not the godlike figure many imagined. Indeed, Rush feared extravagant public adulation would seduce Washington into believing in his own omniscience and making strategic blunders that would lose the war. He had already lost battles at Brooklyn, New York, Brandywine, and Germantown, and he had ceded the national capital without a fight.

Although exposure of Mifflin's malfeasance improved physical conditions at Valley Forge, it failed to rectify conditions in the Medical Department, whose director—Shippen—sat in his comfortable office ordering hospital supplies separately from those ordered by the Quartermaster General in the field.

To Rush's surprise, however, his complaints against Shippen had provoked others to complain—indeed, so many that Congress had little choice but to summon Shippen to answer charges of mismanagement. Encouraged that Congress was at last seeking "to correct the abuses and reform the system of our hospitals," Rush reversed course and heeded Adams's advice against resigning.

"It will be a disagreeable task to accuse him [Shippen] of ignorance and negligence of his duty," Rush wrote to Julia, "but the obligations I owe to my country preclude all other ties. I shall act strictly to the dictates of my conscience, and if the system is altered and Dr. Shippen can be restrained by proper checks from plundering the sick, I shall not resign my commission, but shall serve another campaign. . . . Adieu. Love as usual. Kiss Jack for me."[1]

Most of Julia's early letters to her husband are missing, but if her later correspondence to him is any guide, she had lost patience with his prolonged absences and chided him for ignoring his obligations as a husband and father in his fervor for service to the army. She treasured her moments with him so much that she could not understand the ease with which he dismissed her and their son in favor of political and professional ties.

When Shippen's trial got under way, Rush led a parade of doctors and military aides who testified against Shippen, but Shippen's in-laws, the Lee brothers, had too much influence. Although Congress criticized Shippen because he "did speculate in and sell hospital stores . . . which conduct [was] highly improper and justly reprehensible," it nonetheless acquitted him of all charges. To add to the scandal, Congress yielded to demands by the Lee brothers that it reappoint Shippen to his post. Rush resigned in anger.[2]

"My application to Congress in favor of our hospitals turned out as I expected," Rush raged in a letter to Adams in Paris. "My complaints were dismissed as groundless, factious, &c., and the Director General was honored with the approbation of Congress. Had you been there, I am sure matters would have taken another turn.

> Would you have winked at . . . the Director General having bought six pipes of wine at £150 a pipe . . . and selling them upon his *own* account for £500 apiece? . . . Would you have winked at the Director General being unable to produce a single voucher from the surgeons of the hospital of the expenditure of his stores and medicines? Would you have winked at bills for poultry and other delicate articles bought for the hospital which no sick man ever tasted? Would you finally have winked at false returns of . . . the mortality in the hospitals. No, you would not.[3]

After posting his letter to Adams, Rush wrote a blistering open letter to Shippen, a copy of which he sent to the *Pennsylvania Packet* for publication. His letter all but dared Shippen to sue him for libel and further open the way for Rush to expose Shippen's misconduct in open court:

> Your reappointment, after the crimes you have committed, is a new phenomenon in the history of mankind. It will serve like a high-water mark to show posterity the degrees of corruption that marked the present stage of the American Revolution.[4]

Rush reminded Shippen—and *Packet* readers—that only a month earlier, Shippen's brother-in-law, Benedict Arnold, had defected to the British, who rewarded his treachery with an appointment as a brigadier general in the British army.

"I do not mean . . . to insinuate that [British general] Sir Harry Clinton will ever tempt you as he did General Arnold," Rush wrote to Shippen. "Men have been found in all countries who have prostituted their consciences for much less.

> Your injured country, which you have robbed . . . by your negligence and inhumanity; the parents and children of those brave men whom you suffered to perish . . . in your hospitals; and the graveyards . . . which you have crowded with the bodies of your countrymen, cry aloud for your dismission from office.[5]

Rush then accused Shippen of "selling large quantities" of wine, sugar, and other hospital stores for his own benefit. Although profiting from the sale of army stores was common in the Quartermaster Department, the theft of foods and medicines from wounded soldiers was too ghastly for even the well-connected Shippen to survive, and two weeks later, he resigned. Congress, in turn, ordered implementation of some of the reforms Rush had demanded, including separation of hospital administrative and purchasing functions and the right of doctors to order medicines they needed directly from suppliers.

But the reforms fell short of what Rush considered essential for restoring order to army hospitals and ending what he called the "injustice and injuries" to injured soldiers. "A putrid fever [probably typhus] raged for three months in [Bethlehem, Pennsylvania] hospital," Rush complained to Washington, "increased by the sick being too much crowded and by their wanting blankets, shirts, straw, and other necessities for sick people.

> So violent was the putrid fever that nine out of eleven surgeons were seized with it, one of whom died . . . and many of the inhabitants of the village caught it and died. . . . There have died 200 soldiers [in Bethlehem], in Reading 180, in Lancaster 120, in Princetown [*sic*] between 80 and 90. . . . These returns are only one-fourth of the hospitals . . . within the last four months. . . . Eight tenths of them died with putrid fevers caught in the hospitals.

All but charging Shippen with treason, Rush told Washington that, even as deaths from putrid fever peaked, Shippen wrote to Congress that "no fatal disease prevails at the hospitals, very few die, and the hospitals are in very good order."[6]

Washington, however, was in no position to override decisions of Congress. In an effort to end the bitter controversy, he gave Shippen a certificate of good conduct and a recommendation that allowed him to disappear from public life with honors and resume medical practice in civilian life. But the commander in chief then toured camps himself, and, shocked by the sight of rotting horse carcasses, he ordered all dead horses and all offal in and about the camp to be burned. He ordered immediate distribution of clothes to the men. A few weeks later, the general apparently realized that only benevolent motives had provoked Rush and he invited the young physician to dine, and the two reestablished cordial albeit strained ties. A decade later, Washington would dine at Rush's home in Philadelphia during the Constitutional Convention.

In April 1778, the king of France inadvertently brought a temporary end to the health crisis in the army by recognizing American independence and pledging to send a French army to supplement Washington's forces. Washington declared an official day of "public celebration" at

Both famed and infamous, the skilled surgeon William Shippen sold hospital supplies and medicines for his own profit as director general of the Continental Army Medical Department. Exposed by Benjamin Rush, Shippen escaped punishment because of his marriage into the powerful Lee family of Virginia.

Valley Forge, followed by an enormous banquet, piled high with enough food and drink for the entire army to forget the thirst, hunger, and mistreatment they had suffered over the winter.

After his resignation from the medical service, Rush took stock of his career in the military. Recognizing his own "indiscreet zeal"—a passion for justice that made political compromise seem obscene—he all but retired from public life. He went to live with Julia and their increasingly unruly two-year-old John at Morven, his father-in-law's Princeton, New Jersey, home.

At thirty-two, Benjamin Rush was out of work, his career in the military ended, and, with the British army occupying Philadelphia, his civilian practice a distant memory. His father-in-law, Richard Stockton, a signer of the Declaration of Independence with Rush, suggested that Rush consider studying law. Stockton, by then, had recovered from the trauma he had suffered as a prisoner of war and had resumed practicing law. He had also won election to New Jersey's Executive Committee and was an Associate Justice of the state Supreme Court. He envisioned nothing but success emerging from a law partnership of two signers.

Before Rush even opened a law book in Stockton's library, however, he received news that the British were evacuating Philadelphia. The threat of a French invasion had forced the British to consolidate northern forces at their main base in New York City. As British troops led a long wagon train northward out of Philadelphia through New Jersey's blistering summer heat, Washington's forces charged off their Valley Forge mountaintop and followed, harassing the British rear. After a week, exhausted Redcoats encamped for the night at Monmouth Courthouse (now Freehold, New Jersey).

The next morning, Washington attacked, triggering a day of exhausting heroics by both sides, but the fighting proved indecisive. As darkness set in, Washington's troops bedded down for the night, and, as they slept, the British quietly slipped away to Sandy Hook, a spit of land on the northern New Jersey shore at the entrance to New York Bay. Transport ships waited to carry them away to New York, ceding New Jersey to the Americans. Washington claimed victory in a letter to his brother John, calling the battle at Monmouth Courthouse "a glorious and happy day." It had cost the British "at least 2000 men of their best troops," he declared. "We had 60 men killed."[7]

The British evacuation of Philadelphia reawakened passions that Rush still harbored for treating the sick and helping the disadvantaged. Abandoning all thoughts of studying law, he all but leaped onto his horse and spurred the beast toward Philadelphia to reenter the lists in combat against disease and injustice.

"The filth left by the British army in the streets," Rush fretted, "created a good deal of sickness . . . [I] quickly recovered my business, with a large accession of new patients."[8] Many in the city worked to clean streets of rubbish and debris, Rush reported, but he counted at least 1,000 businesses standing empty "and all the mechanics and laborers who are dependent upon them unemployed." Property values had plunged to about one-third their pre–Revolutionary War values.

"Bankruptcies were numerous and beggars were to be seen at the doors of the opulent in every street of our city," Rush noted in his diary. "Taxes were heavy and subscriptions for the relief of the poor still more oppressive."[9] Making matters worse, the College of Philadelphia had closed, along with most schools at every level, leaving children and adolescents and an entire class of young men and women idle as well as hungry.

As he trudged through debris-laden streets to find and treat the ill, he raged at the crushing poverty that surrounded him and, as in the past, he sounded his trumpet of protest before Philadelphia's officialdom. Rush now envisioned nothing less than a new, second revolution in the United States to cure not only the diseases that infected individuals but those that infected American society as a whole.

Irate at the apathy of some political leaders, Rush acted on his own, remodeling a space he found on Strawberry Alley, near present-day Chestnut Street, and, with financial backing from Benjamin Franklin, he opened the Philadelphia Dispensary for the Poor. He and a second volunteer physician spent the noon hour three days a week treating the poor and dispensing medicines free of charge. During the first five years of its existence, Rush treated more than 7,000 indigent patients at his own expense.

"The revolution is not over," he warned state legislators as he renewed his pre–Revolutionary War cry for ending slavery. To his call for abolition, he now added pleas for comprehensive prison reforms, an end to the death penalty for noncapital crimes, and an end to forced convict-labor along the roads. Exploding with anger, he described conditions in Philadelphia jails to anyone who would listen. He told of boys and girls, men and women, crowded together in dark, filthy, unlit, unheated cells, without means to avoid fouling themselves and their surroundings. He said the food, when available, was inedible at best, rotten at worst. He reported jailers—all from society's lowest ranks—robbing inmates of their clothing and abusing them physically and sexually. Rush urged replacement of jails with "houses of repentance," each with a chapel, along with gardens and shops to teach inmates trades.

"Laws which inflict death for murder," he pleaded with a gathering at Benjamin Franklin's house, "are as unchristian as those which tolerate revenge. . . . The power over human life is the sole prerogative of Him who gave it." Rush cited as a truism Euclid's declaration: "Murder is propagated by hanging for murder."[10]

Rush condemned all public punishment—the gallows, stocks, whipping posts, forced labor, and other punishments—charging that it left scars that "disfigure the whole character." Criminals punished in public, he said, leave prison hating their jailors and showing little or no remorse or even memory of the crimes they committed or their victims.[11]

But his demands did not end with prison reforms and changes to the criminal code. He called for sweeping changes in almost every area of American society.

"How can a nation be free and happy when the common people are ignorant," he demanded. Answering his own question, he called for establishment of "free [elementary] schools in every township or district consisting of one hundred families.

"Let children be taught to read and write!" he demanded.

Free schools, he argued, had raised standards of living in Scotland. "In the small state of Connecticut," six hundred such schools had promoted "morals, manners, and good government."*[12]

He then provoked roars of angry disbelief and disapproval in the legislature by insisting that schools open their doors to females as well as males—that *universal* education include women as well as men. Rush called it essential for "our ladies" to obtain "a suitable education . . . for instructing their sons in the principles of liberty and government." He described the core of that education as "knowledge of the English language . . . an acquaintance with geography . . . history, biography, and travels . . . with the principles of chemistry and natural philosophy

---

*Connecticut was actually the second colony to establish free public schools in America. In 1647, Massachusetts had passed a "School Act," requiring every town with fifty householders or more to open a petty, or elementary, school and every town with one hundred families or householders to open both a petty school and grammar (middle) school. Connecticut followed suit in 1650.

In his quest to expand education in America, Benjamin Rush founded Dickinson College in Carlisle, Pennsylvania.

[physics]. . . . " He denigrated objections to education of women as "the prejudice of little minds"[13] and called for equal rights for women under the law. "Polygamy of husbands is a crime in women," he snarled, "but plurality of wives not so in men."[14]

To rouse public support for his schemes, he published a small pamphlet, *A Plan for the Establishment of Public Schools and the Diffusion of Knowledge in Pennsylvania; To Which Are Added Thoughts upon the Mode of Education, Proper in a Republic.* The "Plan" was the first in American history to urge establishment of a state-supported, universal education system. To the furor his pamphlet created, he added more controversy with a second pamphlet, *Thoughts upon Female Education.*

Nor was that all. In addition to free, universal public education and equal education for women, he urged establishment of four "colleges" to provide a mixture of secondary-school and higher education, "one in Philadelphia, one in Carlisle, a third for the benefit of our German fellow citizens at Lancaster, and a fourth some years hence in Pittsburgh. Let there be one university [then, a combination of higher education and graduate studies] in the state, and let that be established in the capital."[15]

After Philadelphia's college had reopened, Rush began organizing supporters to establish a second college at Carlisle, Pennsylvania—to offer higher education to the growing rural population too far west of Philadelphia to travel into the city. He attracted two of the state's wealthiest men as benefactors. One was Quaker patriot John Dickinson, by then state president (governor). Although Dickinson's twelve *Letters from a Farmer in Pennsylvania* had helped incite the Revolution, he had tried reconciling differences with the British by writing the Olive Branch Petition, which George III rejected. Dickinson nonetheless refused to sign the Declaration of Independence and objected to the war against Britain. Although he lost all influence in Congress, he remained a popular figure in the huge antiwar Quaker community that dominated the rural sections of Pennsylvania around Carlisle. After Dickinson and his wife pledged to donate their immense library to the new college, Rush named it Dickinson College rather than Rush College, as some benefactors had suggested. Rush realized the Dickinson name would draw more students and benefactors than his own name.

Two years later, after continually pressing the state legislature to expand higher education, Rush succeeded in founding a second college he named Franklin College,* in honor of Benjamin Franklin, in Lancaster, a center of German-speaking Pennsylvania.

Rush's vision for education reforms stretched beyond state borders, however, embracing a concept from Plato's *Republic* that was espoused by both George Washington and Thomas Jefferson: a national university from which every candidate for high office would have to graduate—to ensure the nation a source of well-educated leaders. Calling government "a science," Rush pointed out,

> We require certain qualifications in lawyers, physicians, and clergymen before we commit our property, our lives, our souls to their care. . . . Why

---

*In 1849, to bolster their sagging finances, Franklin College and Marshall College would merge to form today's Franklin and Marshall College.

then should we commit our country, which includes liberty, property, life, wives, and children, to men who cannot produce vouchers of their qualifications. . . . The nation should educate men specifically for government service . . . history, the law of nature and nations, civil law, the municipal laws of our country, and the principles of commerce . . . the principles and practice of agriculture and manufactures of all kinds.[16]

Nor did that end his dream for the nation—or his demands on lawmakers: "For the purpose of diffusing knowledge . . . every state, city, country, village, and township in the union should be tied together by means of the post office," he declared. "It should be a constant injunction to the postmasters to convey newspapers free of charge. . . . They are not only the vehicles of knowledge and intelligence, but the sentinels of liberty of our country."[17]

As Rush was inciting a social revolution in Philadelphia, Washington was in Yorktown, Virginia, putting an end to the political and military revolution with a savage charge by American troops that crushed British resistance. Two days later, on October 16, 1781, Lord Cornwallis, the British commander, proposed "a cessation of hostilities," and three days after that, he signed the articles of capitulation. With his surrender, fighting in the American War of Independence all but ended, allowing soldiers and civilians alike to return to normal peacetime pursuits.

"How the mighty have fallen," Rush rejoiced in a letter to Major General Nathanael Greene. "Cornwallis . . . is fallen, fallen, fallen. How honorable is our illustrious General [Washington]! Accept, my dear sir, my humble thanks as well as congratulations upon your successes in the South."[18]

Oddly enough, Rush failed to write to his friend John Adams, who was still serving as ambassador to France. Diplomatic obligations gave Adams little time to write personal letters to anyone but his immediate family. Indeed, over the next eight years, successive ambassadorial appointments to France and Great Britain would shrink the normally prolific Adams correspondence with Rush and other close friends to occasional short notes—usually introducing a British traveler to America who might need assistance.

Portrait and sketch of fifty-six-year-old Benjamin
Rush, M.D., as first Professor of Medicine at the University of Pennsylvania Medical School in 1802.

A month after the American victory at Yorktown, Benjamin Rush resumed teaching chemistry at the University of the State of Pennsylvania,
which the legislature had chartered to replace the old College of Philadelphia and which would later evolve into the now-private University of
Pennsylvania. By then, Julia had given birth to two more Rush children,
Anne Emily in 1779 and Richard in 1780. To Julia's immense distress, her
father, Benjamin Rush's good friend Richard Stockton, had succumbed
to cancer, and the Rushes named their third born after him.

    With an expanding brood, Rush gladly accepted a second post at the
university as professor of the institutes of medicine and clinical medicine

and later added a third professorship teaching the practice of physic (medicine). Over the next two decades, he would teach and train more than 3,000 students and physicians, more than any other medical school professor of his era in America. His theories of medicine and medical treatment became gospel to all he taught or who otherwise fell under his spell. Each student paid about $24 for the course—the theoretical equivalent of $750 today, in the early twenty-first century. In addition to classroom students, Rush accepted six apprentices a year as private students, with each paying about $100 a year (about $3,000 today) for a three-year apprenticeship. Rush also assumed charge of the university's medical clinics, where he taught and influenced several generations of apprentices.

Often called the "Sydenham of America," Rush did not limit his lectures to medicine and science. He devoted one lecture to the "Duties of a Physician," counseling future doctors, "Never give up hope. Hundreds of patients have recovered, who have been pronounced incurable, to the great disgrace of our profession." He urged his students to continue adding to their medical knowledge with further study and research.

Rush also lectured on medical ethics, warning students never to act against the interests of their patients. Although he said doctors were entitled to appropriate fees from those who could afford them, excessive fees often drove patients to consult quacks, whose ill-conceived treatments often threatened patient lives. He urged them to embrace simplicity "in your manners, dress and general conduct." He called the formal, pompous manners of some doctors reflective of little minds. "There is more than one way of playing the quack," he warned his students.

> A physician who assumes the character of a madman or a brute in his manners, or who conceals his fallibility by an affected gravity and taciturnity in his intercourse with his patients . . . like the quack, imposes upon the public.[19]

"He was uncommonly eloquent, correct, and interesting," one student remarked, while Dr. David Ramsay, a South Carolinian who had served in Congress, said Rush "mingled the most abstruse investigation with the most agreeable eloquence—the sprightliest sallies of imagination with the most profound disquisitions, and the whole was enlivened with anecdotes both pleasant and instructive."[20]

Rush warned students against drinking while on duty. "A physician in sickness is an always welcome visitor," he pointed out, "hence often solicited to partake of the usual sign of hospitality in this country . . . a draft of some strong liquor.

> Let me charge you to lay an early restraint upon yourselves. . . . Many physicians have been innocently led by it into habits of drunkenness. You will be in the more danger of falling into this vice from the great fatigue . . . to which you will be exposed. . . . But . . . strong drink affords only a temporary relief from those evils.[21]

Rush's practice, meanwhile, mushroomed, from eighteen patients in July 1778, his first month back in Philadelphia after quitting the military, to sixty-two patients in August and eighty in September. Soon he was seeing patients from dawn to dusk, adding six apprentices by the end of the year to help him care for patients. He ordered all drugs from reliable London pharmacies and held firm to the centuries-old belief that bloodletting and purging would rid the body of disease.

The second-century Greek physician Galen of Pergamon had asserted that human health depended on the proper balance of four "humors," or bodily fluids, which the fourth-century B.C. Greek physician Hippocrates had described as blood, yellow bile, black bile, and phlegm. Indeed, when blood sat undisturbed in a glass container for a length of time, it settled into four distinct layers: a dark layer at the bottom ("black bile"), a red layer above it ("blood"), a whitish layer above the blood ("phlegm"), and a yellowish layer Hippocrates had called "yellow bile" at the top.

Galen concluded that bloodletting corrected imbalances in the four humors by draining "bad" or infected blood from the body—along with the illnesses and diseases it carried.

In the last years of the eighteenth century, Rush and most other physicians still believed in Galen's theories, and many would continue to do so until the late nineteenth century. Although the invention of the microscope 200 years earlier had permitted discovery of bacteria in the blood,

Iatros [Greek: physician] using the bleeding technique advocated by the great second-century Greek physician Galen.

scientists assumed they were integral to blood structure and contents. Not until after Rush had died in 1813 did an Italian scientist recognize the "little worms" he saw through the microscope lens swimming in blood as independent microorganisms. And another fifty years would pass before scientists recognized the cellular structure of blood and bacteria as alien entities and potential disease carriers.

But throughout the 1700s and most of the 1800s, America's most renowned physicians found nothing to disabuse them of their belief in bloodletting and purging as virtual cure-alls, and parents routinely gave children with fevers emetics and purgatives to clean out their stomachs and intestines.

The fourth-century B.C. Greek physician Hippocrates is considered to this day to have been "father
of medicine."

"If your rheumatism be attended with a full or tense pulse," Rush
would advise his friend Timothy Pickering, who became secretary of state
late in Washington's second term, "lose ten ounces of blood [about one-
half pint of blood], and the day afterwards, take a smart purge . . . an
ounce of salts or fifteen grains of jalap* and ten of calomel.†" It was standard Rush.[22]

---

*A powerful purgative prepared from the root of a Mexican plant related to the
morning glory.
†Mercurous chloride, a powerful purgative which, unbeknownst to doctors then,
caused mercury poisoning when taken over long periods.

A late nineteenth-century daguerreotype shows how recently in the history of medicine American physicians continued using the bloodletting techniques developed by Benjamin Rush.

He and others often recommended less harsh treatments, of course—mostly for minor aches and pains produced by ordinary life-labors that were routine in the age before machines materialized to relieve humanity of its deadliest daily toil. He urged "riding on horseback" to cure "complaints of the breast" by a judge's wife. "Take her with you to all your courts. The more she roughs it on these journeys, the better."[23] And he counseled a gout patient to submit to "three or four punctures . . . in each foot with a lancet to drain off the water" from his swollen feet and legs—again, a common treatment then.

Unlike most of his colleagues, however, Rush was a century ahead of his time in many ways, treating the entire patient rather than limiting his ministrations to symptoms alone. A methodical observer, he took assiduous notes, which he collected, filed, and later combined into a historic, four-volume work on diseases and medical practice called *Medical Inquiries and Observations* (see Appendix B).*

Among the many startling advances in his work was his recognition of one of the most important phenomena in the history of modern medicine: "the influence of the will over the human body." Now recognized as psychosomatic medicine, he first described it informally to his apprentices and later in a 1789 lecture to medical students. Although he admitted he had yet to determine the full extent of that influence, he insisted, "The facts clearly prove the influence of the imagination and will upon diseases."[24]

As a corollary, Rush urged his apprentices and students not to ignore or dismiss the use of harmless folk remedies. Indeed, he kept a special notebook to list any and all folk remedies he found patients using—oil of amber on a lump of sugar for hiccoughs; salt in spirits for sties; salt dissolved in vinegar for warts. Rush told students he often used such remedies when a patient was "confident, bordering upon certainty, of their probable good effects. The success . . . has much oftener answered than disappointed my expectation.

> I have been disposed to attribute their recovery to the vigorous concurrence of the *will* in the action of the medicine. Does the will beget insensibility to cold, heat, hunger, and danger? Does it suspend pain? . . . I have only time to hint at this subject. Perhaps it would lead us, if we could trace it fully, to some very important discoveries in the future of diseases.[25]

Without knowing it, of course, Rush had also discovered the benefits of placebos and was laying the foundations of psychiatry—a century

---

*Rush published volume 1 in 1789, volume 2 in 1793, volume 3 in 1794, and volume 4 in 1796.

before Freud and other European physicians first considered the ties between mind and body. As almost all his professional contemporaries readily admitted, he was indeed the "greatest physician" in the land.

"His prescriptions were not confined to doses of medicine," a renowned colleague of Rush explained, "but to the regulation of the diet, air, dress, exercise, and mental action of his patients, so as to *prevent* disease and to make healthy men and women from invalids."[26]

In the first public acknowledgment by any physician of hypochondriasis, Rush told one patient, "I am disposed to believe [your case] to be of the hypochondriac disorder.

> The first remedy I would recommend is a total abstraction from business of all kinds for a few months . . . now and then join in a country dance. . . . Your diet should consist only of solid food. Beef and mutton . . . wild fowl, venison, and oysters. . . . Three or four glasses of sherry, Madeira, or Lisbon wines . . . every day. . . . Your belly should be frequently rubbed. . . . Your feet should be kept warm . . . assisted by the company of the ladies. . . . P.S. By following all the above directions, I think your recovery is certain."[27]

Rush went on to explore what he called "the reciprocal influence of the body and mind upon each other," or what is now recognized as behavioral medicine. Urging future physicians to note patient behavior as well as physical symptoms, he insisted that observation of the "various modes of combination and action between body and mind" were central to the "rescue of mental science from the usurpation of schoolmen and divines."[28]

Rush noted many instances of the mind acting on the body—especially in older patients. When the aging General Horatio Gates, erstwhile hero of Saratoga, complained of aches and pains, Rush warned Gates, "Old age has no cure." He nonetheless suggested "a warm bath three times a week or daily [and] . . . a clove of garlic every morning and evening" and urged Gates to "go to bed early."[29]

That America's greatest physician relied on such folk remedies as garlic shocked some patients, including Thomas Jefferson, who charged that doctors "destroy more of human life in one year than all the Robin Hoods,

Cartouches,* and Macheaths† do in a century." Jefferson argued that physicians "succeed each other like the dresses of the annual doll-babies from Paris, becoming . . . the vogue of the day. . . . The patient, treated on the fashionable theory, sometimes gets better in spite of the medicine."[30]

Undiscouraged by his friend's admonitions, Rush pursued his explorations of mind-body ties, examining the psychology and physiology of dreams, nightmares, and somnambulism—again, a century before Freud. With little or no earlier scientific research to examine, Rush, however, assumed dreams were pathological—manifestations of an underlying disease, or perhaps a disease themselves.

"As dreams are generally accompanied with distress," he told medical students, "their cure is an important object of the science of medicine. Their remote causes are an increase or diminution of stimuli upon the brain." Rush defined the stimuli as both corporeal and mental, with the former "an excessive quantity of aliments or drink or of both, of an offensive quality to the stomach." He listed other corporeal stimuli as unaccustomed head position, cold, heat, noises, a tight collar, fever, opium, a full bladder, and "inclination to go to stool." He cited the mental stimuli of dreams as "disquieting passions," difficult studies begun at bedtime, or an undue weight of business. Rush said diminution of habitual stimuli—deprivation of food, drink, exercise, work, etc.—could also produce dreams.

As for nightmares, he asserted, "This disease is induced by a stagnation of the blood in the brain, lungs, or heart. It occurs when sleep is more profound than natural." As with conventional dreams, he recommended bleeding or gentle purges as the best remedies.[31]

Thomas Jefferson continued objecting, however, telling Rush he did not believe in doctors or their medicines. Nature, he said, was the controlling force in human maladies—reestablishing order in the ailing human body "by exciting some salutary evacuation of the morbific matter.

"She brings on a crisis, by stools, vomiting, sweat, urine, expectoration, bleeding, &c.," Jefferson asserted, "which, for the most part, ends in the

---

*Nickname for French highwayman Louis Dominique Garthausen who, like Robin Hood, stole from the rich to aid the poor.
† A fictional chivalrous highwayman in John Gay's *The Beggar's Opera.*

restoration of healthy action." Jefferson said he believed that scientists would eventually find cures to diseases then thought incurable, but until then, physicians had best cease what he called "experiments on those who put their lives into [the physician's] hands."[32]

With his arrival at the pinnacle of the medical profession, Rush reaped rewards appropriate to his position, moving to a larger home and enlarging his family. Julia longed for more daughters, and, to their delight, their fourth child was indeed a girl—a fragile little baby they named Susanna. To their parents' distress, she died after only four and a half months.

Undeterred, the Rushes resolved to have another child, and, in 1783, Julia gave birth to another daughter, Elizabeth, who met the same tragic end as Susanna—in the same amount of time, four and a half months. Finally, a year after Elizabeth's death, their family misfortunes ended with the birth of robust little Mary and, two years after Mary's arrival, a strapping little boy they named James emerged as their fifth surviving child.

By the time Mary was born, however, the value of the money her father earned each month—often as much as £500 (arguably, about $30,000–$40,000 in the early twenty-first century)—was deteriorating rapidly, often losing half its face amount in thirty days. Rush, being the *famous* Dr. Rush and a *Founding Father*, sent an angry open letter to Congress via Philadelphia's leading newspaper, signing it with the pseudonym Leonidas, the legendary Spartan leader who fought and died in the Second Persian War.* Few congressmen doubted the author was anyone but Rush.

"I presume . . . to address you as servants of the public," he railed. "You have committed the expenditure of your money to too many hands . . . been too negligent in the choice of officers to whom you have committed the treasury of your country . . . neglected to call for frequent settlement of accounts."

Rush charged Congress with paying commissions to suppliers in exchange for bribes and opportunities for embezzlement that allowed congressmen to acquire fortunes. And by printing money instead of taxing the states to pay government bills, Congress, he said, had produced evils

---

*Prominent Americans signed letters and essays to periodicals with pseudonyms to avoid alienating friends and family and, just as important, to avoid libel suits and challenges to often deadly duels.

so great in number that "had I a thousand tongues, they would not be sufficient to exhaust the subject.

> You have established iniquity and unrighteousness. . . . See yonder poor widow surrounded with a family of children. . . . Her orphans are crying for bread, and she has none to give them. She has spent the last dollar of a handsome principal . . . at the rate of one shilling to the pound. . . . Let it be your first care to do justice to the widow and orphan. . . . Acknowledge the depreciation of your money . . . stop your presses.[33]

It was vintage Rush, "meddling in matters foreign to my profession" and taking pride in describing his revolutionary humanitarian efforts. But after treating the poor each day—after watching them die crushed by deprivation—he could not control his anger at a government made up of privileged men who profited from their public service while tolerating oppression and destitution. His anger increased as his own household began feeling the effects of the depreciation of money. His wife Julia, with five children by then and a sixth on the way, was having trouble paying her household expenses—as were tens of thousands of others in middling economic circumstances.

Across the nation, a majority of Revolutionary War veterans were mired in poverty, with most barely able to fill the needs of their families. Adding to the harsh effects of the plunging dollar were the crushing property taxes that state governments had imposed to pay for public services that the British government had provided before independence.

As farmers fell in arrears, sheriffs moved in, seizing untold numbers of properties for nonpayment of taxes. Growing numbers of farmers saw their lands, homes, livestock, and personal possessions—even tools of their trade—confiscated and auctioned off at prices too low to clear their debts. Hysterical wives and terrified children watched helplessly as sheriffs' deputies dragged their husbands and fathers off to debtors' prisons, where they languished indefinitely—unable to earn money to pay their debts and without tools to do so even if they won their freedom.

By 1786—five years after Yorktown—enraged farmers across the East took up pitchforks and rifles to protect their properties, firing at sheriffs who ventured too near. Reassembling their wartime companies, some set fire to debtors prisons, courthouses, and offices of county clerks. In western Massachusetts, former captain Daniel Shays, a destitute farmer struggling to keep his property, organized an army of 500 other farmers and marched to Springfield. Shouting "Close down the courts!" they shut the state supreme court before marching on the federal arsenal to arm themselves with more powerful weapons. Their battle cry echoed across the state, provoking farmers to march on courthouses in Cambridge, Concord, Worcester, Northampton, Taunton, and Great Barrington—and shut them down to prevent more foreclosures.

The farmer uprising in Massachusetts spread to other states. New Hampshire farmers marched to the state capital at Exeter, surrounded the legislature, and demanded forgiveness of all debts, return of all seized properties to former owners, and equitable distribution of property. A mob of farmers in Maryland burned down the Charles County courthouse, while farmers in Virginia burned down the King William County and New Kent County courthouses, east and north of Richmond.

As popular dissatisfaction swelled, some states were on the verge of warring with each other over conflicting territorial claims and economic disputes over international trade. "Different states have . . . views that sooner or later must involve the country in all the horrors of civil war," Secretary at War Henry Knox warned his old friend George Washington, whom he had served as chief of artillery during the Revolutionary War. "We are entirely destitute of those traits which should stamp us *one nation*."[34]

Discontent had built like seismic pressure beneath a steaming volcano, ready to erupt and spread its flesh-eating lava across the political landscape. The Rush demands for social and fiscal reforms had angered tens of thousands of his countrymen. As Rush had warned, the revolution was not over. It was just beginning.

CHAPTER 5

My Friends in Jails

JUST AS THE shots at Lexington had echoed in London's Parliament, the shots at Springfield reverberated in Congress and state capitols, even jolting the champions of state sovereignty into realizing the need to forestall the spread of anarchy by strengthening central government.

"It is indispensable," Washington had warned when he resigned his commission after the war, "that there should be lodged somewhere a Supreme Power to regulate and govern the general concerns of the Confederated Republic, without which the Union cannot be of long duration.

> There must be a faithful and pointed compliance on the part of every state with the demands of Congress . . . that whatever measures have a tendency to dissolve the Union . . . ought to be considered as hostile to the liberty and independency of America and the authors treated accordingly.[1]

Washington now pressed state leaders to act to save the nation in peace as they had in war. "There are errors in our national government," he complained to New York's John Jay, the influential Secretary for Foreign Affairs of the Confederation Congress. "Something must be done!"[2]

A number of those whom Benjamin Rush called "our enlightened men" in Congress had already given up hope for salvaging a union of all thirteen former colonies and were whispering proposals for separate

Eastern, Middle, and Southern confederacies united only by a defensive military alliance. New York and the New England states seemed ready to form an Eastern Confederacy with close ties to Britain, while New Jersey, Pennsylvania, Delaware, and Maryland favored a nonaligned Middle Confederacy. States to the south seemed ready to embrace a Southern Confederacy with an economy based on slave labor that would orbit within the French sphere of social and economic influence.

By late autumn 1786, however, "the commotions in New England," as Benjamin Rush called Shays's rebellion, had subsided, and after Congress reconvened early in the new year, it issued a call to all states to meet "for the sole and express purpose of revising the articles of confederation . . . [and] render the federal constitution adequate to the exigencies of government and the preservation of the union."[3]

On May 17, 1787, the first delegates appeared in Philadelphia to revise the Articles of Confederation—a tissue-thin document that had served as a constitution of sorts since the end of the revolution. Although state legislatures had elected more than seventy delegates to the convention, not enough arrived in Philadelphia to make up a quorum until May 25, when twenty-nine delegates appeared and elected George Washington the convention president.

Conspicuously absent from Benjamin Franklin's Pennsylvania delegation was the celebrated physician Benjamin Rush, M.D. Though beloved by Philadelphians, he had earned too much enmity among state legislators for constantly assailing their failure to improve the health, education, and welfare of Philadelphia's poor. The lawmakers punished him for his impudence by not only rejecting his proposals for free public schools and equal education rights for women but by denying him a seat at the Constitutional Convention. Personal tragedy compounded his political disappointment when Julia gave birth to a boy who emerged struggling for every breath for ten agonizing weeks before gasping his last. Baby William was their eighth child.

The insults the legislature had hurled at Rush and his social-reform proposals now spurred him to bypass what he called the "little men" who ruled the state by organizing or encouraging the organization of independent groups to further important social causes. In 1786, after the

Benjamin Rush, M.D., was a founder of the Philadelphia Dispensary (above), the first institution in the United States to offer free medical care to the poor.

legislature failed to act, Rush and a group of like-minded physicians and nurses opened the Philadelphia Dispensary, the first free clinic in America and the first dedicated solely to full-time medical care of the poor. Over the next five years, he and the other physicians at the Dispensary would treat nearly 8,000 patients free of charge, not including those too sick to leave their beds and requiring home care. His work at the Dispensary cut sharply into his time treating paying patients and reduced his income accordingly.

As the number of physicians with formal M.D. degrees increased, twenty-three of them joined Rush in organizing a formal medical society— the College of Physicians—to distinguish its members from the swarm of less-educated practitioners with minimum training or no training at all. Indeed, the college barred admission to many skilled physicians whose only training had been as apprentices, and it refused to consider untold numbers of untrained "empirics"—quacks peddling patent medicines and otherwise preying on the public.

Elected one of four directors, Rush gave a talk "On the Means of Promoting Medical Knowledge" at one of the society's first meetings in February 1787. Twenty-nine physicians joined the society during the first year, paying initiation fees of $8 each and annual dues of $2. It remains the oldest medical society in the United States, housing one of the world's most important medical libraries.*

With the Dispensary for the poor and the medical society on firm footings, Rush turned his attention to the antislavery society he had joined in 1774, the Pennsylvania Society for Promoting the Abolition of Slavery and the Relief of Free Negroes Unlawfully Held in Bondage. It had lain dormant during the British occupation of Philadelphia, and Rush now set about reviving it, convincing Benjamin Franklin to lend his prestige by serving as president. Rush would succeed Franklin as president after the latter's death.

In addition to social-action groups he sponsored or joined, Rush did what he did best: he walked Philadelphia's streets and back alleys— treating not only poor white patients but the free blacks he saw sitting against the walls of the meanest dwellings. Although freed by their masters, many former slaves—even the skilled—wandered Philadelphia idle and gripped by poverty, barred by deep-seated prejudices from jobs and other privileges of freemen, barred from praying in or even entering white churches to participate in services. Astonished and unable to comprehend such prejudice, Rush immediately meddled in the lives of African Americans, suggesting that they found a formal African Church to serve as an anchor for free-black society.

"Met about a dozen free blacks," Rush noted in his diary. "Read to them sundry articles of faith and a plan of church government which I had composed for them."[4]

---

*Although not founded until 1781, the Massachusetts Medical Society is the oldest continuously operating medical society in the United States.

After winning their approval, he fired a battery of fund-raising letters that reached across the Atlantic to Britain and attracted a £14 14s contribution from the British social activist Granville Sharp, who had just helped found Britain's Society for Effecting the Abolition of the Slave Trade and won election as its first president.

"The African Church goes on swimmingly," Rush wrote to Julia. "The President of the United States and Mr. Jefferson have both promised to send a contribution to it . . . and many others have subscribed liberally. *All will end well.*"[5] As usual, Julia and the children had fled Philadelphia's oppressive summer heat to the shade of the towering elms at her parents' home in Princeton, New Jersey. To Julia's growing annoyance, even war's end had not ended Rush's summertime absences from his family. He seemed to "meddle" in every conceivable service to society but that of his own family.

Five years after Rush had started raising funds, workers would complete the exterior of the African Episcopal Church of St. Thomas—the first Episcopal church in America for blacks—and Rush would note in his diary, "Attended a dinner to celebrate the raising of the roof of the African Church." He stood to give two toasts: "Peace on earth and good will to man" and "May African churches everywhere soon succeed African bondage." Diners responded by cheering three times for the second toast.

"To me," he wrote to Julia after completion of the African Church, "it will be a day to be remembered with pleasure as long as I live. In order that my other class of friends, the criminals in the jails . . . might sympathize a little in the joy of the day, I sent them a large wheelbarrow full of melons."[6]

While he was spearheading the drive to build an African church, Rush stepped up his earlier demands on the state legislature for prison reforms and joined the newly founded Philadelphia Society for Alleviating the Miseries of Public Prisons. Meeting with the society in Benjamin Franklin's house—a site that attracted members with substantial political power—Rush again assailed capital punishment as unchristian and called for ending all public punishments.

"A man who has lost his character at a whipping post has nothing valuable left to lose in society," he argued. "Public punishments leave scars which disfigure the whole character." He reserved much of his vitriol for so-called wheelbarrow laws—the use of forced convict labor for road building and other government construction projects. He called wheelbarrow laws harmful to society by making hard labor appear disreputable.

"We had a high scene before our doors," he wrote to Julia in Princeton. "One of the wheelbarrow men (who were all at work in cleaning our street) asked me for a penny.

> I told him I had none, but asked him if a draught of molasses beer would not be more acceptable to him. He answered in the affirmative . . . drank and commended it. A second asked to partake of it—and a third—till at last the whole company consisting of 12 or 13 partook of it to the amount of three jugs full. The keeper of the poor fellows stood by and in a good-natured way indulged them in a little rest while they drank their beer.[7]

Arguing that loss of liberty and contacts with family, friends, and society were punishment enough for most crimes, Rush sought inclusion of a house of worship in each prison, along with one or more gardens and workshops to teach prisoners trades and ensure their useful employment on release. The goal of prison, he contended, should be reformation. "The infamy of criminals is derived not so much from the remembrance of their crimes as from the recollection of the ignominy of their punishments."[8]

As delegates to the Constitutional Convention straggled into Philadelphia, Rush turned his attention back to national politics. Although he had not won election to the convention, he compensated for his absence on the floor by opening his dinner table to delegates. He was a Founding Father after all, and his views on government carried weight among others who had risked their lives with him by signing the Declaration of Independence and fighting in or actively supporting the war. His guests on June 24 included his old friend, Benjamin Franklin, and a new one, James Madison of Virginia. The guest of honor at his and every other table in town was always convention president George Washington, when he chose to appear.

"Dr. Franklin exhibits daily a spectacle of transcendent benevolence by attending the Convention punctually and even taking part in its business and deliberations," Rush wrote to his friend Richard Price, a Welsh minister and political radical who favored American independence and corresponded regularly with several American Founding Fathers. "He says it is the most august and respectable assembly he ever was in his life.

"You must not be surprised," Rush warned Price, "if you should hear of our new system of government meeting with some opposition. There are in all our states little characters whom a great and respectable government will sink into insignificance. These men will excite factions among us, but they will be of temporary duration. Time, necessity, and the gradual operation of reason will carry it. We are traveling fast into order and national happiness."[9]

The "new system of government" that convention delegates finally adopted represented a coup d'état. After four months of often-heated debate, the delegates ignored instructions from Congress to revise the Articles of Confederation and discarded them all in favor of a new constitution that created a new and powerful federal government. Three of the forty-two delegates still in attendance when the convention ended refused to sign, however. Thus, the 4,500-word finished document bore only thirty-nine signatures—scarcely representative of the original number of delegates, let alone "We the People," who, the preamble insists, created the seven articles of the document.

The first three articles defined the shape and powers of the three branches of the national government—the legislature, the executive, and the judiciary. Article IV forced the states to recognize each other's laws, give all citizens rights of citizenship in every state, and guarantee "a republican form of government" in every state.

Article V provided for amending the Constitution, and Article VI ranked laws by category, with the Constitution and US laws and foreign treaties ranking highest, state laws next, and local laws lowest. For the Constitution to take effect, Article VII required ratification by popularly elected conventions in at least nine of the thirteen states.

In the end, every state won a little and lost a little. No state won everything it sought, and, except for white adult male property owners, the vast majority of Americans obtained only a few benefits—despite its opening words of homage to "We the People." Women and children remained chattel, most blacks remained slaves, and most poor whites remained indentured or without properties of their own. Voting rights remained in the jurisdiction of the states, which barred women, blacks, and those who owned no property from voting and holding public office. To keep the South in the Union, the North agreed to prevent the new federal government from interfering with the slave trade for twenty years.

Few of the Founding Fathers—the signers of the Declaration of Independence—viewed the finished document as a triumph for man. Rush was an exception. "Our new federal government . . . will certainly be adopted . . . by *all* the states," he predicted in a letter to John Coakley Lettsom, an English physician, philanthropist, and abolitionist. "When this shall happen," he effused, "a citizen of the United States . . . will be a citizen of the freest, purest, and happiest government upon the face of the earth. . . . In the year one thousand eight hundred and eight there will be an end of the African trade in America."[10]

The only reservation Rush expressed about the final document was its failure to establish "an office for promoting and preserving perpetual peace in our country." Never wanting for quixotic fantasies to benefit mankind, Rush envisioned a cabinet post headed by a Secretary of Peace who would work to promote "universal and perpetual peace . . . and equal liberty."[11]

With the last signature on the Constitution, Franklin raced into the Pennsylvania state assembly to coax it to call a ratification convention before other states could act. If Pennsylvania was first to ratify the Constitution, he reasoned, Philadelphia would become the logical choice as the national capital—and enrich the city's entrepreneurs.

Rush made his presence felt in both the city government and the state assembly. Citing Franklin's efforts to make Philadelphia the national capital, Rush pressed the local city council to embrace social reforms that would make Philadelphia a model city and attract investments from around the world. To Rush's delight, Philadelphia's council responded.

"I have the pleasure of informing you that, from the influence of our Prison Society," Rush wrote somewhat optimistically to Lettsom, "a reformation has lately taken place in the jail of this city. . . . Our wheelbarrow law will probably be repealed. This I hope will pave the way for adoption of *solitude* and *labor* as the means of not only punishing but reforming criminals."[12]

Although translation of the Rush demands into state laws would take nearly seven years, Pennsylvania's legislature revised its criminal code to conform to many Rush suggestions. By 1794, the state had eliminated public punishments, converted parts of its prisons into reformatories, and eliminated the death penalty for all crimes but deliberate homicide. The reforms represented startling changes for eighteenth-century America.

Not all of America's Founding Fathers, however, were as sanguine about the new constitution as Rush. "This Constitution has been formed without the knowledge or idea of the people," Virginia's George Mason complained as the convention neared its end. "It is improper to say to the people, 'Take this or nothing,'" he declared in refusing to sign the document.[13] Virginia's Patrick Henry agreed. "What right had they to say, '*We, the People*?'" Henry demanded. "My political curiosity . . . leads me to ask who authorized them to speak the language of *We, the People* . . . The people gave them no power to use their name."[14]

"The Constitution is not free from imperfections," Washington conceded in rebutting Henry, "but there are as few radical defects in it as could well be expected considering . . . the diversity of interests that are to be attended to. As a constitutional door is opened for future amendments and alterations, I think it would be wise in the people to accept what is offered."[15]

For the new constitution to take effect, each state had to call a popularly elected ratification convention, and at least nine states would have to vote in its favor. As one of the most popular and visible men in Philadelphia, Rush easily won election to Pennsylvania's ratification convention. Although he found federalists held a large enough majority of votes to ensure ratification, they had not enough to silence furious opposition by antifederalists from western farm lands and keep them from postponing the inevitable longer than anticipated.

From the first, the antifederalists stalled voting on each amendment with endless and often heated arguments that spilled into the streets outside the State House and provoked violent brawls between mobs of federalists and antifederalists. In the convention hall, antifederalist delegates delayed attempts to vote by arguing that the Constitution, beginning as it did, "We the people," was a compact between individuals and "not between separate states enjoying independent power."[16]

"Ah-ha," rang the unmistakable brogue of Ben Franklin's friend, the Scottish-born James Wilson, who stood to rebut. "The secret is now disclosed, and it is discovered to be a dread that the boasted state sovereignties will under this system be disrobed of part of their power. Upon what principle is it contended that the sovereign power resides in the state governments? . . . My position is that the sovereign power resides in the people. They have not parted with it. . . . This Constitution stands upon this broad principle."[17]

Benjamin Rush agreed, all but shouting, "We stand here as representatives of the people. We were not appointed by the legislature. . . . The sovereignty of Pennsylvania is ceded to the United States. I have now a vote for members of Congress." Then pausing between each word for dramatic effect, he declared, "I am a citizen of every state."[18]

"I never heard anything so ridiculous," scoffed the Irish-born John Smilie, a staunch antifederalist from Fayette County in western Pennsylvania. Smilie argued that farmers in the West were threatening to secede from what they called "the state of Philadelphia." Wilson and Rush were "not the voice of the people of Pennsylvania," he insisted, "and were this convention assembled at another place . . . the sentiments of the citizens are different indeed."[19]

Infuriated, Wilson demanded to know how "the honorable gentleman from Fayette [County] claimed for the minority the merit of contending for the rights of mankind. . . . Who are the majority in this assembly? Are they not the people? Were they not elected by the people as well as the minority?"[20]

As cheers broke out across the hall, Rush also stood to answer Smilie. Visibly angry, he tried to control his emotions. Unlike Smilie, he had risked his life and fortune to proclaim his allegiance to American independence and was again risking his professional future by publicly supporting the Constitution.

Rush waited a moment too long, however. Before he could utter a word, the shout for a motion to vote echoed through the hall, ending the debate. With a two-thirds majority that included Rush, federalists ratified the Constitution on December 12, 1787, forty-six to twenty-three. To Franklin's disappointment, however, the debate had delayed ratification so long that it prevented Pennsylvania from being the first state to ratify. Tiny Delaware ceded its sovereignty to the new United States federal government on December 7, a week before Pennsylvania, and was the first state to join the Union. Its small size and disproportionately long shore-line had made union with other states essential to its defense and survival against foreign attack.

By February 1788, six states had ratified—Delaware, Pennsylvania, New Jersey, Georgia, Connecticut, and Massachusetts. In the spring of 1788, Maryland and South Carolina became the seventh and eighth states to ratify, and in June, New Hampshire and Virginia provided the decid-ing votes that made the new union of American states a reality.

With that, Benjamin Rush, M.D., decided again to abandon politics and return to full-time medicine. "I had resolved and repeatedly declared that I would close my political labors with the establishment of a safe and efficient general government," Rush affirmed. "I sought no honors and repeatedly refused the offer of profitable offices. . . . I was animated con-stantly by the belief that I was acting for the benefit of the whole world and of future ages."[21]

Although elated by ratification, Rush expressed bitterness about the political process needed to achieve it. In contrast to men in battle who "kill without hating each other," he said, political office-seekers "hate without killing, but in that hatred they commit murder every hour of their lives. . . . The first wish of my heart," the forty-four-year-old phy-sician avowed, "will be to devote the whole of my life to the peaceable pursuits of science and to the pleasures of social and domestic life."[22]

In March 1787, however, the aging Franklin asked Rush to assume a new post as secretary of the Pennsylvania Society for Promoting the Abo-lition of Slavery and the Relief of Free Negroes Unlawfully Held in Bond-age. Unable to resist a call to public service from the great Franklin, Rush again had to put aside his resolve to abandon politics. Within a year, his efforts on behalf of the society forced the Pennsylvania Assembly to relax its abolition law by ending the slave trade, if not slavery itself. Rush hailed the new law with a dramatic act: He purchased a slave and immediately announced his intention to emancipate him:

I, Benjamin Rush . . . having purchased a Negro slave named Wil-liam . . . and being fully satisfied that it is contrary to reason and religion to detain the said slave in bondage beyond such time as will be a just compensation for my having paid for him the full price of a slave for life, I do hereby declare that the said William shall be free from me and from all persons claiming under me on the twenty-fifth day of February . . . one thousand seven hundred and ninety-four.

The Rush declaration, of course, meant he would postpone William's emancipation for six years, but he did so because the youngster was "a drunkard" and illiterate, without means of independent self-support. In the six years that followed, Rush saw to William's education, but when the day of his emancipation arrived, William refused to leave the Rush household. He opted instead to stay on as a paid servant and gardener, remaining for ten years before finally going to sea to earn more money.

"He lived with me afterwards," Rush boasted, "and after returning from sea, always made my home his home."[23]

On July 2, 1788, Rush learned of his friend John Adams's return from Europe.

"Permit an old friend," Rush wrote with excitement, "to congratulate you upon your safe arrival in your native country. I rejoiced in reading of the respectful manner in which you were received by your fellow citizens." Indeed, Adams had no sooner returned to his farm in Braintree (now Quincy), Massachusetts, than his townsmen reelected him to his old seat in Congress—only to learn too late that the old Congress—and Adams's seat—had disappeared with ratification of the Constitution.

"I owe more than I can express to you for your excellent volumes upon government," Rush continued his effusive welcome, referring to an epic three-volume work Adams had written and published in London in 1787: *A Defense of the Constitutions of Government of the United States of America.*[*] One of the English-speaking world's classic works on government, it served as the basis for constitutions in nine of the thirteen American states after independence from Britain.

---

*The publisher of the first London edition in 1787 was cited as "C. Dilly in the Poultry." A subsequent edition was published in Philadelphia in 1797 by William Cobbett, publisher of *Porcupine's Gazette* [q.v.].

"They [the three volumes] shall be the *Alcoran* [Koran]* of my boys upon the great subject of political happiness," Rush told Adams.

> You have laid the world and posterity under great obligations by your remarks. I am not more satisfied of the truth of any one proposition in Euclid than I am of the truth of the leading propositions in government. Go on, my dear friend in removing the rubbish of ignorance and prejudice from the minds of your fellow citizens.[24]

Rush told Adams that the New Englander's "labors for your country are only beginning. I hope . . . I shall see you in one of the first posts of the new government." And Rush was sincere, adding the "compliments and congratulations to Mrs. Adams" from "my dear Mrs. Rush" and signing it, "your affectionate old friend and humble servant."[25]

Two days after writing to Adams, Rush participated in Philadelphia's enormous Federal Procession on July 4, 1788, "to celebrate the birth of a free government," as Rush put it. Church bells had greeted the dawn of the nation's new government, and, by 9:30, 17,000 marchers, representing every profession and trade, began the procession. Rush marched the three-mile route with a group of physicians—all of them M.D.s he had known and worked with for most of his professional life. Although New York staged a similar procession, it did not match Philadelphia's, which, according to Rush, produced "such a tide of joy as has seldom been felt in any age or any country.

> It was not to celebrate a victory obtained in blood . . . no city reduced to ashes . . . no news of slaughtered thousands brought Philadelphia together. It was to celebrate a triumph of knowledge over ignorance, of virtue over vice, and of liberty over slavery.[26]

---

*The *Alcoran*, a French translation of the *Koran* in 1647, was considered the definitive western translation of the Koran. It was translated from French into English in 1649.

Leading the procession was a gigantic float drawn by ten white horses carrying the "Federal Edifice," a dome supported by a circle of thirteen Corinthian columns, all but three of them eleven feet tall. Three shorter, unfinished columns represented New York, North Carolina, and Rhode Island, which had yet to ratify the Constitution. Atop the finished columns rose the four-foot-high dome, itself topped by a five-foot-tall cupola on which stood the figure of "Plenty," carrying a cornucopia.

The most remarkable aspect of the procession, Rush found, was the "solemn silence" of both marchers and spectators. The patriot, he said, "enjoyed a complete triumph, whether the objects of his patriotism were the security of liberty, the establishment of law, the protection of manufactures, or the extension of science in his country. The benevolent man saw a precedent established for forming free governments in every part of the world. The man of humanity contemplated the end of the distresses of his fellow citizens in the revival of commerce and agriculture."[27]

In the early afternoon of April 30, 1789, George Washington took the oath as the first President of the United States at Federal Hall in New York City. John Adams had already claimed his seat as Vice President in the Senate, no oath having been required by the Constitution. The new office gave Adams no executive or legislative powers, however, except the right to cast a vote in the Senate in event of a tie. He was not happy.

"My country," Adams barked, "has in its wisdom contrived for me the most insignificant office that ever the invention of man contrived or his imagination conceived."[28] His friend Dr. Rush was no happier. Elated at first by Adams's election to what seemed to be the second-highest office in the land, he soon grew disillusioned—and lonely: the adjournment of the Constitutional Convention had left Philadelphia a relative ghost town. The entire federal government had moved to New York—the President and the executive branch, along with both houses of Congress, and the hangers-on who sought favors from those in high places.

Only silence now filled Philadelphia streets where Washington's army had marched, where British and Hessian troops had caroused, where thousands of Americans had feted ratification of the Constitution—and where Rush now walked, a solitary figure, black satchel in hand, into the dark alleys of the poor to care for the sick and forgotten. For a brief time,

Rush became Philadelphia's elder statesman and de facto political leader to whom local officials turned for advice.

With Congress anchored in New York, Philadelphia's port and commerce suffered—along with Rush's medical practice. The majority of his wealthy patients, who usually paid their bills on demand, were congressmen and government officials, along with the professionals, businessmen, and contractors who derived their livelihoods from the government. Rush joined Benjamin Franklin and banker Robert Morris in writing to leading federal officials urging them to return the seat of government to Philadelphia.

"My principal objection [to New York as the seat of government]" Rush wrote to his friend Vice President Adams, "is the influence which a city contaminated by having been for seven years a garrison town to a corrupted British army must have upon the morals and manners of those men who are to form the character of our country. The citizens of Pennsylvania are truly republican. . . . I think this the most eligible spot in the Union for the present residence of Congress."[29]

Adams's reply startled Rush: "The influence which you may suppose I may have as President of the Senate will be found to be very little. My situation, where I was placed by the people at large not as the members were by their [state] legislatures, instead of giving me an influence, as you suppose, will prevent me from having any." He went on to call his election to the vice presidency "a curse rather than a blessing. . . . I never served the public one moment in my life but to the loss and injury of myself and my children, and I suffer as much by it at this moment as ever."[30]

Adams refused to suffer long, however. After calling the Senate to order, the irrepressible New Englander was unable to keep silent when the Senate began considering the question of how to address the President. Infatuated by the pomp of European courts he had visited as American minister, Adams jumped into the debate, suggesting "Your Highness" or "Your Most Benign Highness" as appropriate titles for the President. Although several senators protested Adams's blatant violation of accepted procedures by intruding in the debate, others directed themselves to the central question, stating that the President was neither a king nor an emperor and entitled to no title but "George." Certainly not George I, a few voices grumbled. Vice-President Adams suggested that the Senate and House name special committees to resolve differences. He warned that the United States would earn "the contempt, the scorn and the derision" of Europe's monarchies if Congress failed to give the President a distinctive title.

"You may depend on another thing," he warned. "The state government will always be uppermost in America in the minds of our own people 'till you give a superior title to your first national magistrate."[31]

When details of the debate reached Philadelphia, Rush could not contain himself: "I find you and I must agree to disagree or we must cease to discuss political questions," he wrote before going on to accuse his friend of "aping the corruptions of the British court.

> That you may never mistake any of my opinions or principles in my future letters, I shall add . . . that I am as much a republican as I was in 1775 and 6, that I consider hereditary monarchy and aristocracy as rebellion against nature, that I abhor titles and everything that belongs to pageantry in government. . . . To this detail of principles, I have only to add one . . . that I am, with as much affection and respect as I was in 1775 (notwithstanding our present contrariety of sentiment) your sincere friend and humble servant.[32]

Adams protested that he, like Rush, remained as much a republican as he had been in 1775, but insisted that, unlike Rush, but citing Rush's words, "I do not 'abhor titles nor the pageantry of government.'

> For there never was and never will be, because there never can be, any government without titles and pageantry. There is not a Quaker family in Pennsylvania governed without titles and pageantry; not a school, not a college, nor a club can be governed without them. . . . I really know not what you mean by aping the corruptions of the British court.

"No," Adams promised, "you and I will not cease to discuss political questions, but we will agree to disagree whenever we please." And he signed his letter pledging to remain "yours . . . with real friendship."[33]

An intimate friend of Benjamin Rush, John Adams won election to the new nation's second-highest office—only to find that the vice presidency was "the most insignificant office that ever the invention of man contrived or his imagination conceived." (HARVARD ART MUSEUM)

After more days of Senate debate, one member stunned his colleagues into puzzled silence by reminding them that the Constitution prohibited titles. After considerable throat clearing, members finally adopted the republican simplicity of "Mister President" as the proper form of address. Even Washington, after a dozen years of being addressed as "Your Excellency," seemed relieved, telling his son-in-law, "Happily the matter is now done with, I hope never to be revived."[34]

For John Adams, however, the matter was not done with—especially his argument with his friend Dr. Rush. "Without waiting for an answer to my last," he wrote to Rush, "I will take a little more notice of a sentiment in one of your letters. You say you abhor titles. I will take the familiar freedom of friendship to say I don't believe you.

> What would you say or think or feel if your own children, instead of calling you Sir or Father or Papa, should accost you with the title of "Ben"? Your servant comes in and, instead of saying "Master," cries "Ben!". . . . The principles of government are to be seen in every scene of human life. There is no person and no society to whom forms and titles are indifferent. . . . Family titles are necessary to family government; colonial titles were indispensable to colonial government, and we shall find national titles essential to national government.[35]

Before Rush could reply to Adams, Thomas Jefferson returned to America from France to serve as Washington's secretary of state and stopped in Philadelphia and met with Rush before traveling on to New York. Their meeting solidified a relationship formed at the signing of the Declaration of Independence and based on common, deeply held political and social beliefs. With their reunion in Philadelphia, their friendship grew almost as important to Rush as his friendship with Adams.

"We both deplored your attachment to monarchy," Rush wrote to Adams of his meeting with Jefferson, "and we both agreed that you had changed your principles since the year 1776." Rush cited as proof a letter Adams had written praising monarchical systems of government that was published in a Philadelphia newspaper. Adams denied ever having written the letter, and it has yet to be found.

"To the accusation against me," Adams protested to Rush, "I plead not guilty. . . . I deny an 'Attachment to Monarchy' and I deny that I have changed my principles since 1776."

During his meeting with Rush, Secretary of State Jefferson described his fellow Virginian, Congressman James Madison, as "the greatest man in the world," and Rush immediately made a point of reestablishing contact with Madison as part of an effort led by Benjamin Franklin to coax Congress into moving the federal government back to Philadelphia immediately.

In the meantime, a decline in his income left Rush no choice but to push politics aside to focus on sustaining his medical practice and fulfilling his teaching responsibilities. As usual, he rose at dawn and worked until late evening. Without other means of communication, patients and their relatives often left notes under his door to summon his help. In addition to patients in Philadelphia, Rush treated dozens of patients across the nation by mail.

"Calculating upon your charity," wrote a patient from Petersburg, Virginia, "I avail myself of this method of stating to you my case. . . . I have been too long acquainted with your tenderness of heart and too often heard of your attention to the afflictions of your fellow creatures to doubt your readiness to give me your advice and direction." The supplicant complained of having suffered persistent headaches for seven years.

Besides patients, other doctors—many of them former students—often wrote to Rush describing symptoms they were unable to diagnose.

"My business continues to be extensive," Rush wrote on July 6, 1789, to his cousin Elisha Hall, also a physician, "but . . . constant public and private pursuits since the year 1774 have nearly worn me out. . . . My dear Mrs. Rush on the 3rd of this month added a 4th boy in my family. We now have six children living . . . John 12 years old, Emily 10, Richard 8, Mary 5, James 3, and Benjamin 3 days old. We have buried three children . . . Susan, Elizabeth, and William."[36]

Three weeks later, Rush and his wife would bury baby Benjamin as well. Although he had been with his wife at Benjamin's birth, Rush continued spending most of his summer alone in Philadelphia much of the time, while Julia and the children took shelter from summer in the cool of her family's country home in Princeton, New Jersey. Knowing how annoyed she grew at his long, continuing absences, Rush wrote to her almost every night during their separation.

"Solitude," he wrote, citing a French author, "would be delightful had I anybody with me to whom I might impart the pleasure I derive from it.

I feel the force of it every hour of the day. To a mind like mine . . . it is a peculiar hardship to lose at once a domestic friend, a wife, and five children to most of whom I had been in the habits of imparting every thought as soon as it rose in my mind. . . . Adieu, thou dear right side of my heart. . . . With love as usual.[37]

Without her father or husband to manage the house and property—Julia Rush seized the reins at Morven, limiting her letters to her husband to short, light-hearted family matters, implying that she was learning to do quite well running the estate and raising a family without a husband. "Dicky [three-year-old Richard] coughs very much, but he looks very well and he has a great appetite," she wrote to her husband. "The family all join in love to you. Let me hear from you very often."[38]

In his effort to lure the federal government back to Philadelphia, Rush scored another triumph in his continuing war against social injustice by rallying a group of powerful Philadelphians to support his plan for free universal education that would elevate skills levels of the city's workforce.

"We met last night about our free schools," he wrote to Julia: "A plan was adopted that cannot fail (heaven continuing to smile upon the undertaking). . . . O! Virtue, Virtue, who would not follow thee blindfold! . . . Methinks I hear you cry out after reading this, 'Alas! My poor husband! He is as crazy as ever.'"[39]

In 1791, the College of Philadelphia merged with the University of the State of Pennsylvania to become the University of Pennsylvania, and the new institution named Rush professor of the institutes of medicine and clinical medicine (professor of medicine in twenty-first-century terms). Among the thousands of students he would teach in the years that followed were two of his own sons, John and James.

"There are three ways of acquiring medical knowledge," Rush opined to his students, "reading books, hearing lectures, observing diseases as they occur. . . . Diseases are much more instructing than books; as well might a man attempt to swim by reading as practice medicine from books. . . . The good physician . . . combines observation and reasoning."[40]

In addition to lecturing, Rush began collating his notes and writing and publishing definitive works on diseases and their treatments. He had started keeping notebooks a decade earlier, detailing each patient and his or her disease and treatment. He noted every environmental factor that could possibly have affected the outbreak and medical response—the time of year, the weather, condition of crops, tides, conditions in the streets, the patient's residence and neighborhood, etc.

Rush noted that the incidence of disease in Philadelphia increased as filth and stagnant water accumulated in the streets, and he noted a commensurate decline after the city cleaned its streets. Ironically, Rush associated accumulation of stagnant water in streets with outbreaks of disease after the spring and early summer rains, but he did not link either the stagnant water or the increased incidence of disease to the emergence of mosquitoes and other insects after the rains. Disease, he continued to believe, was carried by foul air via the respiratory system into the human body, emerging as fever.

By 1791, he expanded the scope of his work to include treatment of injuries, hygiene, medical care in general—even moral behavior—and, in 1792, he published the second volume of what would grow into his four-volume epic, *Medical Inquiries and Observations*. It would become the basic text—indeed the Bible—of medical practice in the United States for the next century.

In addition to practicing medicine and writing his classic text on medicine and medical practice, Rush continued hectoring the Pennsylvania legislature for social reforms. He added cleaner streets and other public health measures to his list of demands on government, along with improved treatment of prisoners. After a visit to one jail, he expanded the scope of his demands to include reforms in the treatment of the insane. Until then, Philadelphia authorities had sent the homeless poor and any of the insane who "raised the devil" to prisons, almshouses, or the Pennsylvania Hospital. The mildly insane were left to wander the streets on their own if they left others alone, did no damage to property, and showed no evidence of behaving under the spell of Satan or other evil spirits.

Founded in 1751 by Benjamin Franklin, the original Pennsylvania Hospital had been the first hospital in America to designate a specific area for treatment of the poor and insane, but when Rush joined the hospital, he found the treatment area nothing but a filthy basement prison. Basement cells, he scolded hospital directors, were frigid in winter, insufferably hot in summer, unventilated and malodorous the year-around, with patients often manacled or chained by their waists to iron rings embedded in the floors or walls of cold, damp basement cells. Lying in their own excreta, half-starved, and whipped for violating hospital rules if they complained, they either sank deeper into black holes of mania or died. Attendants shaved patient heads regularly to keep them from tearing at their scalps to scratch lice. Keepers also bled and purged hyperactive inmates into insensibility to tranquilize them. Often, the guards charged fees to curious passers-by to open the cellar doors and let them stare at or even poke the helpless maniacs.

Rush called the hospital's treatment not only cruel but useless. Worse, he called the treatment "dishonorable both to the science and the humanity of the city of Philadelphia." Eager to build the reputation of the hospital as America's premier facility, the directors finally yielded to the Rush demand for reforms.

Responding like a maniac himself, Rush charged down the cellar stairs, ripped whips from the hands of aides and ordered them to unchain all but the most violent patients. Rush was about to stage another of his revolutions. Even the maniacs stood silent, staring at the enraged physician, uncertain what he would do to them.

Until Benjamin Rush put vast reforms in place, the insane sat chained and manacled in dark cellars, wallowing in their own filth, subject to whipping by sadistic guards.

CHAPTER 6

Murder by War

To CALM RUSH's evident anger, embarrassed directors of the Pennsylvania Hospital in Philadelphia gave him full charge of its almost three dozen maniacal patients. Whatever the outcome, they reasoned, it would be his responsibility, not theirs, and necessarily end his criticisms.

"I have lately obtained the exclusive care of the maniacal patients in our hospital," Rush boasted to British philanthropist John Coakley Lettsom. "They amount at present to 34. The remedies on which I place my chief dependence are the warm and cold baths. . . . I shall carefully record the effects of these and other remedies upon my patients."[1]

Not content with simply ending cruel treatment of the mentally ill, Rush established the first standards of hygiene in the hospital, ordering attendants to bathe patients regularly and keep beds and linens spotlessly clean. He dismissed aides who would not or could not respond to patients with care and kindness. He introduced and integrated recreational activities—quoits, chess, checkers, etc.—for his patients, and, for the first time in American medical history, he developed and provided occupational therapy—spinning, sewing, and churning for women; carpentry and other crafts for men—as an integral part of treatment.

As he studied his patients, he developed "a new theory of mania" that he described to a colleague in London: "I suppose it [mania] in nearly all cases to be accompanied by inflammation in the brain. This, the water, blood, pus, and hardness found in the brain after death all demonstrate. . . . The hardness is a real scirrhus [tumor]. In consequence of the adoption of this theory, I have lately cured three deplorable cases of madness by copious bleeding (100 ounces in one case [more than six pints']). It was aided afterwards by cold baths."[2]

His work with maniacal patients spurred him to begin classifying different types of mental illness, thus taking the first, hesitant steps in an entirely new field of medicine that would later be called "psychiatry."

Rush, however, was far from satisfied with the progress he was making in treating the insane. As a deeply committed humanitarian, he saw reforms in the physical treatment of the mentally ill as only one step in a broad sweep of reforms in the treatment of all the disadvantaged—women, children, the chronically ill, the addicted, the poor, and the enslaved, as well as the mentally ill. "The commerce in African slaves has breathed its last in Pennsylvania," he crowed to Jeremy Belknap, the Harvard-educated Boston clergyman.

> My next object shall be the extirpation of the *abuse* of spirituous liquors. I am encouraged by the success that has finally attended the exertions of the friends of universal freedom and justice to go on in my romantic schemes (as they have often been called) of serving my fellow countrymen. . . . The effects of this perseverance begin already to show themselves in our state. Associations are forming in many places to give no spirits at the ensuing harvest. . . . Many storekeepers among the Quakers now refuse to buy or sell spirituous liquors.[3]

In effect, Rush intended bypassing reluctant state legislators by effecting his "romantic schemes" through popular action.

---

*The average adult has about ten pints of blood in his body. Loss of six pints would probably leave the otherwise maniacal patient in hemorrhagic shock—weak, sweating, compliant, and probably too subdued to display manic behavior. Death can ensue, however, after the loss of as few as four pints of blood (40 percent of the body's blood supply), depending on other factors such as the rate of blood loss.

In 1790, Rush reissued his tract, *An Inquiry into the Effects of Spirituous Liquors upon the Human Body and Their Influence upon Society*, retitling it *An Inquiry into the Effects of Spirituous Liquors on the Human Body and the Mind*.[4] Sneered at during its first appearance, the book received a huge welcome from the expanding temperance movement and the growing Quaker communities across the north. Quakers alone would buy more than 170,000 copies in the decades following its publication.

"Spirituous liquors destroy more lives than the sword," Rush thundered. "War has its intervals of destruction, but spirits operate at all times and seasons upon human life. . . . A people corrupted with strong drink cannot long be a free people." Acknowledged after his death as "instaurator" of the temperance movement, he hoped to make drunkards as "infamous" in society as liars and thieves "and the use of spirits as uncommon in families as a drink made of a solution of arsenic or a decoction of hemlock."[5]

Rush's campaign against hard liquor coincided with his determination to require Bible study in schools. In the winter of 1790 he wrote the pamphlet *A Defense of the Use of the Bible as a School Book*. Insisting that the Bible was appropriate for study in a secular society, he declared, "This divine book, above all others, favors equality among mankind, respect for just laws, and all those other sober and frugal virtues which constitute the soul of republicanism."[6]

A year later, Rush helped found the Sunday School Society, which opened the first nonsectarian Sunday school in the United States. An English institution founded in 1780, the Sunday School Society sought to provide both secular and religious education to lower-economic-class children who worked in factories during the week and could not attend England's secular common schools. Sunday schools first appeared along the American frontier in the 1790s, when churches were the first public buildings and ministers were among the few literate community members with time to spare from the fields to teach children. Sunday schools quickly became the only schools in rural America, and, in 1808, Rush introduced the institution into Philadelphia slums, which was as much an educational wilderness as the frontier. He then helped found the Philadelphia Bible Society, whose seminary would train young men for the ministry, for teaching in Sunday schools, and for ministering to prisoners. He reported his progress in each area of social reform in regular letters to English philanthropist John Howard, a pioneer of British prison reforms.

"I . . . have the pleasure to inform you," he told Howard in one report, "that such have been the effects of the numerous publications and religious associations . . . respecting the mischievous consequence of spirituous liquors . . . that not more than one-half the quantity of them is consumed now that was consumed four or five years ago in the middle and eastern states of America."[7]

Rush was overoptimistic, however. In attributing the decline in alcohol consumption to his temperance crusade, he ignored the effects of Treasury Secretary Alexander Hamilton's imposition of a 25 percent tax on liquor distillers. After Hamilton had taken office in 1789, Congress ordered him to study and report on the new government's finances. He found it had inherited foreign debts of more than $11.7 million from the Revolutionary War and domestic debts of about $42.4 million, including back pay owed to Revolutionary War veterans, debts to wartime suppliers, unpaid interest, outstanding bonds, and outstanding currency. Debts of individual states totaled an additional $12.7 million, bringing the total national debt to nearly $70 million. The result was a collapse in the value of the American dollar, or "continental," to about two and one-half cents.

Arguing that the Revolutionary War had been a national enterprise, Hamilton proposed that the national government assume all state war debts and put each of the states on a sound financial footing. The states could then reduce property taxes and calm the political, social, and economic turmoil that had spawned Shays's Rebellion. To cover some costs of assuming state debts, Hamilton suggested a new 25 percent federal tax on liquor distillers—the first national tax in the new nation. The "whisky tax," he reasoned, would win widespread support from forces supported by Rush, namely, the antiliquor churchgoers, the growing temperance movement Rush had spawned, and those physicians who, like Rush, saw spirits as a danger to public health.

He was wrong on all counts.

Rush startled Hamilton by opposing the whisky tax and, in effect, contradicting his own previous efforts to outlaw "spirituous liquors." His contradictory stand stemmed in part from his need to retain support of congressional republicans for his other humanitarian projects. House leader James Madison, Secretary of State Thomas Jefferson, and other republicans who had exhibited tacit support for most of Rush's humanitarian projects all opposed the whisky tax, while Hamilton and other Federalist leaders who supported the tax had consistently opposed the Rush projects as impractical and dangerous to the nation's social fabric. In opposing the whisky tax, Rush cemented his ties to Madison but alienated the sensitive Hamilton, who never forgot a political slight and would soon return the favor.

After Madison moved for an indefinite postponement of a vote on Hamilton's scheme, Rush wrote to Madison, congratulating him and predicting that the next congressional election would oust those who favored Hamilton's whisky tax. Whisky, he reasoned correctly, was fundamental to the western farm economy. Without roads to transport grain in bulk across the Appalachian Mountains to eastern markets, farmers to the west of those mountains distilled their grain into whisky, which they could carry in kegs and jugs by packhorse or mule on mountain trails to the East. Hamilton's 25 percent tax, however, threatened to siphon all the profits from even the most efficient stills. For most farmers, the whisky tax was nothing less than legalized government theft: it would bankrupt them and allow bankers to foreclose on their farms and reap the profits from reselling the land.

"Congratulations for the honor you have done to the claims of justice and patriotism by your motion," Rush wrote to Madison after the Virginia congressman postponed the voting on Hamilton's tax. "The small number of the minority that rose to support it does not lessen its merit. The decision upon that great question will leave a stain upon our country. . . . History will decide very differently upon it."[8]

With Hamilton and Madison at an impasse over the whisky tax, Secretary of State Thomas Jefferson came up with a compromise. Congressmen and Senators from southern states had found travel north to New York so difficult that many refused to attend unless Congress relocated at a more convenient site. With George Washington lurking in the shadows, Madison reluctantly agreed to support Hamilton's unpopular economic plan, including the whisky tax, if Hamilton agreed to support moving the capital to a point midway between north and south. For that purpose, Maryland and Virginia agreed to cede to the federal government an uninhabitable, wooded marsh bordering the Potomac River on the border between the two states. Hamilton agreed, and, despite angry objections by many members, a majority in Congress passed the whisky tax and voted to return south to Philadelphia until 1800, when a new capital city would be ready to host the government on the banks of the Potomac River.

Across the West, farmers refused to pay the tax, however, and President Washington prepared to send troops across the Alleghenies to crush tax revolts. Nor were farmers alone in their opposition to the whisky tax. Whisky was the most widely consumed beverage in America—not just for pleasure but for "medicinal" purposes. Quack doctors peddled whisky-based patent medicines from horse-drawn wagons that passed through every town, village, and hamlet in the nation, and even M.D.s like Rush occasionally prescribed whisky for its calming effects on certain patients. Whisky, moreover, served as a form of currency. Small towns and rural areas without access to specie functioned by bartering goods and services, with buyers and sellers routinely trading "white lightning" in various-sized jugs for dry goods and other provisions as well as services. In the end, Hamilton's whisky tax would affect almost all but the wealthiest Americans.

"What was it that caused the Revolution if it was not this?" railed an angry "Republican" to Philadelphia's *National Gazette*.

Although angry Congressmen continued posting objections in the days that followed, their complaints suddenly ended when news arrived to cast a pall of silence across the capital and the entire nation: Benjamin Franklin was dead.

"April 18 [1790]," the entry in Rush's diary began.

> Last evening at 11 o'clock died the venerable Dr. Franklin . . . in his 85th year. . . . To record all the exploits of his [Franklin's] benevolence and the discoveries of his genius would employ a volume. . . . He possessed his reason to the last day of his life . . . Dr. Franklin's last publication was to ridicule a defense of slavery of Negroes by [James] Jackson, a member of Congress [from Georgia].[9]

Three days later, Rush joined 20,000 other mourners at Franklin's funeral, but not before visiting Franklin's house to view the corpse. "It was
much reduced, but not changed. Had his beard been shaved after his
death, he would have looked like himself. . . . I obtained a promise of a
lock of his hair, which I afterward procured and sent . . . some of it to the
Marquis of Fayette."[10]

Apart from the emotional loss, Franklin's death presaged an economic
loss for Philadelphia and the vast farmlands and wilderness that stretched
westward to the Allegheny Mountains. For years, Franklin had been the
chief promoter of European emigration to Pennsylvania, promising untold wealth to those who risked sailing the Atlantic to establish businesses
or buy land in Pennsylvania. As he did with many of Franklin's philan-
thropic activities, Rush stepped in to fill the void, writing and publishing
a remarkable portrait of America to attract potential settlers from Europe.

Called *Information to Europeans Who Are Disposed to Migrate to the
United States*, the Rush pamphlet is a historic landmark of sorts, standing
alone as a description of the young nation by one of the few Founding
Fathers who were not members of the elite, wealthy, slave-owning, landed
gentry. A farmer's son who had metamorphosed into a scientist and activist humanitarian, he had worked among and befriended the poor and
the working class, and he begins his essay by urging "men of independent
fortunes . . . not to come to America."

Instead, he called on "cultivators of the earth" to come, along with
"mechanics and manufacturers of every description . . . laborers . . . persons willing to indent themselves . . . gentlemen of the learned professions . . . [and] schoolmasters of good capacities and fair characters."
He promised liberty and opportunity for those with habits of "sobriety,
industry, and economy," and, he added, a recent act of Congress had
reduced to two years the time of residence "to entitle foreigners of good
character to all the privileges of citizenship.

"No state in the Union afforded greater resources than Pennsylvania,"
he declared. "There can be no doubt that Pennsylvania will always maintain the first rank for national prosperity and happiness in the United
States."[11] Left unsaid was the prosperity that incoming settlers would reap
from the return of the federal government to Philadelphia.

Although New England congressmen were less than pleased by the government's plan to move southward to Philadelphia, southerners were delighted—as was John Adams's wife, Abigail. Not only did she find a fast friend and intellectual peer in Julia Rush, she found Benjamin Rush "a kind friend as well as physician. . . . I am upon such an intimate footing with the doctor since his practice in our family."[12] For Secretary of State Jefferson, the return of government to Philadelphia allowed him to renew his ties to the American Philosophical Society, which he had joined when he was a member of the Confederation Congress in the early 1780s. His discussions with Rush at society proceedings cemented an intimate friendship between the two that would last until Rush's death in 1813.

With the federal government's return to Philadelphia, however, came the first great international crisis of President George Washington's administration: the outbreak of the French Revolution. Although intervention in the American Revolution had nearly bankrupted the French government, the French king had hoped American victory and independence from Britain would allow France to replace Britain as America's most important trading partner. But American merchants and many of their clients were largely British in origin, and they preferred British goods to French goods. Moreover, most American merchants were too used to dealing in a language and currency they understood. They often found it too difficult to deal with the French—and impossible to speak the language.

A decade after the Franco-American victory at Yorktown, the French had accumulated a trade deficit with the United States of 65.5 million livres, which combined with the 140 million livres spent on the American Revolution to collapse the French economy. In addition to the economic price the French paid for the American Revolution, they paid a steep social price when French soldiers, sailors, and public officials returned home from America having witnessed and experienced individual liberties for the first time. As British statesman Edmund Burke put it, "They imbibed a love of freedom nearly incompatible with royalty."[13]

With tens of thousands of Frenchmen unemployed and facing starvation, mob frenzy engulfed France. Rioters raged through cities, towns, and villages, looting and burning chateaux, manors, and any other structures that smacked of aristocratic plenty. Thomas Jefferson called the French Revolution "an illumination of the human mind,"[14] while Rush—usually an outspoken champion of republicanism—postponed judgment.

The frenzy of the French Revolution did not stop at the frontier of mainland France.

Inspired by slogans and songs of the revolution in metropolitan France, black Haitians slaughtered every white man, woman, and child they could find on their island in the Caribbean. By mid-summer of 1791, former slaves controlled one-third of the French colony and cut off the flow of sugar to mainland France. The violence set loose a tide of refugees who fled as far as they could run, sail, or swim.

As some washed onto South Carolina sands, they carried tales of mass butchery, of the fiery destruction of the city of Cap François, and of a raging yellow fever epidemic that was felling thousands. A boatload of refugees spilled its human cargo onto Philadelphia piers, along with enough cases of influenza and scarlet fever to unleash epidemics of both diseases. As Benjamin Rush scrambled from house to house bleeding and purging the stricken, quacks by the dozens trotted into town selling patent medicines that were nothing more than "white lightening" flavored with fruit or herbs. A healthy dose left many patients dead drunk—if not dead—in city alleyways.

In the end, relatively few died of influenza, scarlet fever, or patent medicines, and city leaders hailed Rush as a brilliant and heroic physician who had put himself at risk stamping out the deadly diseases. Adding to his joy from accolades in 1791 was the birth of another boy—a healthy child this time, whom he and Julia again named Benjamin.

The French Revolution, however, disrupted trade between France and the United States, further undermining the French economy and impoverishing the French people. After a brief flirtation with a constitutional monarchy, a swarm of madmen who called themselves Jacobins smashed their way into the French National Assembly, seized control of government, and imprisoned the king and royal family. To ease food shortages at home, they sent armies across French borders into Belgium and Germany to strip farmlands of fruits, vegetables, and livestock for transport to the starving French population.

"We will not be satisfied until Europe—all Europe—is aflame," screamed the revolutionary leader of the moment, Jacques-Pierre Brissot de Warville, a mediocre journalist and pamphleteer who envisioned himself a prophet. "France has been called to lead a gigantic Revolution [and] worldwide uprising to liberate the oppressed peoples of the world," he screamed. "All Europe, as far as Moscow, will be Gallicized, communized, and Jacobinized."[15]

Thomas Jefferson embraced the new French dictum, even proposing "mutual naturalization" of French and American merchants to permit them to buy and sell goods duty-free in both countries as citizens of both nations. "The liberty of the whole earth depends on the success of the French Revolution," Jefferson proclaimed. "I would have seen half the earth devastated rather than it should have failed."[16]

Rush was less enthusiastic. Although not oblivious to events in France, he faced so many daily obligations he had little time to visit, let alone discuss international affairs, with his political friends. Vice President Adams and his family were exceptions, of course, and Rush's presence proved a comfort to Abigail, whose rheumatic agonies spurred the doctor to administer periodic bleeding. In the winter of 1792, a bout with "a violent fever" combined with her rheumatism to lay her low for six weeks, during which Dr. Rush bled her so often she complained, "I have scarcely any flesh left in comparison to what I was."[17] It was only after three months and the arrival of warm spring weather that she began to recover and, at the first opportunity, fled to her beloved Massachusetts farm near Boston, far from the lancet stings of her friend Dr. Rush.

By then, Rush's medical practice—if not his income—had expanded again. In addition to lecturing at the university, he attended to the poor at the Dispensary, took charge of treating the insane at the hospital, saw and treated prisoners at the jail, attended board meetings of Dickinson College and Franklin College, hectored Pennsylvania Hospital trustees to support new and different treatments for the insane, and lobbied state legislators to provide universal free public education, expand reforms in prisons, and improve the lot of the poor by subsidizing hospitals and health care and cleaning city streets of sewerage and garbage. The number of his meetings and visits each day seemed endless. He was everywhere, bobbing up at every corner in the city, sprinting in or out of every doorway to see if all was well and whether he could help.

In 1791, the state legislature finally succumbed to his campaign to further ease the plight of the insane by appropriating $15,000 to construct a separate building for them at the Pennsylvania Hospital. In an equally startling surrender to Rush, the legislature subsequently voted to begin establishing the free schools he had proposed.

Just as the first such schools opened in Philadelphia, the French Revolutionary government in Paris took two steps that threatened to set Philadelphia streets ariot. It ordered the execution of King Louis XVI and declared war on Britain. Britain responded by blockading French ports and seizing every American and other foreign ship bound for those ports. In seizing American ships, the British impressed hundreds of American seamen and English-speaking passengers into the British navy.* France responded by blockading British ports and seizing American and other foreign ships trying to deliver goods to British ports.

Americans immediately divided into two camps, with many outraged by British impressments of American citizens and others outraged at the French for killing a king who had helped Americans overthrow British rule a dozen years earlier. Jefferson deplored "as much as anybody" the death of innocents, but argued that "the tree of liberty must be refreshed from time to time with the blood of patriots and tyrants."[18]

Initially, Rush called Louis XVI "the best king in Europe" and condemned his execution as "unjust, unconstitutional, illegal, impolitic, and cruel in the highest degree."[19] Unwilling to alienate his friend Jefferson, however, the doctor qualified his condemnation of French regicide by adding, "One wicked act does not justify another. We deplore and reprobate likewise the interference of Great Britain in the dispute."[20]

As a Founding Father, Rush was still a powerful behind-the-scenes activist, walking in and out of the Statehouse at will, mingling with and chatting with federal and state officials—all without playing a visible

---

*Impressment—the physical abduction of men for forced service in the navy—began along British waterfronts and evolved into that nation's eighteenth-century equivalent of the modern military draft.

on-stage role in the political theater. The first indication that he might return to center stage, however, came when he charged Secretary of War Henry Knox*—and by implication President Washington—with plotting "murder by war" against France.

Although Washington's cabinet had split on the subject, Knox and Hamilton favored American intervention on the side of Britain. Rush took dead aim at the Anglophile Knox.

"He seems to consider man," Rush said of Knox, "as created not to cultivate the earth or to be happy in any of the pursuits of civilized life but *to carry a musket, to wear a regimental coat,* and *to kill or be killed.* [His italics.] Half the money demanded by General Knox, [if] spent on establishing free schools and in teaching our young people industry and morality, would extirpate war forever from the United States."[21]

Couched in his attack on Knox, a longtime intimate of Washington, were Rush's lingering doubts about the President's executive abilities. Still puzzled about Washington's unwillingness as commanding general in the Revolutionary War to address military-hospital scandals, Rush now saw Washington's obeisance to Knox as further evidence of his inadequacies.

"Last night I had a visit from Dr. Rush, whose tongue ran for an hour," Vice President Adams wrote to his wife Abigail, who now lived in their home near Boston. Like many wives in Washington, the novelty of capital life had worn thin, and she had abandoned Washington City's cold political environment and returned to the warmth and familiar family heirlooms of home. "He got disaffected to Washington during the war," Adams's letter to Abigail continued. "His old griefs and prejudices still hang about him."[22]

As the Franco-British war intensified, the British stepped up their attacks on American shipping, with consequent increases in the number of American sailors impressed. Groups gathered outside newspaper offices to read the latest news—or hear it read by the most literate in their number. Half sided passionately with their ancestral Anglo-Saxon motherland, while the other half demanded—just as passionately—that the American

---

*A close personal friend of President Washington, Knox had been a major general in charge of the Continental Army artillery in the Revolutionary War.

government support its Revolutionary War ally against America's former oppressor. Newspaper editors sensed an opportunity to increase profits by fanning the flames of war. The pro-English press urged breaking ties with France, while the opposition press assailed Anglophiles as monarchists and traitors.

What began as street-corner debates deteriorated into brawls that spread down alleys and avenues in major cities and exploded into full-scale rioting. Rush placed a bold-lettered sign with the word "DOCTOR" on his carriage to avoid confrontations with any mobs he passed.

All but forgotten in the national mayhem, President George Washington espoused neutrality and pleaded for national unity behind his policy, saying it would be "unwise in the extreme . . . to involve ourselves in the contests of European nations."[23] Anticipating far more sales and profits from war news than peace, newspapers all but ignored his pleas. In the spring of 1793, the French Government intensified the crisis in American streets by sending a new ambassador to the United States—Citizen Edmond-Charles-Edouard Genet. He arrived with two sets of instructions from his government. Publicly, he was to offer Congress a new treaty "in which the two nations should amalgamate their commercial and political interests and establish an intimate concert, which would promote . . . mutual nationalization of French and American citizens."[24] His secret instructions, however, ordered him to foment revolution and bring the United States under the political control of France.

When Genet arrived, Jeffersonian newspapers whipped Francophilia into mass hysteria that soon engulfed daily life in Boston, New York, Philadelphia, Charleston, and other cities. Genet's first stop in America was Charleston, where pier-side crowds had prepared a thunderous welcome. Waving the French banner of worldwide revolution, Genet assailed President Washington and called his Federalist supporters monarchists who sought to restore ties to England.

"In the United States," Genet cried out, "men still exist who can say, 'Here a ferocious Englishman slaughtered my father; there my wife tore her bleeding daughter from the hands of an unbridled Englishman,' and those same men can say, 'Here a brave Frenchman died fighting for American liberty; here French naval and military power humbled the might of Britain.'"[25]

Initially, Genet's arrival had little effect on Rush—or his routine rides through Philadelphia. He continued his daily letters to his wife, who, as usual, had gone to Morven with most of the Rush children for the summer. While there, she gave birth to a daughter they named Julia to give each parent a namesake among their many children.

Several years earlier, when Richard, their second son, was ten, he convinced his parents to let him remain at his father's side and spend the summer learning how to be a doctor. With Benjamin Rush facing a lonely summer without his wife and children, they agreed. In 1793, however, it was the turn of their aggressive six-year-old John to insist he was enough of a man to join thirteen-year-old Richard and remain at his father's side healing the sick. Neither Julia nor Benjamin could resist. Julia admitted she could no longer control the unruly little boy. Rush believed he could manage John—especially after Rush's mother and one of his sisters agreed to move into his house to help supervise the boys.

In Charleston, meanwhile, Genet built on his base of support by organizing a fleet of privateers to prey on Anglo-American commerce between the British West Indies and the Atlantic coast. Antifederalist governors in the South, intent on weakening presidential powers and restoring state sovereignty, opened their harbors to Genet's ships, which sailed in and out at will with captured British cargo vessels. Luring hundreds of unemployed American shipbuilders back to work to refit cargo carriers as warships, Genet soon had a fleet of more than eighty vessels that patrolled American coastal waters and captured scores of British merchant vessels—many inside American territorial waters.

As the summer of 1793 approached, Genet's plans were complete. "I have prepared the revolution of New Orleans and Canada," he wrote to the French foreign minister in Paris. "I have destroyed the maritime commerce of the English in these waters."[26]

With his privateers marauding British ships along the coast, Genet left Charleston in a coach-and-four and began what metamorphosed into a triumphal procession toward the American capital in Philadelphia to present his credentials to the President. Church bells tolled his arrival in each town, cannons boomed, French flags flapped in the wind, and when he arrived at the outskirts of Philadelphia a few weeks later, 500 coaches filled with ardent Francophiles waited to escort him into the city. Thousands rushed into the streets to cheer and march; an estimated 5,000 supporters rallied outside his hotel window and set off demonstrations that raged through the night into the next day—and the next—and the next.

Vice President John Adams described "the terrorism excited by Genet in 1793, when 10,000 people in the streets of Philadelphia, day after day, threatened to drag Washington out of his house and effect a revolution in the government or compel it to declare war in favor of the French Revolution and against England." Adams said he "judged it prudent and necessary to order chests of arms from the war office" to protect his house.[27] Washington feared for the safety of his wife and grandchildren and made plans to send them to the safety of Mount Vernon.

Adding to the turmoil Genet had unleashed was the sudden arrival of a French fleet from the Antilles. Genet ordered gangways lowered to let French seamen swell the Jacobin mobs raging through the crowded streets.

"The town is one continuous scene of riot," the British consul wrote in panic to his foreign minister in London. "The French seamen range the streets by night and by day armed with cutlasses and commit the most daring outrages. Genet seems ready to raise the tricolor and proclaim himself proconsul. President Washington is unable to enforce any measures in opposition."[28]

The intensified street disturbances did not deter Dr. Rush from making his daily rides across town to treat the poor, however—and find time to continue promoting abolition and the cause of black Americans. With chaos raging around him, Rush calmly approached Pennsylvania's comptroller-general with "an idea of offering 10,000 or more acres of state lands for sale on moderate terms . . . for a few years to *Africans only* who have been brought up as farmers. . . . I think the offer would succeed and thereby a precedent be established for colonizing, in time, all the Africans in our country."[29]

President Washington, meanwhile, responded to the chaos with a demand for Genet's recall. Genet quickly hopped aboard the flagship of the French fleet and ordered all ships to sail to New York—ostensibly for repairs and resupply.

The first minister plenipotentiary of the French revolutionary government, Citizen Edmond-Charles-Edouard Genet had secret instructions to overthrow the government of George Washington.

After Genet's fleet reached New York Harbor and docked at the city's piers, more than 5,000 French sailors and marines spilled over the rails into the welcoming arms of local Jacobins and Francophiles. Together, they set off on an endless orgy of drunkenness and violence that all but leveled New York's tumbledown waterfront warehouses. Within days, Tories and their families had fled the city, and a week later, on August 7, Genet stepped ashore in an adjutant general's uniform to mobilize the cheering Americans to unseat President Washington. The hysterical mobs did nothing to dissuade him, chanting, "Genet to power!" and "Down with Washington!" and serenading him with revolutionary airs, while cannons and church bells sounded their explosive welcomes.

"The whole of America has risen to acknowledge me," Genet exulted. At thirty years of age, he was ready to raise the French flag over New York, reclaim New France [Canada], and restore his nation's glory in the Americas.

The next morning, however, the church bells failed to resume their song; nothing but silence embraced the ship and surrounding quays. Genet came topside and looked over the rail. The waterfront was deserted; the air still and silent. He disembarked and walked toward a nearby inn. A servant awaited, his bag packed to leave. Genet demanded an explanation. The answer struck like a dagger:

"Yellow fever, *Monsieur*."

CHAPTER 7

The Hundred Days of Doom

"The coolest and firmest minds," John Adams recalled later, "have given their opinions that nothing but the yellow fever . . . could have saved the United States from a fatal revolution of government."[1] Had the epidemic arrived a month later, Adams believed, Genet's armies of followers would have seized control of New York, Boston, and Philadelphia and unseated President Washington.

On August 15, however, the terrible, swift disease sent New Yorkers and Philadelphians—Jacobins and non-Jacobins alike—fleeing by the thousands to the perceived safety of the countryside. Life came to a standstill in both cities. Federal, state, and city governments shut down in Philadelphia, and the handsome Washington carriage—its huge Belgian brays unaware of impending doom—prepared to carry the President and his family home to the safety of Mount Vernon. With the tide of refugees from Haiti lapping the shores of South Carolina, Governor William Moultrie, a heroic general of the Revolutionary War, closed the state to ships and boats from the islands to try to block entry of yellow fever into the United States. Holding to the universal belief that the disease was contagious, other governors quickly followed suit.

Their efforts came too late.

On August 5, a doctor's little girl in Philadelphia fell ill with "bilious remitting fever," a catch-all term at the time that sometimes referred to what was probably typhus. Just as often, however, it meant any and every illness that produced fever and nausea and left the patient feeling—and looking—sickly and spent. This particular child's skin turned yellow the next day and she died the following day.

"A malignant fever has been generated in the filth of Water Street," Secretary of State Jefferson wrote to his friend Congressman James Madison, who was spending the summer between sessions of Congress in the safety of his isolated plantation in Orange County, Virginia, north of Charlottesville.

"About seventy people died of it two days ago," Jefferson reported, "and as many more were ill of it.

> It comes on with a pain in the head, sick stomach, then a little chill, black vomiting [blood] and stools, and death from the second to the eighth day. Everybody who can is flying from the city, and the panic of the country people is likely to add famine to the disease. . . . It is still spreading, and the heat of the weather is very unpropitious. . . . Hamilton is ill of the fever. . . . The President goes off the day after tomorrow . . . Knox then takes flight. . . . I would . . . go away . . . but I do not like to exhibit the appearance of panic.[2]

Jefferson said the fever had emanated from the trash and raw sewage that covered many streets along the waterfront, brought there by refugees from Haiti and by French sailors. Philadelphians across the city walked in the middle of the streets to avoid touching other pedestrians, Jefferson reported. A century would pass before anyone would conceive the notion that an insect could infect humans with a disease. With one of America's most perceptive scientific minds, Benjamin Rush noted the noxious odor that permeated the air on Water Street as he approached the Delaware River. A load of overturned coffee on the dock had putrefied and was emitting a nauseating odor that affected all those living within one hundred yards. Rush was of the Sydenham school of physicians who believed all diseases were transmitted through the air as a "miasma" that invaded the respiratory system and ultimately infected the rest of the body. Adding to the nauseating fumes of the rotting coffee were the normal summer odors from open sewers and rotting offal at open-air markets.

At the same time the first little girl was dying of the bilious fever, a lady developed similar symptoms. Rush treated her with two bleedings and a dose of calomel cathartic, and although her skin turned yellow, she recovered. But then two young men a few houses away developed the symptoms and after two bleedings and a purge with calomel, both youths died, their skin having turned a ghastly yellow.

And so it went over the first ten days of the fever's outbreak. Rush learned that several others in the neighborhood had died—all lived nearby and had passed the pile of putrefying coffee.

"As yet," he wrote to Julia at Morven, "it has not spread thro' any parts of the city which are beyond the reach of the putrid exhalation [the coffee odor] which first produced it. If it should, I shall give you notice that you may remain where you are till you receive further advice and information from me."[3] Julia and the children normally returned to town in September, after the last of the summer heat waves had ebbed.

Four days later, after eleven neighbors had died—two of them his own patients—Rush confessed to his wife, "The fever has assumed a most alarming appearance. . . . I need hardly request you to remain for a while with all the children where you are. Many people are flying the city, many by my advice. . . . I shall confine John and Richard to the house and oblige them to use precautions against the disorder. My mother and sister are so kind and attentive as to prevent all our wants and wishes."[4]

And a day later: "It is indeed a serious time. Dejection sits upon every countenance. . . . Five persons died this morning, and five more are expected to die tonight. [One] lies on the corner of Walnut Street." Recalling an outbreak of a similar illness he had seen thirty years earlier as an apprentice—yellow skin and all—Rush now added the word "yellow" to the name of the disease. Most other doctors adopted Rush's terminology, and the disease now became "bilious remitting yellow fever," or, more simply, "yellow fever." Like Rush, they agreed it was contagious.

There were a few dissidents among the Philadelphia physicians, however. Scoffing at the Rush pronouncements, they insisted the fever was nothing more than normal, albeit mythical, "autumnal fevers" that gripped many Americans with the sharp autumn drop in nighttime temperatures. Although few eighteenth-century physicians agreed on a common definition of "autumnal fever," the symptoms they described indicate a wide range of possible diseases, including typhoid, cholera, dysentery, influenza, croup, and common colds. Many physicians perpetuated the concept of autumnal fevers into the late twentieth century, citing increases in flu and other communicable diseases among children when they returned to school and came into daily contact with larger numbers of children in confined quarters.

To prevent a fall-off in business, Philadelphia civic leaders quickly joined the skeptics, blustering denials that their city could ever have spawned such a dreadful disease. A few conceded it might have originated in Dock Creek—a disgraceful open sewer that sliced through the heart of the slums—but they insisted that foreigners had imported the disease. Some even renamed it Barbados Fever, others Siamese Fever, or Burmese or Indian. Rush, however, combed the city's archives and found that the city had hosted many yellow fever epidemics—some more widespread than others—beginning as early as 1699 and recurring regularly almost every two years until 1762, after which the city experienced an unusual respite of thirty years.

As the death toll increased, Rush decided to send his sons John and Richard to Julia and the safety of Morven's rural isolation, but, fearing they might come into contact with infected victims en route, he hesitated.

"I feel very much for the safety of both the boys," he wrote to Julia. "They are both indisposed with the headache and by no means in a condition to travel." But of the two dangers his boys faced—remaining in town or risking travel—he decided travel was less dangerous.

"Our neighborhood," he warned Julia, "will be desolate in a day or two. . . . Adieu. My love to each of the children. Tell them all that the best proof they can give of their affection for their Papa is to pray for his health and life, and to be dutiful to their Mama and kind to each other."[5]

Day by day, the news from Rush to Julia grew worse:

The disease has raged with great virulence this day. . . . Its symptoms are very different in different people. Sometimes it comes on with a chilly fit and a high fever, but more frequently it steals on with headache, languor, and sick stomach. These symptoms are followed by stupor, delirium, vomiting, a dry skin, cool or cold hands and feet, a feeble slow pulse. . . . The eyes are at first suffused with blood, they afterwards become yellow, and in most cases a yellowness covers the whole skin on the 3rd or 4th day. Few survive the 5th day, but more die on the 2d or 3rd days. . . . One of my patients stood up and shaved himself on the morning of the day he died. Livid spots on the body, a bleeding at the nose, from the gums, and from the bowels, and a vomiting of black matter [blood] . . . closed the scenes of life.[6]

Rush posted his letter the following morning, but not before adding, "Another night and morning have been added to my life. I am prepared to set off for my daily round of duty and feel heartily disposed to say with Jabez, 'O! that the hand of the Lord may be with me,' not only to preserve my life but to heal my poor patients."[7]

When she received his latest letter and learned he was treating victims at home—in his and her family house—Julia snapped: "I have endeavored to keep up my spirits through the whole of this calamity," she fumed as she wrote from Morven, "and all my friends say I have done it wonderfully—but your last letters have been too much for me.

I think for the sake of your poor children you should have kept your own house free from infection. . . . I fear your mother and sister have gotten it by nursing those that have been so much worse . . . to hear that those persons are ill under your roof. . . . I have not slept above three hours for two nights past. . . . I must request you will get your mother or sister to give a little heed to my clothes. I ordered my chest of clothes to be locked. . . . If that room is a hospital and black nurses about the house, I shall have a poor account of them I fear. I hope you will not take any more into the house. If you get sick yourself, which I very much fear, what shall I do when I come to you with a house full . . . of so many sick and dying . . . a perfect horror. The boys are much affected. They fear they shall lose both their parents.[8]

Deeply immersed in his struggle with the epidemic, Rush replied almost nonchalantly that he had been contemplating "moving out of the house I now occupy before you come to town . . . [but] I cannot promise to visit and escort you to town." With that, he sent his "love to each of the children" and assured her, "I remain . . . your ever faithful friend."[9]

When the death toll on Water Street approached forty, Rush grew still more convinced that the rotting coffee on the dock was responsible for the epidemic. He now identified the disease with certainty as "bilious remitting yellow fever," a deadly and, in his opinion, a highly contagious disease that he had seen thirty years earlier as an apprentice.

A few physicians and civic leaders continued to scorn—even ridicule—Rush as a panic-monger, but enough Philadelphians believed him to quit the city. Even those who did not flee crossed the street when they saw him approaching to avoid touching him. As the disease spread ever more widely, the criticisms and ridicule of Rush subsided, and the College of Physicians acknowledged that a serious infection had gripped the population. It advised a quarantine of the infected and urged healthy citizens to avoid all contact with the sick. It condemned as dangerous the suggestion of empirics that street-corner fires would ward off the disease, but conceded that burning gunpowder might be useful. Homeowners nonetheless lit bonfires outside their doors. The committee urged the use of smelling bottles containing camphor to prevent catching the disease and to sprinkle their clothes and all interior linens—sheets, drapes, etc.—with vinegar, then commonly used as a disinfectant.* City officials seized the circus enclosure to house the homeless sick, only to have the first seven patients lay unattended and die. As their bodies began rotting, a mob of neighbors threatened to burn the circus down and forced government officials to order removal of the foul-smelling remains. The officials then took control of a mansion outside of town, which volunteers converted into a hospital for the sick without homes or lodging.

What had been a stream of citizens pouring from the city turned into a torrent—on carts and wagons, on chairs and carriages, on horseback and on foot. One-third of the city's population of about 55,000 abandoned Philadelphia, including most government workers. The President and his cabinet members had long earlier retired to their homes, and the few federal officials they left behind moved the remnants of the national government to Germantown, Pennsylvania. Foreign emissaries fled. Churches

---

*Vinegar contains acetic acid, an effective disinfectant by itself but not present in modern vinegar (5 percent) in large enough quantities to kill disease-causing bacteria.

either closed or stood deserted. The city library, the court, and most local and state government offices closed, as did three of the city's four newspapers—one, because of the editor's death. Most banks and businesses also closed and, in doing so, created a shortage of cash that forced townsfolk to barter to buy goods or services. As seamen contracted the disease or simply fled for fear of catching it, ships lay idle in port or tied up wharfside, unable to unload cargoes or sail elsewhere. Other cities declared themselves off limits to Philadelphians and others who had visited Philadelphia. Rhode Island, North and South Carolina declared statewide quarantines to prevent the disease from infecting their citizens.

"All the schools in town," Rush wrote to his wife, "are either broken up by design or moldering away by the daily desertion of scholars into the country. It is indeed a serious time."[10] Even the London Coffee House and its slave market had closed. Serious indeed.

Local government collapsed as officials, judges, clerks, and other public employees either fled or died. Almost half the houses stood empty, many deteriorating into derelicts each day, as looters ripped clapboards off their exteriors and left gaping holes and menacing splinters where families had once lived. People walked in the middle of the street to avoid infections emanating from houses where others had died.

"The old custom of shaking hands fell into disuse," wrote Mathew Carey, publisher of *The Pennsylvania Herald* and the respected *Columbian Magazine* and *The American Museum.** "The smoke of tobacco being regarded as a preventive, many persons—even women and small boys—had cigars constantly in their mouths. Others placing full confidence in garlic, chewed it almost the whole day; some kept it in their pockets and shoes."[11]

Those who remained in town tried to keep indoors, spending their idle time scrubbing and whitewashing their walls and floors, purifying them with vinegar, burning gunpowder, smoking tobacco, breathing camphor

---

*Born in Dublin in 1760, Carey became a dissident journalist and fled to Paris, where he went to work in Benjamin Franklin's printing office. He emigrated to the United States in 1784, where the Marquis de Lafayette underwrote his bookshop and publishing business. Successful editions of the Bible allowed him to expand into political tracts and the first American atlases. His map of Washington, DC, was the first to name the land west of the Capitol "The Mall."

fumes. Terror gripped the city, with many citizens fearing to breathe the air, fearing that each whiff carried hidden sources of death into their bodies.

Husbands deserted their sick wives, Carey reported. Wives fled their homes, abandoning their husbands and children at the first hint the disease had infected any of them. More than 200 urchins roamed the streets pleading for food or drink, many of them deserted by their parents, others having been orphaned after their parents succumbed. Some formed vicious gangs, surrounding passers-by and threatening to touch them and transmit the disease unless their targets surrendered their cash and valuables. Many of those who fled the city—even children—were denied food and shelter miles away in other states—some even thrown off stages midroute and left "to perish in the woods" when fellow travelers learned they had come from Philadelphia.

"The frightful scenes that were acted seemed to indicate a total dissolution of the bands of society," Carey reported. The epidemic had transformed the most elegant, grand dame of American cities from riches to rags. Carey's on-the-scene tales of horror included that of a woman whose husband and two children lay dead in the room with her as she went into labor. The city's midwives had either died or fled. The woman's cries attracted the attention of a carter of dead bodies in the street below.

"With his assistance she was delivered a child, which died in a few minutes, as did the mother, who was utterly exhausted by her labor. . . . And thus lay, in one room, no less than five dead bodies, an entire family, carried off within a few hours. To relate all the frightful cases of this nature that occurred would fill a volume. . . . To pass them over wholly would have been improper."[12]

The disease seized rich and poor, young and old, often killing entire families—ten in one family, a minister and his wife and two children in another home, five members of a third family, and six of another, eight, ten . . . and twenty unrelated boarders in another house. Seven of eight who died lived in poor neighborhoods, according to publisher Mathew Carey, "without a human being to hand them a drink of water, to administer medicines, or perform any charitable office for them." The dead lay everywhere, in their beds, on floors, in the streets. "The extraordinary public panic," Carey reported, "produced scenes of distress and misery of which parallels are rarely to be met. . . . A man and his wife, once in affluent circumstances, were found lying dead in bed, and between them was their child, a little infant, who was sucking its mother's breast. How long they had lain thus was uncertain."[13]

Carey cited particularly high death rates among "tipplers, drunkards, and gourmands and persons of a corpulent habit of body.

> To the filles de joie it had been equally fatal. The wretched, debilitated state of their constitutions rendered them an easy prey to this dreadful disorder, which very soon ended their miserable careers. The inhabitants of dirty houses have severely expiated their neglect of cleanliness and decency by the numbers of them that have fallen sacrifices. Whole families in such houses have sunk into one silent, undistinguishing grave. The mortality in confined streets, small alleys, and close houses, debarred of a free circulation of air, has . . . exceeded in great proportion that in the large streets and well-aired houses.[14]

Carey reported thirty-two deaths in the thirty houses that filled narrow Pewter Alley, but only thirty-nine deaths in the one-hundred seventy houses of spacious Market Street.

As August ended the number of deaths rose to twenty a day—only to spike to forty-two and then forty-eight a week later. Then doctors began to fall—ten by the end of the first six weeks of the epidemic. Each had a different remedy; most tried a variety, ranging from the mild to the extreme; Rush tried them all. None succeeded. The mildest in the range of treatments was the so-called French cure concocted by Dr. Jean Devèze, who combined small doses of laudanum with gargles, lemonade, chicken broth, skimmed milk, baths, wine, and tea, among other standard home remedies. At the other end of the range was the "purge-and-bleed" approach espoused by Rush, who combined repeated bleedings of ten or more ounces each with a traditional "Ten and Ten" purgative—ten grains each of the cathartics calomel and jalap.

Despite all his efforts and those of other Philadelphia doctors, the death toll kept rising, with carters harvesting fifty to one hundred bodies a day in September and transporting them to burial pits. Only occasionally did they err in their mission. After one carter lifted a dead sailor he found in the street into a coffin, the sailor suddenly rose from the dead, emerging from his drunken stupor, sitting straight up, and demanding to know where the carter was taking him. According to Carey, the terrified black man dropped him and "ran off as if a ghost was at his heels."[15]

"Amidst the general abandonment of the sick," Carey pointed out, "there were to be found many illustrious instances of men and women . . . who in the exercises of the duties of humanity exposed themselves to dangers which terrified men." Foremost in what he called "this noble group," were the few doctors who refused to flee the city. "Scarcely one of the practicing doctors who remained in the city escaped sickness. Some were three, four, and five times confined."[16]

Benjamin Rush led "this noble group"—one of only three, perhaps four (depending on the definition of a physician) who remained in Philadelphia from the beginning to the end of the epidemic. Another member— the youngest—was twenty-five-year-old Philip Syng Physick, a graduate of the University of Pennsylvania who had studied surgery in London and had only just received his M.D. at the University of Edinburgh the previous year. Like Rush when he returned from Scotland, Physick had lacked the wealth and professional connections to launch his practice, but devised a unique solution—in effect, the nation's first medical insurance scheme. For a flat fee of $20 (almost $500 today), Physick agreed to treat each subscribing patient for a year. Embracing Benjamin Rush as a mentor and friend and adopting Rush's treatment methods, Physick soon acquired a reputation as one of the city's most skilled physicians.*

As the epidemic peaked, Rush rose before dawn, seeing upwards of one hundred patients during the day and into the night, convinced that God alone had saved his life to permit his treating the poor. By late October, only Rush among the few doctors left in Philadelphia dared venture into filthy slum neighborhoods, where the living hurled the dead into the streets to rot with the garbage and the contents of their chamber pots.

Exhausted and desperate to halt the spread of the disease, Rush cried out to heaven before retiring one night and then recording his thoughts and prayers in his nightly note to his wife. "Thirty-eight persons have died

---

*Ironically, Physick's name—not Rush's—became synonymous with purgatives until the late twentieth century, when millions of American children blanched at the prospects of their parents administering a "physic."

in eleven families in nine days in Water Street and many more in different parts of the city," he wailed. "I fear we have seen only the beginning of this awful visitation. . . . Help me, my dear Julia, with your prayers."[17]

Julia replied, citing a friend in New York who told her "you are all but prayed for by name in most of the churches. I hope it will please you to hear the prayers that are offered on your behalf, as well as the afflicted among you."[18]

After he had written to Julia, Rush recalled the epidemic he had encountered during the second year of his apprenticeship, thirty years earlier in 1762. "It began in August and prevailed in September, October, November, and December," he recalled, "carrying off for some time twenty persons in a day."[19] Though gripped by fatigue, he shot out of his bed determined to rip open every book in his library and restudy every page that dealt with yellow fever.

Later, as he pored through a 1741 manuscript Benjamin Franklin had given him, a sudden flash of understanding went off in his head. Its author was the famed Virginia botanist John Mitchell (1711–1768), who had studied medicine at the University of Edinburgh and, without receiving a degree, had started practicing medicine. He had reached the conclusion that yellow fever resulted from poor sanitation conditions, which permitted emissions of "putrid miasmata" that infected the humors of the body and could only be "eradicated by timely emptying [of] the abdominal viscera." Mitchell then described curing patients in two yellow-fever epidemics with powerful thrice-daily "purges" using ten grains (¼ ounce) of calomel and fifteen grains (⅜ ounce) of jalap instead of the conventional Ten and Ten. "The evacuation by purges was more necessary in [yellow fever] than in other fevers," Mitchell had written, "and ill-timed scrupulousness about the weakness of the body was of bad consequence in these urgent circumstances." Mitchell warned that physician timidity in administering strong and frequent purges could prove fatal.

The prescription of powerful purges coincided with the theories of the seventeenth-century English physician Thomas Sydenham, whose works Rush had studied and come to revere at medical school in Edinburgh—including Sydenham's exhaustive studies of epidemics. In the light of Sydenham's studies—and indeed the works of Hippocrates and Galen—Mitchell's conclusions now seemed obvious to Rush.[20]

"Dr. Mitchell dissipated my ignorance and fears," Rush proclaimed with joy as he believed he had found why he had failed to cure many of his patients. "I suspected that my want of success was owing to the feebleness of my purges," he rejoiced. "I adopted his [Mitchell's] theory and resolved to follow it. It remained now only to fix upon a suitable purge to answer the purpose of discharging the contents of the bowels." Rush increased the amount of jalap in the conventional Ten and Ten to fifteen grains—a concoction that soon became known as "Rush's Thunderbolts," or, to some, "thunderclappers." In addition, he prescribed three doses of Thunderbolts a day instead of one, each to be given every six hours until they produced four or five "large evacuations."

"The effects of this powder not only answered but far exceeded my expectations," Rush enthused. "It perfectly cured four out of the first five patients to whom I gave it. . . . After such a success . . . I gave it afterwards with confidence."[21]

In addition to explosive purges, Rush prescribed extravagant blood-letting (at least ten ounces several times a day), cool air, cold drinks, "low diet," and applications of cold water to the body. "Never before," he rejoiced, "did I experience such sublime joy as I now felt in contemplation of the success of my remedies." Believing he had found the cure for yellow fever, Rush proclaimed, "The conquest of this disease was not the effect of accident, nor the application of a single remedy; it was the triumph of a principle of medicine."

On September 10, 1793, Rush wrote, "Thank God! Out of one hundred patients whom I have visited or prescribed for this day I have lost none"[22] Rush believed he had found the cure to yellow fever and would save the people of Philadelphia from one of the world's ghastliest diseases. Tens of thousands had died around the world, but Benjamin Rush, M.D., now believed he would make it possible for millions to live.

CHAPTER 8

"You Cannot Die Now, Doctor!"

T HE SELF-PROCLAIMED SUCCESS of Rush's Thunderbolts in curing yellow fever drew crowds of patients to the doctor's home day and night, slipping notes under his door when the doctor was asleep or away treating patients. "Please to come and see my daughter," pleaded William Innes in one note. "Will the humane Dr. Rush condescend to step into the house of mourning?" asked another patient's note. "Another of my family is ill."[1]

Although several doctors remained skeptical, most—especially those in isolated rural areas—embraced Rush's "discovery" and pleaded for his help as earnestly as patients, flooding his home with letters seeking directions on implementing his cure.

Scorning sleep, he rose before dawn each day, answering a few letters, then going downstairs to treat the ill who stood in long lines outside his door, many having arrived in the dead of night. His sister and five of his students lived in his house to help him cope. After treating some patients at home, he climbed into his two-wheeled chair and spurred his horse to a trot that took him to almost every street and alley in town. Although half the houses in the city were deserted, Rush seems to have treated the ill in every structure that still harbored the living. By nightfall, he had often seen as many as 150 patients, while his five apprentices treated twenty to thirty patients each in the Rush house. They, like Rush himself, were—for all they knew—risking their lives, as they treated each patient, but, infected by the Rush fervor to save the sick, they worked as tirelessly as their master. Blood flowed everywhere in and out of the Rush house, covering their clothes and his, as well as floors and walls, even oozing from the ground outside, where they bled patients when rooms in the house grew too crowded.

Rush and other physicians continued to believe yellow fever was contagious, and, as the epidemic grew worse, all but Rush, Physick, and two other doctors had either fled the city or died. Most of the city's wealthy citizens—the only patients who could afford to pay their doctors—had also fled. By staying in town, Rush exposed himself not just to what he believed was a deadly contagious disease but to bankruptcy. Only Julia's willingness to sell 227 acres she had inherited from her father, Richard Stockton, in Princeton, New Jersey, provided her with enough funds to feed herself and her children in their isolation at Morven.

"Sunday and Monday always seem as long as four days," she complained to her husband, "because I do not get my daily letter, which is the only satisfaction I can now have in this state of exile and separation."[2]

In Philadelphia, meanwhile, Rush was unable to meet the demand for his magical Thunderbolts, and he sent instructions on making them to apothecaries around town. He published printed instructions in the *American Daily Advertiser* for those able to obtain and mix the ingredients themselves. In doing so, he deprived himself of still more income making and selling Thunderbolts himself.

In his instructions, he urged patients to take one Thunderbolt mixture "in a little sugar and water every six hours, until four or five evacuations result.

> After the bowels are thoroughly cleansed, eight or ten ounces of blood should be taken from the arm, and more if the tension or fullness of the pulse should continue. Balm tea, toast, and water . . . should be drunk . . . and the bowels kept constantly open. . . . The food should consist of gruel, sago, panada [a sweetened paste of bread crumbs and water], tapioca, tea, coffee, chocolate, wine whey [a cream whisky], chicken broth, and the white meats. . . . The fruits of the season may be eaten with advantage at all times.[3]

Secretary of War Henry Knox reported to President Washington, who was then safely ensconced at Mount Vernon, that "everybody whose head aches takes Rush." He cited one acquaintance who took twenty grams each of calomel and jalap: "Although it cured him of his apprehensions of the yellow fever, it has nearly killed him with the gout [cramps] in his stomach."

Knox lamented "the mortality in the city" as "excessive . . . the numbers buried were not short of an hundred each day—some ever much more, some much less.

> The streets are lonely to a melancholy degree—the merchants generally have fled. Ships are arriving and no consignees to be found. Notes at the bank are suffered to be unpaid. In fine, the stroke is as heavy as if an army of enemies had possessed the city without plundering it. . . . I shall set out for Boston tomorrow. . . . I understand Mr. Jefferson set out yesterday.[4]

After Knox left for New York, he stopped at a tavern on the way, where a man fell sick and, rather than express sympathy, Knox reported, his fellow imbibers "ordered his coffin in his presence."[5]

In mid-September, the *Federal Gazette* published a letter from Dr. William Currie, a prominent Philadelphia physician and a member, with Rush, of the College of Physicians and the American Philosophical Society: "The disease, which Dr. Rush calls the yellow fever and of which [he] says he has cured such numbers by the new method," Currie scoffed, "is only the fall fever. . . . It is time the veil should be withdrawn from your eyes, my fellow citizens."[6]

Currie was not history's first skeptic of bloodletting as a cure for disease. A century before Sydenham, the sixteenth-century German physician Andreas Libau, a chemist who had authored the then-classic text *Alchymia*, published the first known call to replace bloodletting with blood replacement, or, as it is now called, blood transfusion. "Let there be a robust healthy youth full of lively blood," Libau wrote. "Let the master of the art . . . open an artery of the healthy one . . . and the arterial blood . . . warm and full of spirit, will leap into the sick one and immediately will bring him to the fountain of life."[7]

Although Libau did not translate his words into action, interest in blood transfusion gained momentum in 1616, when the English physician William Harvey discovered and described circulation of blood through the human body. Such notable scientists and physicians as England's Sir Christopher Wren, a renowned physician as well as architect, and Robert Boyle, the great physicist and equally accomplished physician, experimented with primitive animal-to-animal, animal-to-man, and man-to-man blood transfers. They used lambs, dogs, even human cadavers as donors—all without success.* Three centuries before the discovery of blood types, however, recipients of such transfusions—both animal and human—almost always suffered adverse hemolytic reactions to incompatible blood and died. Bleeding remained the only apparent cure for the ill.

When Alexander Hamilton and his wife contracted the fever in 1793, however, their physician Dr. Edward Stevens deemed bleeding and purging too debilitating. Instead, he administered large doses of quinine, which helped reduce fever, inflammation, and pain. He also prescribed soothing doses of Madeira wine, whose effects were the same as those of any high-alcohol-content wine. Cold baths numbed his patients still more and helped further reduce body temperature, while opium-based laudanum put them to sleep at night. Rather than purging, he administered a concoction of chamomile, peppermint, and lavender spirits to inhibit vomiting.

When Hamilton and his wife each recovered after only five days of the Stevens treatment, the Treasury Secretary boasted of his newfound health to the entire city and wrote to Philadelphia's College of Physicians praising the Stevens treatment as more effective than the "standard" [read Rush] approach. Hamilton urged members of the College to adopt the Stevens method and put an end to "that undue panic which is fast depopulating the city and suspending business both public and private."[8]

Hamilton's broadside infuriated Rush, who called it politically motivated and charged that if his bleed-and-purge remedies "had been

---

*Both Wren and Boyle practiced two professions. In addition to being a physician, Wren was England's greatest architect, the designer of St. Paul's Cathedral, among other monumental structures. Boyle was both a physician and an experimental physicist, who developed Boyle's Law—namely, that the pressure of a gas in a closed system is inversely proportionate to its volume when the temperature remains constant.

introduced by any other person than . . . a friend of Madison and Jefferson, they would have met with less opposition from Colonel Hamilton.

"My method is too simple," Rush added scornfully. "They forget that a stone from the sling of David effected what the whole armory of Saul could not do. Many hundreds of my patients now walk the streets and follow their ordinary business. . . . Could our physicians be persuaded to adopt the new mode of treating the disorder, the contagion might be eradicated from our city in a few weeks. But they not only refuse to adopt it, they persecute and slander the author of it."[9]

Shortly after Hamilton released his back-handed criticism of Rush, Dr. James Hutchinson, professor of chemistry at the University of Pennsylvania, who, like Dr. Currie, had assailed Rush's treatments, succumbed to the disease. "This evening," Rush wrote to his wife Julia, "Dr. Hutchinson breathed his last.

> It is remarkable that he denied the existence of a contagious fever in our city for above a week after it appeared among us, and even treated the report of it with contempt and ridicule. . . . He continued to object taking my medicine. . . . The reason, I fear, was . . . it came *from me*. . . . Poor fellow! He died as well as lived my enemy.[10]

Julia Rush commiserated with her husband but doubted that, "after risking your life and making such sacrifices for your fellow man . . . it will be in the power of these men materially to injure you. If the citizens of Philadelphia do not show some public mark of approbation and gratitude to you for your . . . exertions, they will not deserve such a man."[11]

Although Hutchinson's death convinced Currie to recant his criticism of Dr. Rush, others continued carping, despite any scientific evidence to prove Rush wrong.

"Besides combatting yellow fever," Rush groused, "I have been obliged to contend with the prejudices, fears, and falsehoods of my brethren all of which retard the progress of truth and daily cost our city many lives."[12]

A few days after Hutchinson's death, the punishing routine that Rush maintained to treat victims finally exacted its toll on him and his household. After the disease had claimed three of his students and infected two others, Rush found himself without enough time to treat the swelling crowd of patients pleading for his care. He was seeing more than one hundred patients a day, some before 5 a.m. He turned many away, some "in tears. . . . But they did not feel more distress than I. . . . Even yet, I recollect, with pain, that I tore myself at one time from five persons who attempted to stop me . . . by suddenly whipping my horse and driving my chair as speedily as possible beyond the reach of their cries."[13]

Rush's efforts to treat the sick raised him to godlike status among most Philadelphians. No physician in memory had given of himself to the sick as Rush had done, even opening his house to them day and night without regard to his personal safety. "He is become the darling of the common people," Philadelphia Circuit Court Judge William Bradford declared, "and his humane fortitude and exertions will render him deservedly dear."[14]

Clearly, Rush had reached the limits of his ability to treat the sick, however, and he finally published an open letter to that effect addressed "To His Fellow Citizens" in Philadelphia's *Federal Gazette* on September 12. "Dr. Rush regrets that he is unable to comply with all the calls of his fellow citizens who are indisposed with the prevailing fever." He went on to urge self-medication where possible, describing a "Treatment for Yellow Fever" for "such of them as cannot have the benefit of medical aid. He urged taking "mercurial purges . . . and to lose ten or twelve ounces of blood as soon as is convenient after taking the purges, if the headache and fever continue.

> The almost universal success with which it hath pleased God to bless the remedies of strong mercurial purges and bleeding in this disorder enable Dr. Rush to assure his fellow citizens that there is no more danger to be apprehended from it when those remedies are used in its early stage.[15]

Because the epidemic had forced the College of Physicians to cancel its weekly meetings, Rush also sent the newspaper an open letter to physicians on the "Use of the Lancet in Yellow Fever."

> I have found bleeding to be useful, not only in cases where the pulse was full and quick, but where it was slow and tense. . . . This state of the pulse

seems to arise from an inflamed state of the brain, which shows itself in a preternatural dilation of the pupils of the eyes. . . . It indicates the necessity of more bleeding and purging. I have found it to occur most frequently in children. I have bled twice in many, and in one acute case four times, with the happiest effects. I consider intrepidity in the use of the lancet . . . to be as necessary as it is in the use of mercury and jalap in this insidious and ferocious disease.

As a final word, Rush told his colleagues, "I lament the contrariety of opinion among the members of our college upon the remedies proper in the disease," and he signed the letter, "From, Gentlemen, your friend and brother, Benjamin Rush."[16]

Ironically, illness finally struck Rush himself on the morning his open letter appeared in the newspaper. Barely able to gather enough strength to leave his bed, he managed to scribble a few lines to his wife: "After a restless night, I am still alive and preparing for the awful duties of the day. . . . I send you these few lines only to let you know that . . . I stand in greater need than ever of the prayers of all good people. Adieu, adieu. . . . "

A friend and fellow physician rushed into the doctor's bedroom to treat him, pleading, "You cannot die now, doctor!" before drawing ten ounces of blood from Rush's arm. Shortly before noon, however, Rush defied his doctor's orders and staggered out of the house, climbed into his horse-drawn chair, and trotted off to treat the ill. In the next two hours, he ministered to more than forty patients before returning home in mid-afternoon, exhausted and feverish. He took a dose of Thunderbolt and bedded down for a few hours before bleeding himself—draining another ten ounces, then taking a second dose of Thunderbolt. After it had worked its worst, he felt faint and fell into his bed, not certain whether he would awaken the next day.

Weakened, but grateful to be alive as dawn's first light entered his bedroom, Rush postponed his morning visits and wrote a thoughtful, somewhat apologetic letter to Julia asking about each of the children in emotion-filled phrases that his previous letters often lacked. He even included a special note to John, their oldest, and asked about the health of baby Julia, who had been ill but had subsequently recovered.

"I was overcome with joy and gratitude," Julia wrote back, somewhat sarcastically.

> You have at last recollected that you have a child . . . worth your atten-
> tion, for a more lovely, engaging child no one ever had. . . . The other
> children are well. John [16 years old] has been much benefited by your
> paragraph. . . . There is an English school in town to which I have put
> James [7]. . . . Mary [9] is at a sewing school. . . . John always desires me
> to give his love to you, as does James. . . . Adieu my dear husband. I trust
> in God that he will 'ere long unite us in that state of sincere and tender
> friendship we have so long enjoyed. The time is ardently longed for by
> your most affectionate Julia Rush.[17]

Rush's insistence on prescribing repetitive doses of debilitating Thunderbolts stemmed from his conviction that the disease accelerated repro-
duction of morbid bile in the intestine, which, therefore, required constant
cleansing to prevent the bile from accumulating. "I have found lately, I
hope, a preventive of the disease as well as a cure," he wrote his wife. "It
consists in keeping the bowels gently open, for in them the disease first
fixes its poison."[18]

His conclusion was logical at the time, given the lack of instruments
and research to prove otherwise. Nearly a century would pass before the
development of statistics would permit scientists to perform controlled
studies of the effects of medical procedures and drugs on large groups of
patients. When disease infected any organ in the body, eighteenth-century
reasoning called for its removal by thorough cleansing of that organ—the
intestines, the stomach, the bloodstream, and any other part of the body.
To that end, Rush often bled patients three times a day, usually limiting
each bleeding to twenty ounces or less, but often draining as much as one
hundred ounces over five days—and he prescribed as many as three doses
of Thunderbolt a day to keep the bowel "open," as he put it.

What neither Rush nor any other physician could know—and had not
the means to know—was that the loss of 20 percent or more of a person's
blood supply—about thirty-two ounces for an average adult—sent the
patient into hemorrhagic *shock*. Such shock can occur when the heart no

longer has enough blood to pump through the body for all its organs to function. Blood pressure and body temperature drop precipitously, with death likely unless the bleeding stops. In the meantime, the person suffers other symptoms, including blue lips and fingernails, sweating, confusion or anxiety, dizziness, abdominal pains and swelling, chest pains, vomiting, and, of course, low blood pressure and possible unconsciousness. To follow one bloodletting with another and then a third only accelerates *shock*—a phenomenon several doctors in Britain and America already suspected at the time of the Rush bleedings.

Both Rush and Thomas Sydenham, a century before Rush, misunderstood many initial symptoms of shock as beneficial. Bleeding necessarily raised the heart rate because the heart had to work harder to pump a reduced supply of blood to the body's organs. But while the heart (and pulse) *rate* quickened, the *strength* of each pulse diminished and, as a result, slowed the rate of hemorrhaging and vomiting. The end of vomiting, in turn, reduced patient pain, eliminated redness in the eyes, and produced other signs of *apparent* improvement. The patient looked better—and seemed to feel better.

"Bloodletting, when used *early* on the first day," Rush concluded logically, but incorrectly, "frequently strangled the disease in its birth and generally rendered it more light and convalescence more speedy and perfect."[19]

Despite the Rush proclamation of a cure to yellow fever, other physicians and a host of empirics claimed that they too had found cures. One doctor claimed to have saved sixty patients by making them sweat for twelve hours, then feeding them tea and molasses, along with a concentrate produced by boiling and reducing to three quarts one gallon of water with twelve turnips, one endive, and eight carrots.

Twenty-five years would pass before London's Dr. James Blundell would produce his landmark "Experiments on the Transfusion of Blood by the Syringe,"[20] in which he introduced fresh blood into patients instead of bleeding them. The death toll from such transfusions, however, would remain high and make them too dangerous until 1900, when Austrian-born scientist and Nobel Prize Laureate Karl Landsteiner would identify the four blood types A, B, AB, and O and their incompatibility with each other. By limiting transfusions to compatible blood, mortality rates would plunge and allow transfusion to replace bleeding as a standard treatment for the sick and injured.*

Meanwhile, untold thousands—perhaps millions—of patients survived bloodletting as promoted by Benjamin Rush. Most believed it had made them well—much as millions believed patent medicines concocted by quacks had made them well. It was—and is—fortunate for both patients and physicians that the human body has so many natural, disease-fighting mechanisms that allow the sick and injured to recover without medical intervention. Indeed, about half the victims of yellow fever today recover without medical intervention of any kind.† Rush claimed that his purge and bleed treatment saved 6,000 lives during the 1793 epidemic, but there is no scientific evidence that it saved a single life, and it probably killed many of his patients. Many who died would undoubtedly have survived had Rush and his acolytes not treated them with poisonous mercury purges and emetics and exposed them to shock by excessive bleeding.

The loss of ten ounces of blood, however, produces few if any ill effects, and there are no scientific reasons to explain why so many patients claimed they felt better after bloodletting other than a possible "placebo" or psychological effect. The comforting assurances of a trusted physician or nurse to a patient that he or she *will* feel better after a painful procedure can produce just such an effect. That was especially true when the soft-spoken, world-renowned physician Dr. Benjamin Rush—one of the nation's Founding Fathers and heroic figures—provided those assurances.

---

*By 1913, surgeons were limiting syringe transfusions to those with compatible blood types, but the process proved slow and cumbersome until Lester J. Unger, M.D., invented a direct-transfusion instrument to convert blood transfusion from an hours-long process with syringes into an efficient ten-to-twenty-minute process. A quarter century later, the development of sterile containers would permit storing blood safely for delivery to patients by gravity without the presence of donors. By the late twentieth century, 150 years after Blundell's first successful transfusion, the process became no more complex than a simple injection.

†According to the World Health Organization, about 200,000 people—90 percent of them in Africa—contracted yellow fever in 2013, with about 30,000 succumbing to the disease.

Also affecting the perception of some patients was the tendency to grow faint from the pain of the lancet slicing through flesh to set off the bloodletting. And as the pain of the lancet masked some discomforts of the fever, the rest all but vanished as violent spasms gripped the patient's gastro-intestinal system, provoking explosive diarrhea and vomiting.

Regardless of how effective bleeding and purging were in masking yellow fever symptoms, however, they had no effect on yellow fever itself. The patients Rush (and other physicians) claimed to have saved either did not have yellow fever or survived despite his (or their) intervention. Any deaths of patients under his care, however, did not—and do not—diminish his standing as one of the greatest, most brilliant physicians in the history of American medicine.

That Rush was so mistaken about the genesis of one disease does not reduce his stature as a giant in his field—any more than the failure of Leonardo da Vinci to convert his concepts and designs into practical parachutes, helicopters, solar power generators, and calculators diminished his stature as a master inventor. When Major Walter Reed, M.D., discovered the mosquito as the carrier of the disease, he benefited from more than a century's worth of accumulated knowledge and results of previous research that Rush lacked when he treated the disease during the epidemic of 1793. Without those resources, Rush and his contemporaries could not imagine any alternative to the traditional one of ridding the body of disease by cleansing its digestive tract and circulatory system.

Only the ignorant dare judge events, actions, or conclusions of those in the past on the basis of current knowledge and conditions. Even today, as I write this book in the early twenty-first century, recent studies show that 40 percent or more of the most advanced medical treatments may well prove to be useless or harmful, supporting the old saw said to have originated at Harvard that half of what all students learn is wrong. The problem in medicine is how to determine which half.

One study released in 2015 listed nearly 150 "modern" medical treatments that subsequent research determined to be of no value to patients and often harmful. Some of the finest scientific minds had prescribed them to their patients because they believed them to be "reasonable" and "logical" treatments—much as Benjamin Rush, M.D., prescribed and administered his purge-and-bleed treatments during the yellow fever epidemic of 1793.[21] Ironically, even if purge-and-bleed treatments had been effective in treating yellow fever, sterilization remained unknown, and septicemia born of bacteria-laden lancets would almost surely have claimed many lives.

Four days after Rush himself had apparently contracted the disease, he emerged from his sick room and stumbled down the stairs, determined to resume what he believed was his divine mission. Believing God had appointed him to heal the sick, he naturally believed that God had also protected him from death. Unfortunately, his fervent beliefs prevented him from questioning his medical theories and treatments more carefully.

"I depend upon divine protection," he insisted to his wife, "and feel that at present I live, move, and have my being in a more especial manner in God alone."[22] In another letter he told her, "My life, so long and so often forfeited to divine justice, is still preserved. . . . I have . . . much work for my divine master to be performed in months and years to come, but if he means to have it completed by other hands, 'his will be done.'"[23]

"God preserve and comfort you, my dearest friend," Julia replied, "prays she who is with the greatest sincerity, your affectionate wife, Julia Rush."[24]

Suffering too much to venture abroad, Rush nonetheless admitted and treated one hundred patients in his home office that day.

By October 1, the epidemic was growing worse, claiming an average of seventy deaths a day over a two-week period and, on October 1, it reached into the Rush household and claimed his sister. She had worked day and night treating patients since the beginning of the epidemic. When Rush had urged her to flee the city, she refused, saying she would stay to help him even if she died of the disease. "My life is of no consequence to anybody compared to his," she said of her service to her brother.

"She was my friend and counselor . . . my nurse in sickness," Rush wrote as he mourned his sister. "She gave her life to save mine." Rush said her last words had been, "A thousand and a thousand thanks to you, my dear brother, for all your kindness to me."[25]

The death of his sister traumatized Rush. He grew noticeably weaker each day. Three days later, on October 4, he resumed riding across the city, but, after visiting almost fifty homes, he fell into a near-faint at the bedside of a patient, and the patient's family had to help Rush home. Although he remained in bed the remainder of the day, he darted out the door the following day, October 5, increasing his activities on the 6th and 7th. And after six other doctors fell ill on the 8th, Rush doubled his activities to compensate for their absence. On the 9th, however, as the epidemic's daily death toll soared above one hundred, Benjamin Rush collapsed, and they carried him home to his bed to die.

CHAPTER 9

Bleed, Bleed, Bleed

S PENT AND SICK, Benjamin Rush struggled into consciousness the next morning and sent for Philip Syng Physick, the young surgeon Rush had mentored. Physick had earned his M.D. at the University of Edinburgh only a year earlier but had proved remarkably skilled, even developing his own unique techniques for performing cataract surgery and tonsillectomies. After Physick had contracted yellow fever a month earlier, he sent for Rush and later credited Rush with having saved his life by appropriate bleeding and purging. Physick subsequently became a staunch advocate of the Rush treatment for his own patients.

Physick sped to Rush's bedside to bleed the legendary physician, and Rush subsequently proclaimed that he owed his life to Physick's bleeding, followed by "one of my purges." He believed he had "proved upon my own body," as he put it to his wife, that his remedy had made yellow fever as easy to cure as a common cold.

"I am now perfectly well," he exaggerated in a letter to Julia two days after his collapse, "so much that I rested better last night than I have for a week past." He warned her against coming to see him, however, saying "the city is a great mass of contagion."[1]

Despite his flirtation with death, he resolved to continue treating the sick as soon as his strength permitted. Too weak to drive himself, however, he hired a driver to help him resume his rounds. On the third day after his collapse he stepped from his house and rode about town, expecting to visit "a dozen to twenty" patients. Describing "the distress which pervades our city," he wrote to Julia of the sick dying alone, without care. "Some perish for want of a draught of water. Parents desert their children as soon as they are infected. . . . Many people thrust their parents into the streets as soon as they complain of a headache.

"Adieu, my dearest and kindest friend," he ended his letter to Julia. "You lie near my heart. . . . Continue to pray without ceasing not only for me but for a distressed and desolating city. Some of the rich suffer, but the weight of the distress and mortality falls upon the poor. May God recompense to them double hereafter for their unparalleled sufferings here."[2]

Slowly, day by day, Rush recovered his health and increased the number of patients he treated, but the seeds of suspicion that Dr. Currie had planted in some minds took root. With only one newspaper left to report conditions in the city, its articles carried information and misinformation. One article claimed that Rush himself had abandoned hope that the city would ever recover from the epidemic.

"'Tis said that 150 were buried in the city yesterday," Elizabeth Drinker, a prominent Quaker, wrote in her diary. A Rush ally in the Pennsylvania Society for Promoting the Abolition of Slavery, Drinker cited Rush as believing that "the disorder was now past the art of man or medicine to cure, that nothing but the power of the Almighty could stop it."[3]

Her claim was untrue, of course, and simply added to Rush's bitterness at the growing number of ugly remarks emanating from physicians without enough courage to remain in the city to treat epidemic victims. "Never before did I witness such a mass of ignorance and wickedness as our profession has exhibited in the course of the present calamity," Rush growled. "Indeed, the principal mortality of the disease now is from the doctors. . . . I almost wish to renounce the name of physician."[4]

Enraged by both the slanders and cowardice of so many fellow physicians, Rush resigned from the College of Physicians that he had helped found. To answer his attackers, he began writing *An Account of the Bilious Remitting Yellow Fever as It Appeared in the City of Philadelphia in the Year 1793.*

"I have kept a diary of everything that related to the disease and in the operation of the remedies which I used to cure it," he explained to his friend James Pemberton, a prominent Quaker abolitionist. "From the success which attended the use of mercury, jalap, and the lancet . . . I am disposed to believe it will never be so fatal hereafter as it has been."[5]

The result was the first comprehensive examination of the epidemic, and although he reached incorrect conclusions about the cause and cure of yellow fever, it became a classic reference work in its time and remains an important historic, if not scientifically accurate, document of that era and the devastating epidemic.

As the epidemic peaked, it claimed among its victims the popular Philadelphia mayor Samuel Powel, who, with his wife, were close friends and neighbors of President and Martha Washington. "Our people heard after meeting . . . 40 persons sent to the hospital and vast numbers buried," Elizabeth Drinker noted in her diary on October 5. "It is said . . . 80 persons were bury'd in the potter's field. If that be true, 'tis indeed alarming to a great degree. . . . The disorder now, 'tis said, still rages."[6]

Though still weak, Rush returned to work full time treating patients—from fifty to as many as one hundred fifty a day—then answering letters and ending his long day with an emotional letter to his wife: "Another day has been added to my life," he wrote at the end of September. "I have tottered up about a dozen pairs of stairs. . . . I have just seen the sexton of the Quaker meeting who [thinks] upwards of an 100 have been buried daily . . . throughout the city and that the mortality increases. . . . Adieu. Continue to pray for us, and for none more than your ever faithful friend."[7]

After regaining his health, however, Rush grew sicker in the days that followed, though probably not from yellow fever. The symptoms he described resemble tuberculosis more closely than yellow fever. "A slow fever attended with irregular chills and a troublesome cough hung constantly upon me. . . . I took a dose of the mercurial medicine and went to bed. In evening, I took a second dose and lost ten ounces more blood. . . . The next day I came down and prescribed in my parlor for not less than an hundred people."[8]

As he grew more feeble and less able to travel, more patients flocked to his door, and, with many collapsing on arrival, his house turned into a makeshift morgue as well as hospital. The epidemic was claiming more than one hundred a day, bringing the total number of deaths by mid-October to more than 4,000 in a city of 50,000.

And then the weather changed.

"It blows hard N.W. and is very cold,"[9] Elizabeth Drinker noted in her diary. And the next day was "a beautiful pleasant fall day" followed by "a delightful cool frosty morning. 'Tis generally agreed that the fever is very much abated," she wrote. A few days later, she noted, "very cold . . . and seems likely to snow. . . . The fever appears to be nearly at an end, for which we cannot be too thankful."[10]

On November 1, 1793, Benjamin Rush, Elizabeth Drinker, and other survivors of the epidemic rejoiced as they read Philadelphia's lone surviving newspaper, the *Federal Gazette*: "It gives great pleasure to the Editor to hear from every quarter of our city that universal health prevails in a degree equal to any formal period in the history of this country."[11]

Later that day Drinker "had the agreeable intelligence from my children that the wagons were taking the people and goods back to the city. It is cleared up this morning with a fine frost. What a favorable reverse, which calls for humility and thanks."

On November 5, Philadelphia celebrated the end of the great epidemic "by firing guns, ringing bells, bonfires," according to Drinker. "Inhabitants were fast moving into the city. . . . 'tis said there were upwards of 20,000 had left their dwellings and retired into the country."[12]

Returning landlords were among the happiest of the Philadelphians. When tenants failed to pay their rents during the epidemic, regardless of whether they were alive or dead, their landlords invariably foreclosed and, on paper at least, they repossessed the dwellings.

By November 13, the epidemic seemed to have ended as abruptly as it began. "When we arose this morning," Elizabeth Drinker smiled, "it was snowing fast, the houses and trees cover'd." Left unwritten in the lady's diary was that the falling snow had smothered swarms of mosquitoes and larvae that had carried the epidemic to the city.[13]

"We may ever remember the Thirtieth of November," Vice President John Adams wrote to his wife, Abigail, "because . . . it was the day on which I entered this City in 1793.

Finding by all accounts that the pestilence was no more to be heard of . . . I drove directly to Market Street and took possession of my old chamber and bed. The principal families have returned, the President is here; several members of Congress are arrived. . . . The greatest mortality appears to have been in bad houses and among loose women and their gallants among the sailors and low foreigners. . . . I hope to convince Philadelphia that all has not been well. Moral and religious reflections I shall leave to their own thoughts: but the cleanness of the streets I shall preach in season and out of season. . . . My duty and love where due/yours forever[14]

As snow fell in Philadelphia, French sailors on Genet's fleet in New York mutinied, seized control of their ships, and sailed home to France. To add to Genet's indignity, the sailors sailed off with his funds and left him unable to pay outstanding debts to merchants in Boston, New York, Philadelphia, Charleston, and elsewhere. The drafts for $100,000 he had issued to New York shipbuilders to refit the French fleet were worthless.

To Washington's relief, a new French ambassador, Jean-Antoine-Joseph Fauchet, arrived in Philadelphia a month later and, after presenting his diplomatic credentials, he displayed a French-government warrant for the arrest and execution of Edmond Genet. Rumors held that a guillotine aboard Fauchet's ship stood ready to carry out the sentence. Although Vice-President Adams despised Genet, he recoiled at the fate awaiting the young Frenchman.

"Poor Genet I fear is undone," Adams wrote to his wife, Abigail. "Bad as his conduct has been, I cannot but pity him. What will become of him, I know not."[15]

By then Genet's friend, Secretary of State Jefferson, had resigned from office and retired to his plantation in Charlottesville, Virginia. His departure ended the deep divisions in the cabinet and forced Genet to plead with a new Secretary of State—Edmund Randolph—not to enforce the warrant. A former Virginia governor and close friend of Washington, Randolph turned to the President for guidance.

"We ought not to wish his punishment," Washington decided, and granted the Frenchman the equivalent of political asylum and the protection of the government he had tried to overthrow.[16] Fearing Fauchet's agents would kidnap him, Genet fled Philadelphia during the night and found his way to a secluded hideaway on a friend's farm in Connecticut. Before leaving, however, he sent word to Benjamin Rush to come to his quarters to bleed and purge him as a precaution against yellow fever.

A year later, substantial funds materialized to permit Genet's purchase of his own farm in Jamaica, Long Island, where he assumed the title of *cultivateur américain* and disappeared from public life amidst his fruits and vegetables.*

The snows that smothered the yellow fever epidemic did not quiet the controversy over Rush's bleed-and-purge methods, however. Indeed, it gained momentum, with some of Rush's colleagues who had fled Philadelphia returning and voicing the most vicious criticisms. One even accused him of murdering patients. Curiously, it was Dr. Hugh Hodge, the doctor whose little girl was the first victim of the epidemic, who most criticized Rush—with no evident reason. "Dr. Hodge leads the list of my calumniators," Rush wrote to his wife. "I gave him no offense. I never intended to begin a controversy with him."[17]

Rush had already resigned from the College of Physicians, but in a spiteful gesture, he now sent the college a copy of Dr. Thomas Sydenham's classic work *On Acute and Chronic Diseases: With Their Histories and Modes of Cure*. A treatise that Rush had studied as a medical student, it championed blood-letting and remained his medical "bible" and that of many hundreds of other doctors in Britain and America.[18]

Although Julia and the children yearned to rejoin him, Rush feared their reunion might be premature. "You cannot be more impatient for

---

*The pro-French governor of New York, George Clinton, sheltered Genet and, when Genet proposed to Clinton's daughter Cornelia, her dowry provided the funds to buy their farm. Genet died at the age of seventy-one, on Bastille Day, July 14, 1834, having fathered two daughters and four sons by Cornelia Clinton. The sons all joined the American military as did their sons, and one of Genet's great-great-grandsons, Edmund Charles Clinton Genet, was the first American aviator killed in battle after the United States entered World War I. Not yet twenty-one, Genet died in the skies over France with the Lafayette Escadrille, a group of American fliers who volunteered to fight on the side of France and her allies before the United States entered the war.

our meeting than I am," he cautioned Julia, "but I dread the thought of seeing you in town till the city is more thoroughly purified from the contagion of the yellow fever." He warned her that many of those who had returned prematurely had become ill and died. But he then added his first playful words after months of penning tales of doom and gloom:

"I do not give up my hopes of being able to pay you a short visit," Rush wrote to Julia. "Will you consent to receive me without the usual modes of salutation among long absent and affectionate friends?"[19] Clearly, Rush envisioned better times ahead.

They arrived sooner than he expected when Julia refused to prolong their separation and embarked unexpectedly for Philadelphia with the children.

"I want words to describe my emotions," he wrote to Julia on November 12, "upon hearing that the dearest person to me on the face of the earth is at last within three miles of me after a long and most distressing separation."[20] In anticipation of their arrival, Rush ordered his surviving servants to scrub every inch of the walls and floors of his Walnut Street home. He ordered windows left open and all the beds and furniture moved outside into the open air.

When Julia Rush and his children finally arrived, Rush lost control of his emotions, abandoning all restraint and greeting them with what he had called "the usual modes of salutation" holding Julia in his arms and kissing her full on the lips. "I have often said that you were an uncommon woman," he whispered. "I can now truly say that you are a great woman. . . . For such a wife and such children, I desire to be thankful."[21]

After spending several days celebrating their reunion, Rush tried resuming his practice, but found the assertions of his enemies had cost him the confidence of his wealthiest patients. Nor did he have the physical strength (or finances) to resume his exhausting—and costly—forays into Philadelphia's poor neighborhoods. Indeed, his devotion to the poor had cost him about $30,000 of his own funds to provide the indigent with medicines (and often food) they needed. Benjamin Rush was on the verge of bankruptcy, and at the worst possible time. Julia had just given birth to their eighth child, Samuel. And, to celebrate the boy's birth, he bought watermelons for all the prisoners in the Philadelphia jail. In return, he asked prisoners only that "they should consider that God, by disposing the heart of one of his creatures to show them an act of kindness, is still their Father and their Friend."[22]

Blessed (or cursed, depending on his mood) with leisure time, he finished writing and published his book *An Account of the Bilious Remitting Yellow Fever as It Appeared in the City of Philadelphia in the Year 1793*. At the same time, he began what would be a long-term inquiry into the causes of yellow fever, temporarily abandoning his diary, or "Commonplace Book."

Indeed, he noted only the arrival and visit to the United States of British scientist Joseph Priestly, the discoverer of dephlogisticated air, or oxygen, and carbonated water. Priestly had been a great friend of Benjamin Franklin and he now joined the American Philosophical Society in hopes of finding new partners in learned conversation.

"He raised many instances of the persecuting conduct of the church and court towards him," Rush explained in noting Priestley's emigration from his native country. The founder of Unitarianism in England, Priestly would eventually leave Philadelphia with his wife to try to found a utopian community in Northumberland County, then a wilderness in central Pennsylvania, about 150 miles northwest of Philadelphia.

At the beginning of summer, Rush rejoiced as he visited Philadelphia's new Walnut Street Prison, where officials had adopted almost all the reforms he had advocated five years earlier. "The prisoners, about 50 from the whole state, convicted on light offenses . . . all busy working . . . sawing marble . . . weaving . . . shoemaking . . . tailoring . . . cutting or chipping logwood." One prisoner earned sixty dollars for his efforts, Rush noted, while another earned enough to make restitution for a stolen horse.

> They work from daylight 'till 6 o'clock. . . . Care of morals: Preaching, read good books, cleanliness in dress, rooms, &c., bathing, no loud speaking, no wine . . . no obscene or profane conversation. . . . Constant work, familiarity with garden, a beautiful one, 1200 heads of cabbage, supplies the jail with vegetables, kept by prisoners.[23]

August 1794 saw the reappearance of yellow fever in Charleston, Baltimore, Philadelphia, New York, and New Haven. Rush sprang into action in Philadelphia. This time he had a formidable ally at his side: Dr. Philip Syng Physick, the young surgeon he had treated for yellow fever with bleed-and-purge therapy the previous year and who had reciprocated by treating Rush the same way. With the return of the disease, Rush wrote to Philadelphia's Committee of Health alerting them to its presence and asserting, "The remedies of bleeding and purging continued to be successful in every case in which they were applied on the first day, and could all the physicians in the city be prevailed . . . to treat it with copious evacuations, there would be no more danger to life . . . from it than from measles or influenza."[24] He said Dr. Physick and three other prominent physicians concurred with him and urged the committee to make the information public.

The effects of the disease were less dramatic than in the previous year— perhaps, in part, because mosquito bites received by those who survived the previous year's epidemic had inoculated them against further infection. Rush, of course, could not know this, but nonetheless took credit for the reduced casualties of the epidemic.

"My success has been much greater this year than last," he boasted, "owing to my patients being so much better attended and nursed. I have bled more freely. . . . From a newly arrived Englishman, I took 144 ounces [nine pints!] of blood at twelve bleedings in six days—four were in twenty hours. I gave him within the course of the same six days nearly 150 grains of calomel, with the usual proportions of jalap and gambage [an explosive emetic and cathartic]."*

It was fortunate indeed for the Englishman that the normal human body replaces most of the fluid, or plasma, lost in a pint of blood in about twenty-four hours. With nine pints of blood in six days, Rush drained the poor man of 90 percent of his blood supply—a bit less if he was a big man of above average height and weight—and sent him into hemorrhagic shock (short of breath, dizzy, sweating) for some of the time.†

---

*Derived from the gum resin of trees found in Sri Lanka, Thailand, and Cambodia, or, in French, *Cambodge* (hence, the similarly pronounced name *gambage*).

†With four bleedings in the first twenty-four hours, Rush may have drained him of as much as 30 percent of his blood supply (forty-eight ounces, or three pints), but the patient's body may have replaced the plasma in at least one of those pints in the ensuing twenty-four hours, for a net loss of only two pints of whole blood (less if he was a big man). Although enough to send him into hemorrhagic shock, a loss

"Such has been the clamor against me," Rush wrote to a friend in London, "that a proposal has been made in a company of citizens to 'drum me out of the city.' I am not moved by insults, but persist in asserting and defending all my opinions respecting the disease."[25]

Rush insisted he had achieved "unparalleled success," having lost only 2 of 120 patients he treated in the early stages of the yellow fever. He said that, in addition to Physick and two other prominent doctors in Philadelphia, doctors in Charleston, Baltimore, and New Haven had adopted his bleed-and-purge treatment "with almost universal success. Physick has in two cases saved his patients by drawing 120 ounces [7.5 pints, or 75 percent of the average person's blood supply]."[26]

Although questions in the press about bleed-and-purge treatments discouraged some of his former patients from seeking his help, a collapse in land values in the fall of 1796 left many Rush patients unable to afford his services and further eroded his practice. Unscrupulous Philadelphia brokers had fueled a boom in land values by selling nonexistent lands or lands with unclear titles to naïve would-be settlers streaming in from Europe. As whispers of fraudulent deals grew in volume, however, investors suddenly stopped buying and sent land prices plunging, dragging legitimate and illegitimate land speculators alike into bankruptcy. Among the casualties were former New York Congressman William Duer and Pennsylvania Senator Robert Morris, a signer of the Declaration of Independence and Superintendent of Finance for Congress during the Revolutionary War.

"A spirit of speculation infected all ranks," Rush noted. "The President of the Bank of Pennsylvania drew $100,000 without accounting for it. . . . Hundreds drew their money from banks . . . to lend it . . . at usurious interest, all of whom suffered more or less by the failure."[27]

---

of two pints may not have put him at death's door. With the eight bleedings that followed in the next five days, Rush extracted twelve ounces a day, while the Englishman's body probably produced sixteen new ounces of plasma a day—enough to replace the twelve drained on that day and four of the thirty-two-ounce deficit from the first day's bleeding. At the end of the five days, the man may have had a net deficit of only one pint of whole blood, of which he would recover the plasma in the ensuing twenty-four hours. Two centuries after the fact, however, it is impossible to know the facts.

Caught in what he called "the great distress [that] pervaded our city," Rush sold more than 8,000 of the 20,000 acres of undeveloped land he had bought as a speculation. "It is said . . . 150 [failures] occurred in six weeks," Rush reported, "and sixty-seven [including Robert Morris] went to jail in two weeks."[28] The death of a colleague, however, allowed Rush to compensate for the shrinkage of his practice by assuming the chair of theory and practice of medicine at the University of Pennsylvania, where one hundred students and six apprentices crowded into his classroom to hear his lectures. Paid directly by students in such courses, he added enough income from his lectures to continue his research into the origins of yellow fever.

Each time he examined and reexamined the literature on the disease and his notes from the epidemic of 1793, he returned to the same conclusion: that it emanated from bad air, or "exhalations" from stagnant water in gutters, cellars, sewers, privies, puddles and ponds of stagnant water on the docks and elsewhere, foul air emanating from the holds of ships, and rotting vegetable and animal matter in markets and other public places. To support his views, he cited the success eradicating bubonic plague by cleaning streets in British and Dutch cities.

Ironically, his conclusions were correct—indeed, tantalizingly close to the actual solution to the yellow fever epidemic. By urging city officials and citizens to clean and remove stagnating water from streets, gutters, ponds, puddles, sewers, privies, and other wet or damp areas, he effectively reduced the number of breeding sites for mosquitoes and, therefore, the intensity of subsequent epidemics. He had no way of knowing, however, that he had overlooked the link that tied stagnating water to the actual cause: the mosquito that had bred in the water and carried the yellow fever virus to humans much as the rat flea carried the bubonic plague.

Although he provoked a citywide cleanup, Rush's public denunciations of the city's filth enraged bankers and land developers, who feared the Rush warnings would drive businesses out of Philadelphia. Rejecting the premise that their city could be the source of so deadly a disease, they fed the press with more criticisms of Rush and his bleed-and-purge treatments and drove still more of his patients away.

Rush used the spare time he accumulated from his shrinking practice to renew his efforts to promote abolition and improve living conditions among Philadelphia's growing population of free blacks migrating from the South. Most, he said, could find employment only as servants or sailors—jobs he deemed demeaning for the better skilled. He proposed buying up western lands and forming a huge farm cooperative where blacks could work the land and profit from their efforts. He then donated some of his own land to get the project under way.

"Most of the black men who come to Philadelphia from New Jersey and the southern states are farmers," he argued. "In order to . . . obtain employment for them more congenial to their knowledge . . . I request the Abolition Society to accept 5,000 [acres of] desirable land in Bedford County . . . for the settlement of blacks."[29]

In January 1795, Rush accepted the presidency of the national convention of abolition societies held in Philadelphia that year. In his opening declaration, he pleaded with delegates to redouble their efforts to repeal slavery laws in their respective states. At the time, only Massachusetts had issued an outright ban on slavery, although Pennsylvania, Vermont, New Hampshire, Connecticut, and Rhode Island had banned the slave trade and introduced gradual abolition. In Europe, Portugal and England had abolished it, and Rush was able to report that France had just declared all blacks free, with full citizenship, in France and all its territories.

Another midsummer outbreak of yellow fever in 1795, however, interrupted Rush's medical research and his work with the Abolition Society. But as he resumed what he called "copious depletions" to treat the stricken, criticisms mounted again in Philadelphia and elsewhere. In New York, where the epidemic raged far worse than in Philadelphia, the noted physician Alexander Hosack charged that the "promiscuous use of the lancet" advocated by Rush had proved "injurious and unsuccessful.

"In the New York Hospital," Hosack reported, "it was frequently employed, but in the majority of cases, the disease terminated fatally. . . . Generally speaking, bloodletting was attended with pernicious consequences. . . . Several of our most respectable practitioners agreed. The more common and successful practice was to procure free evacuation from the bowels . . . by calomel and jalap."[30]

Hosack and other New York physicians, however, were no more successful stemming the epidemic than Rush had been the previous year in

Philadelphia. Indeed, Rush's bleed-and-purge treatments seemed far more effective than Hosack's approach. Physick also boasted of a remarkably high rate of success using the Rush approach. What neither Rush nor Physick understood was that the cumulative effect of two years of epidemics had rendered an ever-growing proportion of Philadelphians somewhat or totally immune to the fever. Those with mild cases, from which they would have recovered with simple bed rest and no medical treatment, nonetheless submitted to bleed-and-purge treatments. When they then recovered, they naturally sang the praises of Rush or Physick or both and sent their friends and relatives for similar treatments.

"Dr. Physick has become a champion for our remedies," Rush wrote to a colleague in London, "and under the influence of the success of his practice . . . he has risen into an extensive and profitable business."[31] Much of Physick's success resulted from his skills as not only a surgeon but as an ingenious entrepreneur. The inventive young Physick's "medical insurance plan"—launched when he first began practicing three years earlier—had become a highly profitable enterprise, with hundreds subscribing at $20 to cover their medical needs for a year. In an era long before the annual medical check-up became a norm, few subscribers ever needed his services.*

As Rush had once shunted the overflow of patients at his office to Physick, Physick now reciprocated, with both profiting handsomely from the 1795 epidemic. "Dr. Physick is established owing in part to . . . his

---

*Called the "Father of American Surgery" by some historians, Physick went on to invent such innovative medical instruments as needle-tip forceps, adaptive splints, and customized traction equipment for various bones. He also pioneered advanced techniques of surgery to remove gallstones and cataracts, as well as tonsils and other diseased body parts. In 1831, he operated on Chief Justice John Marshall, removing about 1,000 gall stones with the forceps he invented and effecting a full recovery for the stricken jurist. [See Harlow Giles Unger, *John Marshall: The Chief Justice Who Saved the Nation* (Boston: Da Capo Press, 2014).] Physick displayed skills as an entrepreneur as well as a physician, buying unmarked bottles of carbonated water from a local pharmacist and reselling them to patients for $1.50 a month to relieve stomach and intestinal disorders and broadening the use of the word "physic" to include such medicines.

having adopted the new principles in medicine," Rush effused, adding that "my enemies have unwittingly made me one of the richest men in the United States."[32]

As late autumn frosts extinguished the epidemic of 1795, a curious parade of "maniacal patients" approached Rush for treatment at the hospital and at his home. "They yield to copious blood-letting," Rush concluded to no one's surprise. "I discharged three patients in one day as cured of that deplorable malady . . . from the hospital. . . . Madness is nothing but the chronic state of frenzy."[33]

Rush's brash display of omniscience, of course, couched total ignorance of the subject—not uncommon behavior among doctors, professors, and thinkers. Rush and other physicians of his era seldom admitted that they did not know the answer to a question. It was—and remains—the curse of many physicians that their patients, often frightened, in pain, or facing death, view their doctors as keepers of knowledge to which they alone in the world are privy—knowledge that can ease fright, soothe pain, and prevent death. Seduced by such abject deference, some physicians begin to believe in their own omniscience and ignore the warning of the great nineteenth-century Canadian physician Sir William Ostler* to his students:

> Medicine is an art, not a trade; a calling not a business; a calling in which your heart will be exercised equally with your head. Often . . . your work will have nothing to do with potions and powders, but with the exercise of the strong upon the weak . . . of the wise upon the foolish.[34]

Fortunately, Julia Rush would not put up with her husband's self-absorption, always questioning (gently) the source of his assertions. Just as fortunately, he was, at heart, humble enough in the quiet of his home to reexamine many of his most outrageous assertions.

---

*Often called the "father of modern medicine," Sir William Ostler (1849–1919) was a Canadian physician and one of four founding professors of Johns Hopkins Hospital in Baltimore, Maryland. He created the first residency program for specialty training of physicians.

"Your letter . . . gave me great pleasure," he responded to one of Julia's gentle reproaches. "I have the deepest sense of your fervent and unabated affection for me. . . . "[35] And in another response to Julia's suggestion that he refer to the 37th Psalm, he replied contritely, "I have been rebuked, humbled, and comforted by reading the 37th Psalm. I find I am a perfect Jew in unbelief. I desire to be humbled into the dust for it."[36]

He did not have to wait long.

When Rush entered the new wing for the insane at the Pennsylvania Hospital a few days later, the incoherent utterings and screams left him shaken, dumbfounded, and in tears. For once, he had no omniscient pronouncement, but his responses would shake the medical world.

CHAPTER 10

The Father of Psychiatry

T HE EPIDEMIC OF 1793 had shut Pennsylvania Hospital, including
the new wing that Rush had badgered the state into financing to
house "cases of chronic madness." With the spread of yellow fever, however, attendants fled, leaving inmates unattended—and unfed. Many of
the unfettered simply left, hoping to find sustenance elsewhere. Others,
along with those who could not free themselves, died, either of neglect or
fever.

When the epidemic began, Rush had been no less guilty of neglecting
his mentally ill patients than attendants, but the demands of patients who
were dying with yellow fever across the city had left him without a moment for his maniacals.

When the hospital reopened, it took months before Rush could find
qualified attendants and almost three years passed before the wing was
functioning as it had before the epidemic. For those mental patients able
to cope and respond appropriately, he introduced two revolutionary
forms of treatment: One was an early form of "talk therapy," or as it is
now called, psychotherapy, which he developed from his own experiences
listening and responding in conversations with patients. The other treatment he had invented earlier but now reintroduced and expanded was
occupational therapy, which he derived by eliciting patient interests and
determining their skills.

To implement early talk therapy, he arranged that "an intelligent man and woman be employed to attend the different sexes, whose business shall be to direct and share in their amusements and to divert their minds by conversation, reading, and obliging them to read and write upon subjects suggested from time to time by the attending physicians."[1]

In designing occupational therapy, he explained, "Certain employments should be devised for such of the deranged as are capable of working." He listed spinning, sewing, and churning for women and, for men, cutting straw, weaving, digging in the garden, carpentry, and grinding corn on the wheel for feed for the hospital's horses and cows.

"My remedies for the recent cases," he wrote to a colleague, "were bleeding to 100 oz. down to 30 oz., strong purges, low diet, kind treatment, and the cold bath."[2] Deeply moved by the sadness and sense of solitude he heard in the ramblings of his patients, he began studying and lecturing on "diseases of the mind," becoming the first American physician to treat mental illness as a disease rather than willful criminal behavior or the work of the devil. He subsequently transcribed his notes into lectures that filled a fifth volume of his monumental *Medical Inquiries and Observations*. Entitled *Medical Inquiries and Observations upon the Diseases of the Mind*, Rush's book was the first, and, for more than a century, the only American study of and text on mental illness.* Rush's findings shook American medicine,

---

*French physician Philippe Pinel (1745–1826)—all but unknown outside his native land—was following a separate, albeit parallel path as Rush in France. A year older than Rush, Pinel had earned his medical degree in Toulouse, France, and found himself shunned as "a provincial" when he tried to practice medicine in Paris. Established physicians at the city's main hospital bumped him into an area they routinely avoided—the insane. Finding his charges at the mercy of untrained, sadistic attendants, he released patients from their chains, substituting more humane treatment for all and straitjackets for the most violent. Like Rush, he concluded that the insane suffered a disease and, in 1794, he published a landmark essay arguing for more humane treatment. Unlike Rush, Pinel did away with bleeding and purging, substituting regular visits and conversations with each patient—all, while taking copious notes. By 1810, however, Rush had yet to see Pinel's work, which had not been translated into English. Simultaneously but separately, Rush and Pinel each asserted for the first time in history—the one in America, the other in France—that mental illness was a disease like any other and neither the work of

politics, and theology to their foundations, awakening some, provoking others, infuriating many, and stunning the rest into silence.

As he developed the lectures that would fill *Diseases of the Mind*, Rush "was aware of its difficulty and importance" and knew he was "about to tread on consecrated ground," but prayed it would prove "the means of lessening a portion of some of the greatest evils of human life."[3] As it turned out, *Diseases of the Mind* would influence millions of patients, physicians, and families of the mentally ill to this day.

In collecting materials for "*medicina mentis*," as he often called his work, Rush pioneered startling advances in treating mental illness, including an early form of psychotherapy, physical therapy, occupational therapy, and medicinal treatments. The American Psychiatric Association honored Rush in 1965 by putting his portrait on its official seal and placing a bronze plaque on his grave, declaring him "Father of American Psychiatry."

In the century that followed publication of *Diseases of the Mind*, Rush's influence on treatment of the mentally ill would eventually reach beyond the hospital to the courtroom. In the last chapter of his book—"Of Derangement in the Moral Faculties"—Rush described several cases of murders by the mentally ill, or, as he called them, "the morally deranged." Ascribing the murders to a "state of mind in which the passions act involuntarily through the instrumentality of the will," he was the first American professional to argue for what is now the widely recognized legal defense of "not guilty by reason of insanity."

Convinced that God was directing his efforts with the insane as with all his other patients, Rush turned to his old stand-by treatments: bleedings and purges, restricted food intake, induced salivation, and cold baths.

When bleedings left patients semi-comatose and calm, Rush evaluated their apparent serenity as evidence of his having cured them. Addressing

---

the devil nor willful criminal defiance of societal morals and mores. In 1798, Pinel published his classic *Nosographie philosophique, ou méthode de l'analyse appliqué à la medicine*, which grouped mental illnesses into five basic categories: melancholia, mania without delirium, mania with delirium, dementia, and idiotism and earned Pinel the epithet as Europe's "father of psychiatry." Like Rush's works in America, they remained central to psychiatric practice in France for most of the nineteenth century.

his students with what became a historic lecture, Rush declared that madness often resulted from "the reciprocal influence of the body and mind upon each other. . . .

> They are part of the unity of disease, particularly of fever, of which madness is a chronic form affecting that part of the brain that is the seat of the mind. The cause of madness is seated primarily in the blood vessels of the brain, and it depends upon the same kind of morbid and irregular actions that constitutes other arterial diseases.[4]

He insisted that mental diseases resulted from abnormally excessive pressure and pulsation of blood vessels in the brain, and the cure—always predictable with Rush—bleeding and purging. As with the cause of yellow fever, Rush again was on the verge of making medical history, identifying two forms of psychologically induced physical ills—one, psychosomatic; the other, hypochondriacal.

"The characteristic symptom [of both]," he told his students, "is distress," which he said can provoke physical symptoms such as hives, sneezing, and lesions, in the case of psychosomatic illnesses. In the case of hypochondriasis, "[The patient] erroneously supposes himself to be afflicted with various diseases, particularly with consumption, cancer, stone, and, above all, with impotence and the venereal disease."[5]

Although he did not—could not—abandon bloodletting and purges as primary remedies, he directed medical students for the first time in the history of American medicine never to suggest that patient complaints are imaginary. "The first thing to be done by a physician," he told his students, "is to treat the disease in a serious manner.

> To consider it in any other light is to renounce all observation in medicine. However erroneous a patient's opinion of his case may be, his disease is a *real* one. It will be necessary, therefore, to listen with attention to his tedious and uninteresting details of its symptoms and cases.[6]

With that declaration, Benjamin Rush unveiled the first, most basic technique of early psychotherapy and set off tectonic changes in the treatment of the mentally ill in the United States.

The Rush tome explored the entire world of madness for the first time in the history of the English-speaking world, examining the most serious forms of "intellectual derangement" or "mania" as well as all-but-harmless forms such as "dissociation"—what the French called *demence.* "Subjects of it in Scotland are said to have a bee in their bonnets," Rush explained. "In the United States, we say they are 'flighty' or 'hair-brained' and, sometimes, 'a little cracked.'" The remedy, he said predictably, was "bleeding, low diet, purges, and all the other remedies for reducing morbid excitement of the brain."[7]

As for intellectual derangement, or, out-and-out madness ("psychosis," in more recent parlance), Rush listed every conceivable cause: injury to the brain; malformation and lesions of the brain; local disorders—tumors, abscesses, etc.; diseases of the brain or of the body that spread to the brain; insolation [sunstroke]; famine; "excessive use of ardent spirits"; great pain; certain narcotic substances; terror; fear; and grief.[8]

Rush grouped the long list of causes into four basic categories: (1) direct trauma to the brain—mostly injuries; (2) indirect trauma through the body—fevers, malnutrition, diseases, etc.; (3) systemic causes—alcohol, narcotics, and so forth; and (4) mental and emotional traumas, fear, etc.

To empirical causes of insanity, such as brain damage, Rush added anecdotal evidence of other possible causes: "An exquisite sense of delicacy produced madness in a school-master," Rush blushed, "who was accidentally discovered on a closet-stool by one of his scholars."

And he said an actor went mad in Philadelphia after the audience hissed him off the stage.

"Africans become insane," he said he was told, "soon after they enter the toils of perpetual slavery in the West Indies." And, Rush said, he learned that "hundreds [of people] have become insane in consequence of unexpected losses of money."[9]

Although he cited no specific cases, Rush claimed that madness could result from "inordinate sexual desires and gratifications" and that "onanism [masturbation]" induced madness in young men "more frequently than is commonly supposed by parents and physicians." Indeed, he added, "the morbid effects of intemperance in sexual intercourse with women are feebleness."[10]

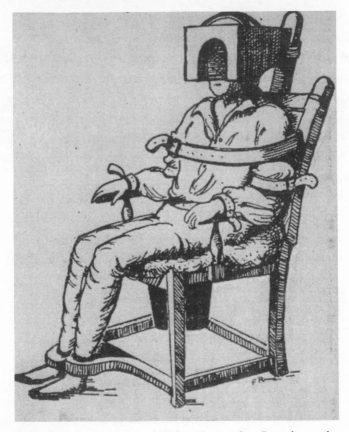

Benjamin Rush designed "The Tranquilizer" to keep the head of a maniacal patient in "a fixed and erect position" and prevent "the interruption of the passage of the blood to and from the brain."

Although bleeding and purging remained his primary treatment, not all his patients responded as he hoped. To try to cure "the violent state of madness" in some patients, he invented what he called a "Tranquilizer"—a chair that held the patient immobile in a sitting position.

He designed the Tranquilizer to replace the straitjacket, or "maddshirt," which he considered cruel. "They often lie whole days and nights, and sometimes in a position which delicacy forbids me to mention," he said of patients in straitjackets.

To obviate these evils, I requested . . . an ingenious cabinetmaker . . . to make for the benefit of the maniacal patients, a strong armchair. . . . By keeping the head in a fixed and erect position, it prevents the interruption of the passage of the blood to and from the brain. . . . It produced muscular inaction and acts . . . in weakening the force of the blood vessels in every part of the body.

Rush said the Tranquilizer made it easier for attendants to apply cold water to the patient's head and warm water to his feet—and to feel the patient's pulse before bleeding and purging. The seat had a large opening beneath which a removable pot with water in it allowed the patient to relieve himself without having to move him from his chair "or exposing him afterwards to the fetor [stench] of his excretions or to their contact with his body."[11]

Rush's studies and conclusions—right *and* wrong—initiated the start of a revolution in treatment of mental illness across the English-speaking world. His passion, eloquence, and vast knowledge attracted a loyal following of students and physicians who dedicated their lives to treating mental illness as a disease and the mentally ill in the most enlightened and humane ways possible at the time.

"For many centuries," he told his students, "they [the mentally ill] have been treated like criminals, or shunned like beasts of prey.

Happily, these times of cruelty to this class of our fellow creatures and insensibilities to their sufferings are now passing away. . . . The clanking of chains and the noise of the whip are no longer heard. They now taste the blessings of air and light and motion in pleasant shaded walks in summer and in spacious entries warmed by stoves in winter. . . . In consequence of these advantages, they have recovered . . . their long forgotten relationships to their friends and the public.[12]

When he had finished writing and publishing it, he considered his *Medical Inquiries and Observations upon the Diseases of the Mind* one of his greatest achievements and inscribed one copy to "My dear Friend John Adams," by then the second President of the United States.

"The subjects . . . have hitherto been enveloped in mystery," he told Adams. "I have endeavored to bring them down to the level of all other diseases of the human body and to show that the mind and body are moved by the same causes and subject to the same laws. . . . If they are not, I shall console myself with having aimed well and erred honestly."[13]

Adams was quick to reply, predicting "your valuable volume . . . will run mankind still deeper in your debt. If I could afford the expense, I would advertise a reward of a gold medal to the man of science who should write the best essay upon the question of whether the writings of Dr. Franklin or Dr. Rush do the greatest honor to America or the greatest good to mankind."[14]

Pleased with the outcome of the presidential election of 1796 and the accession of Adams to the chief magistracy, Rush congratulated his friend personally at a reception at the presidential mansion. He then wrote to his other friend, Thomas Jefferson, to "accept of my congratulations upon your election to the Vice President's chair of the United States and upon your *escape* [his italics] of the office of the President.

> In the present situation, it would have been impossible for you to have preserved . . . republican principles. . . . It has given me great pleasure to hear of Mr. Adams' speaking with pleasure of the prospect of administering the government in a connection with you.[15]

Rush also told Jefferson he was to be named president of the American Philosophical Society, a post he would hold until 1815 and one that would draw him ever closer to Rush. Jefferson, of course, had been away from the capital for three years. Because his pro-French leanings had put him in conflict with President Washington, Jefferson had resigned as secretary of state after the 1793 yellow fever epidemic and the impetuous Genet's attempt to overthrow the Washington administration.

Also missing from the cabinet at the beginning of Washington's second term was Jefferson's political enemy, Secretary of Treasury Alexander Hamilton, who had resigned following disclosures of flirtations with another man's wife in 1791. Feigning outrage, the cuckolded husband, a recidivist blackmailer, demanded a low-level Treasury Department post and payment of $1,000. After Hamilton complied, authorities arrested the blackmailer, James Reynolds, who went to jail for embezzling Treasury funds. Hamilton quit the cabinet rather than muddy the President and his cabinet with scandal.

After reorganizing his cabinet, President Washington alienated the French government by sending Chief Justice John Jay to restore trade relations with Britain. The French government responded by ending its alliance with the United States and sending naval vessels to scour the seas and seize American vessels and cargoes bound to and from England.

By the time Adams took his oath as second American President in 1797, the French had seized more than 340 American ships with cargoes valued at more than $55 million. Hundreds of American seamen were languishing in prisons in Brest, Bordeaux, and the French West Indies. President Adams called an urgent meeting of his cabinet and a special session of Congress to respond.

"France has already gone to war with us," the President barked. "She is at war with us but we are not at war with her."[16] Accordingly, Adams asked Congress for funds to reinforce coastal defenses, build a navy, arm merchant ships, and call up an army of 15,000 men to guard the shores against a possible French invasion. Vice President Jefferson called the President "insane," triggering a personal political feud that would last for more than a decade, with Rush one of the rare Founding Fathers who managed to retain close ties to both men.

When the feud began, though, Rush tried staying clear of political disputes. "I was once a republican," he admitted to a physician-friend, "but residence in a large city and a wife and eight children have degraded me into a mere physician. I once vented good feelings in favor of France, but I now hear her called by a thousand hard names without daring to say a word in her favor. . . . Her arms will soon settle the fate of the world."[17]

Before President Adams could begin building his new navy, another yellow fever epidemic swept into Philadelphia in July 1797 but proved "much less dreadful than in '93," according to Philadelphia publisher Richard Folwell.

"Citizens were more early aware of their danger than in '93 and fled into the country quickly," Folwell reported. "The subject has lost much of its novelty. The silent desolation of our streets one year displays a close resemblance to the same scene in another year."[18]

For once, the entire Philadelphia community—its physicians, politicians, and ordinary citizens—willingly followed Benjamin Rush's entreaties. Once opposed to Rush's bleed-and-purge treatments, Dr. William Currie now proclaimed to the medical profession: "The disease almost invariably gives way to judicious bleeding and mercurial purges when application is made soon after the attack." And the College of Physicians urged city officials and ordinary citizens to pay "the most scrupulous attention to cleaning and watering the streets, particularly washing out gutters, habits of temperance, caution as to clothing, fatigue of body, and exposure to sun and night air."[19]

By October 15, sixteen physicians had contracted the disease; eight died. One of the most tragic deaths was that of Dr. Jacob Thompson, who had wed, gone to bed with his bride, and, Folwell reported, "within two hours felt the symptoms of the disorder approaching. . . . The bridegroom died on the third day, leaving his wife at once a widow and a bride."[20]

The epidemic claimed almost 1,000 victims before it ended after an early October frost. Although Rush was able to boast, "I have as yet not lost a single patient," his success, he claimed, provoked "a revival of the old clamors and prejudices. . . . Testimonies will I hope be produced . . . which will amply refute the calumnies.[21]

Some of the calumnies Rush referred to were on display in a letter of Samuel Hodgdon, the superintendent of military stores and former quartermaster general to Secretary of State Timothy Pickering. "Rush behaves like a madman escaped from bedlam," Hodgdon wrote to Pickering.

> He has told two gentlemen of my acquaintance . . . to fly, for contagion was everywhere and that respiration could not be performed without the utmost hazard. . . . Good God, can the people be any longer deceived by a mountebank and resign all their comforts into the bloody experiments and inconsistency.[22]

The renewed criticisms damaged his practice again—and his income. "I had no new families except foreigners," Rush reported, "and many of my old patients deserted me.

Even the cures I performed added to the detraction that had taken place against my character. . . . No ties of ancient school fellowship, no obligations of gratitude . . . were able to resist the tide of public clamor that was excited against my practice. My name was mentioned with horror in companies.[23]

When Rush's friend the President learned of the doctor's precarious financial condition, however, he appointed Rush Treasurer of the US Mint—essentially a sinecure that even Rush admitted only "employs a few minutes of my time three or four times a week." It nonetheless paid him a then-lavish annual salary of £750 (about $100,000 today).

Although Adams knew Rush was a republican who had voted for Jefferson, he said he had "known, esteemed, and loved [Rush] these three and twenty years. . . . All things considered, my judgment inclines to Dr. Rush on account of ancient merits and present abilities . . . integrity and independence."[24]

Rush used some of his added income to buy a rundown twelve-acre farm two and one-half miles north of the city—just near enough to permit him to make quick, brief escapes from the diseased city air to the healthy, fresh country air. He called his country home "Sydenham" and its dilapidated house "Sydenham Hut."

"The noise of rural insects," he wrote to Julia, who had, as usual, taken the younger children to the safety of Morven, "the sight of domestic animals . . . the purity and coolness of the air, a pleasant and frugal supper of fruit and milk created for a few hours a flow of peaceful and happy feelings. . . . I forgot for a while the disputes and convulsions which now agitate our country and the globe. I forgot the persecutions of my enemies and felt as if I could welcome the most inveterate of them to partake of the simple fare of our little cottage."[25]

Discouraged by the growing volume of complaints and criticisms in Philadelphia, Rush wrote to a colleague at Columbia University's College of Physicians and Surgeons in New York applying for and winning a post on the medical school faculty. Trustee Alexander Hamilton, however, vetoed the appointment because of Rush's friendship with and political support for Jefferson.

Rush being Rush, he again emerged from his personal miseries by helping those more miserable than he. Three days before Christmas, he joined two wealthy ladies he knew and an equally well-off eccentric, Peter Brown, in sending a "request" to prisoners in the new jail "under sentence of confinement and labor to accept of a dinner of turkeys as a proof that they are still remembered in their present suffering condition by some of their fellow creatures." Peter Brown had accumulated a small fortune as a superb blacksmith, then built himself a regal coach, whose doors he adorned with a picture of an anvil and powerful bare forearm poised to strike. Beneath it a motto proclaimed, "By this, I got ye'."[26]

As criticism of Rush's bleed-and-purge treatments swelled again, John Fenno, the fervent Federalist editor of the *Gazette of the United States*, launched an attack on Jefferson and his republicans by targeting Rush, who seemed the most vulnerable of Jefferson's inner circle. In a barrage of "letters to the editor" that Fenno composed himself, he published vitriolic complaints about Rush and his "lunatic system" of treating yellow fever victims.

His charges, however, sparked equally angry replies defending Rush as "our American Hippocrates." Into the fray jumped the now-prominent Dr. Philip Syng Physick, one of the few physicians who had stayed in Philadelphia with Rush in 1793 to treat victims of the epidemic. A devoted disciple, Physick stormed to Rush's defense, recounting how Rush had saved Physick's own life during the epidemic of 1793.

"With a view to inspiring confidence in bloodletting in the cure of yellow fever," he wrote to the *Gazette of the United States*, "I take this method of informing my fellow citizens that I lost during my last attack of that fever one hundred and seventy-six ounces of blood by twenty-two bleedings in ten days. The efficacy of this invaluable remedy was aided by frequent and copious evacuations from my bowels and a moderate salivation."[27]

The furious back-and-forth exchange of letters boosted sales of Fenno's newspaper but so angered Rush that he sued the editor for libel.

"Assault on Liberty of the Press," Fenno's front-page headline fired back in the October 3 edition of the *Gazette*. He went on to intensify his assault on Rush, comparing the doctor's bloodletting to the guillotines of the French Revolution.

Ironically, Rush's libel suit would never reach a courtroom because Fenno, his wife, and newborn daughter contracted yellow fever during the epidemic of 1798 and died after Fenno publicly scorned an offer of treatment by Rush.

"The way is now open and smooth for my usefulness," Rush wrote to his wife. "Public confidence is again placed in me, and my opinions and advice have at last some weight."[28]

The demand for his services, however, was not nearly as great as it had been. Fenno's assaults had damaged his practice, and Rush claimed the public had paid the costs, with three to four thousand succumbing to the disease—almost as many as in 1793. Although thousands had fled the city, the mortality rate had actually climbed, with the disease claiming almost as many lives as it had from a much larger population in 1793. Rush blamed the increased mortality rate on "publications having excited general fears and prejudices against . . . the use of the lancet.

> Such was the influence of these publications that many persons who had recovered from this fever in former years by the use of depleting remedies [i.e., bleeding and purging] deserted the physicians who had prescribed them and put themselves under the care of physicians of opposite modes of practice. Most of them died.[29]

Reduced demand for Rush's treatments left him enough time to retreat to a shady grove of stately elms at Sydenham Farm each evening during the hot summer months and ride into the city each morning to treat patients. He spent especially hot days entirely at Sydenham making improvements "to surprise as well as please" Julia, who had yet to visit. His hope was to replace Morven with a similar retreat closer to town and allow the family to be together more often during summer months.

> I have built a neat brick kitchen, 16 by 12, with a convenient garret room above it. . . . I have added a story and a half to the old brick house, by which means we shall have two comfortable lodging rooms. . . . Ample space has been left everywhere for closets. . . . The building when finished will be convenient, cool, tight, and large enough to accommodate all such of our family as it will be proper to leave the city in warm weather.[30]

Instead of the respite from criticism that Rush had anticipated, Fenno's death spurred even more vicious press attacks on Rush, with the venomous English social critic William Cobbett all but lusting for Rush's republican blood. An obsessive malcontent whose personal beliefs vacillated wildly between monarchism and populism, Cobbett said he despised Americans for reasons that, depending on his mood, sometimes focused on their laziness and other times on their treacherous, treasonous break with Britain.

Cobbett sailed to America, where he published pro-Tory pamphlets until 1796, when he found a shop on Third Street in Philadelphia and began publishing a venom-filled newspaper he called *Porcupine's Gazette*. Printing 3,000 copies a day, he assaulted any and every republican he could think of—dead or alive. He lashed out at Vice President Jefferson, Benjamin Franklin, Tom Paine, Noah Webster, Lafayette, and, finally, Benjamin Rush, M.D. Rush, however, was more vulnerable than other Founding Fathers. He held no public office, owned no printing establishment, and had no public platform or rhetorical weapons to defend himself against the press.

Taking full advantage of First Amendment press freedoms, Cobbett became the consummate newspaper bully, slinging "mud, filth and venom" under the pseudonym "Peter Porcupine," according to Benjamin Russell, the editor-publisher of Boston's respected *Columbian Centinel*.[31] His relentless editorial assaults in *Porcupine's Gazette* "attacked and blackened the best characters the world ever boasted," including the defenseless Founding Father who believed God had put him on earth to heal the sick.

"The remorseless Dr. Rush," Cobbett all but foamed at the mouth, "shall bleed me till I am white as this paper before I'll allow that [he] was doing good to mankind." Cobbett compared Rush to "a mosquito, a horse-leach, a ferret, a pole-cat, a weasel: for these are all bleeders, and understand their business full as well as Dr. Rush." Crazed by an irrational determination to bring down the humanitarian-physician, Cobbett charged that Rush and the physicians who adopted his treatment methods "have slain tens of thousands" and would bleed his patients to the grave if not stopped.[32]

English editor William Cobbett led a vicious campaign
to discredit Benjamin Rush, who sued and won, forcing
Cobbett to flee to his native England. (NATIONAL POR-
TRAIT GALLERY)

In another particularly vicious assault, Cobbett inserted a satirical ver-
sion of an advertisement in one of the articles he wrote:

Wanted, by a physician, an entire new set of patients, his old ones having given him the slip; also a slower method of dispatching them than
phlebotomy [opening a vein], the celerity of which does not give time for
making out a bill.[33]

Nor was Cobbett done. "That his mind was elevated to a state of enthusiasm bordering on frenzy," Cobbett said of Rush, "I had frequent
opportunity of observing; and I have heard . . . that in passing through

Kensington one day, with his black man on the seat of his chaise alongside of him, he cried out with vociferation, 'Bleed and purge all Kensington! Drive on, boy!'"[34]

Deeply wounded, but unwilling to be drawn into an unseemly public controversy. Rush answered only that the Britisher Cobbett had singled him out for having signed the Declaration of Independence "and latterly declared myself a republican."[35]

Cobbett's continuing attacks on Rush, however, infuriated Rush's two oldest sons, twenty-three-year-old John, by then a lieutenant in the US Navy, and seventeen-year-old Richard, just graduated from college at Princeton. "My children were insulted . . . at school and in the streets," Rush complained—so much so that Richard knocked down a doctor who criticized his father, while John decided to confront Cobbett and punish him.

Conspicuous for his erratic behavior throughout his childhood, John had entered Princeton College in 1792, left abruptly in 1794 to become a medical apprentice with his father, but quit just as abruptly in 1795 to join the navy as a surgeon, with the rank of lieutenant. When a doctor on shore criticized Benjamin Rush in a letter to Cobbett's newspaper, Lieutenant Rush wrote to the doctor before confronting him and beating him with a cane. Cobbett responded by assailing young Rush in his newspaper as "an impertinent puppy . . . a liar, and a rascal."[36]

Fearful Cobbett might wait in ambush and kill his son, Rush wrote to New York lawyer Henry Brockholst Livingston, a fellow Princeton alumnus: "This day my eldest son, John Rush, set off in the mail stage for New York to obtain satisfaction of Cobbett for the falsehoods he has published.

> His spirit is uncommonly firm and determined, and his resentments are keen. . . . I tremble therefore for the consequences of a meeting between them. I . . . call upon you as a friend to find him out and by persuasion or the force of law arrest him in his present undertaking. . . . You are a father. Feel and act as you would wish me to do for your children in a similar situation.[37]

Livingston was able to find young Rush and persuade him not to confront Cobbett. Not to be bested, Cobbett conjured a tale of a

"Captain Still," whom Rush allegedly sent in his stead "to call me to account . . . armed *á la mode de Rush* with a bludgeon cane, which, as it had an iron poker to encounter, remained quiet in his hand. And so the noble Captain marched off without beat of drum."[38]

That was enough for Benjamin Rush. He had grown accustomed to personal attacks, but would not tolerate attacks on members of his family. He sued Cobbett for libel.

"Damn him," Cobbett complained. "I will attack him for it."[39]

And he did—in an open letter he published in *Porcupine's Gazette*, Cobbett addressed Charles Willson Peale, whose natural history museum in Philadelphia displayed a mastodon skeleton among other specimens.

> In these degenerate days, dog eats dog and surgeon slays surgeon when he can get no other subject. Take my advice: throw out your snakes and your alligators and replace them with the more venomous brutes above mentioned. . . . Dr. Rush with lancet in his hand should be your doorkeeper.[40]

As more Rush patients turned to other physicians, Rush hoped his suit would quiet his tormentor—but it only spurred Cobbett to more vicious attacks.

"Dying Easy," read the headline in *Porcupine's Gazette*. "Rush having bled a patient within an inch of the grave and being about to give him the finishing stroke, the relations remonstrated, observing that it was useless, for the poor young man was already dying.

"'Very well then,' replied the Quack [Rush], 'it will put him out of his misery and make him die quick.'

"And ought butchers like this to be tolerated?" Cobbett asked. "These monsters look upon every patient that has the misfortune to fall into their hands as a lump of flesh and blood on which they have a right to make experiments. . . . I would caution everyone to avoid the bloody race."[41]

Although friends advised against it, Rush pressed ahead with his lawsuit.

In one of the most sensational trials Philadelphia had ever seen, lawyers for Rush charged Cobbett in the Supreme Court of Pennsylvania in Philadelphia with libel and demanded the then-huge sum of $5,000 (about $100,000 in early twenty-first-century dollars) in damages. It was a daring gambit. Few plaintiffs had ever won a libel suit against any journalist or newspaper in America, and the Rush action would change American journalism and science dramatically.

Historically, truth had never been a defense against libel under British common law. When, however, the governor of New York in 1734 charged the popular newspaper editor/journalist John Peter Zenger with criminal libel for satirical attacks on the governor, a series of dramatic court confrontations resulted in jury acquittals for Zenger. For the first time in America, truth proved a successful legal defense against libel. Although British courts repeatedly reversed the decision—and disbarred Zenger's lawyers—Zenger's jury triumphs established the principle of a free press that Americans incorporated in the First Amendment to the Constitution.

American journalists immediately grew more daring, often cloaking the foulest assertions with First Amendment protection to stimulate newspaper sales. With the Zenger case a precedent, few victims of libel dared challenge journalists who wrote defamatory materials—until Benjamin Rush. In filing his landmark case, Rush and his attorneys were fighting for what they believed to be as sacred a right as freedom of the press—one not mentioned in the Constitution. It was a right that others had defended for centuries before John Peter Zenger's trial—at Galileo's 1633 heresy trial in which the scientist defended his espousal of heliocentrism and, still earlier, at the trial in 399 B.C. of Socrates, who was charged with impiety.

Rush v. Cobbett was a fight for the freedom of scientific inquiry and the freedom of physicians to explore mysteries of disease and ways to heal the sick—free from malicious assaults by the ignorant, the superstitious, and scientifically and medically untrained government and religious officials—and editors such as Cobbett. Although motivated largely by lust for profits from increased newspaper sales, Cobbett, ironically, was no more ignorant than Rush himself—the former, displaying ignorance born of superstition, the latter displaying ignorance born of primitive science.

"Blood, blood! Still they cry more blood!" Cobbett wrote, portraying Rush as more vampire than scientist in an article picked up by newspapers across America. "Our remorseless Bleeder has his partisans in almost every quarter of the country. There is scarcely a page of any newspaper . . . which has the good fortune to escape the poison of their prescriptions. . . . In every sentence they menace our poor veins." Although Cobbett had no training in or knowledge of medical practice, he declared Rush's practice of medicine "preposterous."[42]

After several lengthy postponements, *Rush v. Cobbett* went to trial on Friday, December 13, 1799. Rush arrived with his wife, Julia, tucked by his side, along with their fifteen-year-old daughter, Mary, and their second-oldest son, Richard, who, at nineteen, was the youngest graduate in Princeton University history and had already earned his law degree.

When the Rushes took their seats, Cobbett's lawyers looked about in dismay for their client. After a long wait, they seemed as startled as Rush and his legal team when a messenger brought word that Cobbett had fled to New York. As the trial resumed without its defendant, Rush's lawyers called Cobbett's printed attacks on Rush "the most deadly and violent kind that malice could invent" by an editor who trampled on the rights of others in his greed for added circulation and profits. "The eye of decency can seldom read his pages without offense," the Rush attorney argued, "and virtue turns from them with indignation and disgust. . . . He [Cobbett] accused [Dr. Rush] of murder, of destroying the lives of his fellow citizens, in a time of dreadful calamity."[43]

After entering Cobbett's plea of "not guilty," Cobbett's lawyer responded by citing Cobbett's First Amendment rights as an editor to present different points of view on what was a question under broad discussion by the general public—and, therefore, acceptable for discussion by a free press.

At the end of the second day, Chief Justice Edward Shippen prepared to deliver his charge to the jury. If Shippen ruled against Rush, it would cost the doctor thousands of dollars in court costs and force him and his family into bankruptcy. Rush had every reason for pessimism, for it was he who had brought Justice Shippen's brother, Dr. William Shippen, before a court martial during the Revolutionary War.

CHAPTER 11

On the Causes of Death

To Rush's surprise and Julia's delight, Chief Justice Edward Shippen declared Cobbett's published attacks on the doctor libelous. The only question for the jury, he said, was whether they were defamatory. In his instructions to the jury, he gave the traditional English definition a new, clearly American accent, calling it

> . . . malicious defamation, expressed either in printing or writing, or by signs or pictures, tending to blacken either the memory of one who is dead or the reputation of one who is alive, or to expose him to public hatred, contempt, or ridicule. The charges against the defendant . . . may be reduced in substance to the following; That he repeatedly calls the plaintiff a quack . . . charges him with intemperate bleeding, injudiciously administering mercury in large doses . . . murdering his patients and slaying thousands and tens of thousands.[1]

Shippen went on to recognize freedom of the press as an essential right that should never be abridged in a free country. But, he warned, when it has no basis in fact and "when it is perverted to the purpose of private slander, it then becomes a most destructive engine in the hands of unprincipled men."[2]

The jury deliberated for two hours before declaring Cobbett guilty and awarding Rush the full $5,000 that he had demanded. In addition, the jury ordered Cobbett to pay another $3,000 to cover costs of the proceedings. In effect, the decision balanced the scales of justice in libel proceedings, shifting some of the burden of proof from the plaintiff to the defendant and preventing journalists from knowingly publishing malicious falsehoods. In proving Cobbett's statements untrue and defamatory, Rush (and his attorneys) set a precedent that governs the American press to this day.

The joy of Rush and his family was short lived, however, as they and the rest of the nation plunged into deep mourning the day after the trial: George Washington had died during the night.

Although the United States shut down, Cobbett knew no scruples, taking advantage of national mourning to renew his assault on Rush, all but accusing him of complicity in the former President's death. A physician whom Rush had trained had attended Washington, and Cobbett claimed he had all but murdered the nation's first President with a series of bleedings that had drained nine pints of blood from Washington's body in twenty-four hours.

His new attack had little effect on the court and its award, however. The verdict left Cobbett bankrupt. A sheriff seized all of Cobbett's assets and sold his property and his newspaper supplies and equipment at auction. Cobbett's lawyer met privately with Rush, who said he was unwilling to humiliate his defeated foe and agreed to accept $4,000 as a settlement, which he gave to charity.

Having turned the other cheek, Rush prepared to resume normal family life and medical practice. Not all doctors in Philadelphia had turned against him. "After mentioning the malignity of my enemies," Rush wrote in his autobiography, "it would be criminal of me not to acknowledge my obligations to Heaven for the friendship I experienced from many of my medical brethren in Philadelphia." He went on to list eleven, including Philip Syng Physick. A month after Cobbett had fled Philadelphia, however, another copy of *Porcupine's Gazette* materialized, driving more Rush patients away and shocking him into tears and depression. Published in New York, Cobbett's paper charged Rush with having originated the practice of bleeding patients during the 1793 epidemic and then organizing other doctors in a society of evil "Bleeders."[3] Irate at the result of his trial, Cobbett charged Rush with having fixed its outcome.

"I always had my doubts," Cobbett ranted, "that Rush, that sleek-headed, saint-looking Rush, knew the judges and juries better than my friends did, and the result has, at last, proved that my doubts were but too well founded."[4]

Cobbett's bitterness knew no bounds. Without funds to continue publishing *Porcupine's Gazette*, he managed to print a small pamphlet he called *The American Rush-Light.** The first issue appeared in mid-February 1801 "to assist the publick view" of Rush and those connected with the trial, including the judge and jury. "Rush is remarkable for insinuating manners," Cobbett sneered, "and for that smoothness and softness of tongue, which the mock-quality call politeness, but which the profane vulgar call blarney."[5]

Without a long and costly trip to New York to launch legal proceedings there, there was little Rush could do to stop the Cobbett libel.

In early March, however, Rush finally put Cobbett out of his thoughts as he read of his friend Thomas Jefferson's inauguration as the nation's third president—the first ever held in the nation's new capital of Washington, DC.

"You have opened a new era in the history of the United States," Rush effused to Jefferson after reading the President's March 4th inaugural address.

> Old friends who had been separated by party names . . . for many years shook hands with each other after reading it and discovered, for the first time, they had differed in *opinion* only, about the best means of promoting the interests of their common country. . . . In the third month of the year 1801 we have become "all Republicans, all Federalists."

---

*A play on words. Mature stalks of *rush*, or tufted marsh plants, dipped in grease or beeswax, served as effective torches.

Rush went on to assure Jefferson, "Your new official title has added nothing to my respect for your person. It could not add to my friendship for you."[6]

Like most Americans, Rush was overjoyed not only by the outcome, but by the peaceful exchange of power from the Federalist incumbent to his republican opponent—despite their sharp political differences. Although Rush and Jefferson had known each other for many years, they had grown particularly close during Jefferson's years as vice president. Like Adams when he served as vice president, Jefferson had so few official obligations that he spent as much time as possible with friends in the capital when the Senate was in session or at Monticello, the pretentious mountaintop home he had designed near Charlottesville, Virginia. Far from the nation's capital, his Italianate aerie had allowed him to philosophize by letter with intellectuals he enjoyed, such as Benjamin Rush—and to plot a political campaign to unseat President Adams and the Federalists in the 1800 elections.

"They believe that any power confided in me will be exerted in opposition to their schemes," Jefferson wrote to Rush.

> And they believe rightly, for I have sworn upon the altar of God eternal hostility against every form of tyranny over the mind of man . . . and this is the cause of their printing lying pamphlets against me, forging conversations for me . . . which are absolute falsehoods. . . . But enough of this; it is more than I have before committed to paper on the subject of the lies that have been preached and printed against me. . . . It would be a great treat to see you here. . . . I wish you health and happiness and think of you with affection. Adieu.[7]

Rush himself had seen some of the "lying pamphlets" about Jefferson, some accusing him with sins against Christianity and with blasphemy, heresy, and godlessness. Rush asked Jefferson to send him a definition of his religious creed.

"I have always considered Christianity as the *strong ground* of republicanism," he wrote to Jefferson. "Many of its precepts have for their objects republican liberty and equality as well as simplicity, integrity, and economy in government."[8]

Jefferson replied immediately, saying, "I have a view of the subject which ought to displease neither the rational Christian nor Deists," but not expanding enough to disclose his views. He said that while the Bill of Rights had secured freedom of religion, it had also

> given to the clergy a very favorite hope of obtaining an establishment of a particular form of Christianity . . . as every sect believes its own form the true one, every one perhaps hoped for his own, but especially the Episcopalians and Congregationalists [Puritans]. The returning good sense of our country threatens abortion to their hopes, and they believe that any portion of power confided in me will be exerted in opposition to their schemes. And they believe rightly.[9]

Occupied as he was writing letters to promote his campaign to wrest the presidency from John Adams, Jefferson had failed to answer Rush's question about his religious beliefs. Rush nonetheless voted for his friend from Virginia rather than his friend from Massachusetts in the presidential election.

Jefferson's accession to power was far from smooth, however. A bitter struggle ensued within republican ranks when Aaron Burr, Jr., of New York received the same number of votes in the Electoral College and challenged the Virginian for the presidency. A hero of the Revolutionary War, Burr had been a popular republican Senator, but the Electoral College balloting surprised him as much as it did Jefferson and, indeed, the rest of the country.

At the time, each member of the Electoral College could cast two votes—either both votes for one presidential candidate or one vote for each of two presidential candidates; the candidate receiving a majority of votes won the presidency, the runner-up, the vice presidency. In the unlikely event of a tie, the Constitution required the House of Representatives to break the deadlock. Burr, however, all but precluded that eventuality months earlier by averring, "It is highly improbable that I shall have an equal number of votes with Mr. Jefferson, but if such be the result, every man who knows me ought to know that I would utterly disclaim all competition."[10]

An intimate—and eventual patient—of Benjamin Rush, Thomas Jefferson won election to the presidency in 1801, after defeating President John Adams in the general election, then defeating New York's Aaron Burr, Jr., in a runoff. (WHITE HOUSE)

When, however, Burr won as many votes as Jefferson, ambition got the better of him, and he challenged the Virginian for the nation's highest office. After thirty-five ballots over six exhausting days and nights, Congress mirrored the Electoral College producing thirty-five tie votes. The nation faced a future with no President—until a Delaware Federalist switched his vote and gave the election victory to Jefferson.

Meanwhile, John Adams still raged over his election defeat—impelled as it was by libelous accusations of his preference for monarchy. Severing ties to both Jefferson and Rush, he rode off in the predawn darkness on Inauguration Day to avoid the swearing-in of his successor and the banquet, ball, and other festivities that would follow. He said good-bye to no one—not to Jefferson, not to Rush.

One of Jefferson's first acts as President was the renewal of Rush's sinecure at the Mint—an act that incensed Cobbett and made the Englishman even more determined to injure the doctor. Still working in New York, out of reach of prosecution by Rush, Cobbett published five more issues of *The American Rush-Light* in the spring of 1801, successively calling Rush a "quack," reiterating charges that Rush "slew his patients," and calling Rush's bleed-and-purge treatments one of "the great discoveries . . . which have contributed to the depopulation of the earth."[11] In an article entitled "A Peep into a Pennsylvania Court of Justice," Cobbett again charged Rush with corrupting both judge and jury in the libel case. With the appearance of the *Rush-Light*, lawyers for Rush—and, indeed, Julia and his sons and daughters—began to fear for his safety and urged him to forego practicing medicine for a while. Exhausted by the conflict with Cobbett and with summer approaching, Rush agreed to retire to the farm at Sydenham for the summer months and let his apprentices handle his practice.

Adding to Rush's distress at the time was the departure for Canada of his oldest daughter Anne Emily, who had married a Canadian graduate of Princeton University the previous year. After he decided to stand for Parliament in his native land, Emily agreed to move to Ottawa with their infant child, Rush's grandchild. Julia Rush and her next-oldest daughter, Mary, accompanied Emily and her family as far as New York.

"She [Emily] wept, as did all the servants in my family," Rush wrote of his daughter's departure from Philadelphia in his diary. "My daughter Emily had never once offended me, nor did I ever speak an angry or harsh word to her. Her very infancy and childhood were marked with uncommon gentleness and goodness."[12]

On June 1, 1800, Cobbett ran out of funds and friends. All who had previously befriended him had finally tired of his pointless, irrational assault against an American Founding Father who, despite some failings, was unquestionably the greatest physician in American history. Forced to extract his ink-smeared claws from his American prey, Cobbett sailed off to his British homeland to torture his own countrymen, leaving Benjamin Rush, M.D., deeply hurt and, for the first time in his life, discouraged about his mission to heal the nation's wounds.*

With his practice depleted, Benjamin Rush decided to give up medical practice as he had known it and spend more time at Sydenham farm,† improving the land and structures, reading and rereading great works of medicine, philosophy, and history, and writing and rewriting his own scientific works.

"My persecutions have arrested or delayed the usual languor of 55 in my mind," he explained to President Jefferson. "I read, write, and think with the same vigor and pleasure that I did fifteen years ago." He said the slander he had suffered had "excited our faculties into vigorous and successful exercise.

> I had sometimes amused myself in forming a scale of the different kinds of hatreds. They appear to me to rise in the following order: *odium juris-consultum, odium medicum, odium philologicum, odium politicum,* and *odium theologicum.* You are now the subject of the two last. I have felt the full force of the 2nd and 4th degrees of hostility from my fellow creatures.[13]

Rush turned to lighter matters in what was an especially long letter to his friend who was a passionate gardener. "I send you herewith some muskmelon seeds of a quality above the common melons . . . as a

---

*Two years after his return to Britain, Cobbett started the weekly *Political Register* (mocked as Cobbett's two-penny trash) and railed at everything he—often he alone—found wrong in England. After going to jail for two years for advocating the overthrow of English government, he again fled to the United States, where he spent three years in quiet isolation on a Long Island farm. He returned to England in 1819, all but bankrupt, his influence as depleted as his funds. He scratched out a living writing articles and books, won election to Parliament in 1832, and, after a dismal performance in Parliament, died from influenza in 1835 at the age of seventy-two.

†Sydenham farm stood on and about what is now the intersection of Sydenham Street and Packer Avenue.

pineapple is superior to a potato. . . . They are, when ripe, a little larger than a child's head, round, and have a green rind. They are never mealy, but juicy, and cannot be improved by sugar, pepper, salt, or any other addition." Rush then added a last thought: "When you see [Secretary of State] Mr. Madison, please to tell him he is still very dear to *his* and *your* sincere and affectionate friend, [signed] Benjn. Rush."[14]

Although he was still deeply interested in politics, the exertions demanded by seven consecutive years of epidemics had combined with the Cobbett conflict and advancing age to wear Rush down. Quite simply, he needed rest. For a mind like his, however, "rest" meant research, writing, and teaching. In 1801, he delivered "Six Lectures . . . Upon the Institutes and Practice of Medicine," to medical students at the University of Pennsylvania. Among other topics, Rush expounded on the "connection between observation and reasoning in medicine"; on physiology, pathology, and therapeutics; and on the character of Dr. Sydenham. In one of his most important—and controversial—lectures, however, Rush discussed the "vices and virtues of physicians," "the causes which have retarded the progress of medicine," and "the causes of death in diseases that are not incurable."

Citing incompetence of physicians as the primary cause of patient deaths from *curable* diseases, Rush attributed such incompetence to "incapacity or a want of proper instruction." He went on to cite a litany of irresponsible acts by physicians that cost patients their lives, among them failure to make a thorough examination and consider all the patient's symptoms. He criticized doctors who failed to respond promptly to calls by patients for help, and he accused many of charging such high fees they discouraged patients from seeking medical help until it was too late. He charged physicians with writing prescriptions so illegibly at times as to produce errors in compounding medicines. He also condemned itinerant quacks for selling fraudulent medicines.[15]

Rush did not, however, absolve patients themselves or the general public of responsibility for deaths from curable diseases, ailments, and injuries. He cited ignorance, superstition, neglect, and failure to seek immediate help as primary causes of death from curable illnesses, along with failure to follow physician instructions. He listed fear of the unknown, costs, and irrational shyness at self-exposure as other factors inhibiting patients from seeking often-vital medical care.[16]

From his first day of practice, Rush had never stopped jotting down his thoughts on diseases and their treatments to organize into lectures for his students. From 1789 to 1796, he had compiled them into a massive, four-volume work he called *Medical Inquiries and Observations*—a work that stunned the medical world. It was the broadest, most modern, and most forward-looking work on health and medical care ever seen. Except for its obsessive advocacy of bloodletting, *Medical Inquiries and Observations* influenced and advanced the world of medicine and science for the next century and more, with the first expositions and studies of preventive medicine, personal hygiene, public sanitation, personal diet and health care, geriatrics, and a broad code of ethics for doctors. Even when off-target medically and scientifically, Rush influenced countless thousands of future physicians to think and act charitably, as humanitarians rather than professional profiteers. Because of Rush, responsible doctors never charged the poor until the advent of medical insurance, and they only charged those with financial resources what they could afford. Nor did any doctors except quacks patent and profit personally from pharmaceuticals they developed and instruments they invented until after World War II.

Medical Inquiries also replaced the accepted theories of disease origins proposed by England's Sydenham and Holland's Boerhaave with Rush's own new theory of disease unity. All fevers and diseases, Rush argued, resulted from a disturbance of the bloodstream, mostly in the arteries. Regardless of symptoms—inflammation of the throat, stomach, liver, intestines, or other organs—all resulted from but *one* disease, and, depending on the patient's pulse, treatment fell into one of two categories: stimulants or depressants.

"Fire is a unit," Rush explained, "whether it be produced by friction, percussion, electricity, fermentation, or by a piece of wood or coal in a state of inflammation." So too, disease was a "unit" and the cause of inflammation, wherever it appeared.[17] "The physician who considers every different affection of the different systems in the body or every affection of different parts of the same system, as distinct diseases resembles the . . . savage who considers water, dew, ice, frost, and snow as distinct essences."[18]

In applying his "unitary system" of medicine, Rush was the first American physician to report demonstrable links between ailments in different parts of the body—including a link between infected teeth, for example, and a variety of ailments such as arthritis, dyspepsia, and even seizures. "When we consider how intimate the connection of the mouth is with the whole system," Rush explained, "I am disposed to believe . . . the teeth, when decayed . . . are often the unsuspected causes of general . . . diseases. . . . I cannot help but think that our success in the treatment of all chronic diseases would be very much promoted by directing our inquiries into the state of the teeth of sick people and by advising their extraction in every case in which they are decayed."[19]

As usual in the dawn of modern medical practice, Rush was right and wrong. Decades ahead of his time in recognizing tooth decay as a progenitor of some illnesses elsewhere in the body, he overreached by blaming tooth decay for too many diseases. Nonetheless, given the absence of laboratory methods and equipment, his application of the "unitary system of medicine" proved brilliant in many instances, including the reach of tooth decay.

By 1800, Dr. Rush—tired and aging—was ready to revise *Medical Inquiries*, eliminating some articles, revising others, and adding new ones. Already a pioneer in preventive medicine with his scheme for free smallpox inoculations and, later, vaccinations for Philadelphia's poor, Rush expanded his studies to a wide range of diseases he encountered with greater frequency in poor neighborhoods, for example, measles, colds, and tuberculosis and other pulmonary diseases. Although the results of his research would seem mixed by today's standards, his work was monumental at the time, given the absence of resources for scientific research. His inquiries inspired generations of researchers who followed him and converted many unsuccessful Rush inquiries into successes.

Compiled over twenty-five years from lectures to thousands of medical students and dozens of apprentices, the nearly twenty Rush lectures in Volume 1 of *Medical Inquiries* included ground-breaking studies on diseases of old age, cures for cancer, and comparisons of diseases of North American Indians with those of "civilized nations," as he called white regions.

Volume 1 often went beyond the realm of medical practice to include advances he had pioneered in personal hygiene and community sanitation measures, which he called essential to disease prevention. He recommended warm baths, appropriate dress for each season—even the use of umbrellas by men as well as women*—to preserve individual health. His article on public health described the results of his campaigns for municipal garbage collection in Philadelphia, for wider, cleaner streets, for stricter quarantine of incoming ships from foreign lands, and, above all, for proper sewerage disposal systems "to convey when practicable, to running water, the contents of privies and the foul water of kitchens."[20]

One landmark study Rush had conducted and included in Volume 1 of *Medical Inquiries* was the first look at the then-unknown field of geriatrics—fifty years before any subsequent, scientific studies. Entitled "An Account of the State of the Body and Mind in Old Age, with Observations on Its Diseases and Their Remedies," it described the physical and mental deterioration and disabilities of the aged and suggested possible remedies. It called heredity, or "descent from long-lived ancestors," the primary determinant of old age. "I have not found a single instance of a person who has not lived to be 80 years old in whom this was not the case," Rush wrote.[21]

After studying the aged, Rush became the first physician to declare exercise—particularly walking, running, and swimming—as beneficial to the elderly, along with skating, jumping, tennis, bowls, quoits, and golf. He had first embraced golf as a medical student in Edinburgh and now claimed "a man would live ten years longer for using this exercise twice a week."[22]

He called temperance in eating and drinking a second factor in promoting health and long life, followed by "moderate exercise of the understanding," by which he meant applying the mind to "business, politics, and religion." He urged keeping calm, warning that "violent and irregular action of the passions tends to wear away the springs of life." And he

---

*By tradition, European men had never used umbrellas and parasols, regarding them as feminine accoutrements.

called marriage essential to long life, saying he had met but one unmarried person who lived to be older than eighty.

He mixed personal beliefs with scientific findings in some lectures, discussing the influence of a person's morals and tastes on health in one lecture and, in another, the effects of alcohol and excessive drinking. Other chapters focused strictly on scientific studies, such as attempts to cure cancer with arsenic or the ingestion of various medicines to rid the intestines of worms.

Rush also reported on diseases he encountered in military hospitals during the Revolutionary War—a report that would influence the medical care of American service personnel for the next century. And for the first time in the history of American medicine, he developed moral and ethical codes for doctors, expounding "the duties of the physician" and methods of improving medical care in America. The Rush code of ethics would guide American physicians with M.D.s for more than a century until state legislatures passed laws forbidding "quacks" without proper degrees to call themselves "doctor," add "M.D." to their names, or practice medicine and dispense medicines.

Volume 2 of *Medical Inquiries* added almost fifteen more lectures, half of them dealing with the symptoms and suggested remedies for specific diseases—haemoptysis (spitting blood), pulmonary consumption (tuberculosis), dropsies (edemas), gout, hydrophobia (rabies), cholera, cymanche trachealis (croup), scarlet fever, measles, and flu. Without modern laboratories or advanced equipment to ferret out the etiology of diseases, Rush could only use his extraordinary gift for detail and his remarkable intuition to note and collate symptoms that differentiated one disease from another. He described the pains of yellow fever as "exquisitely severe in the head, back, and limbs. The pains in the head were sometimes in the back parts . . . other times . . . only the eyeballs. In some people, the pains were so acute in the back and hips that they could not lie in bed."[23] The severe skeletal pains provoked the then-popular term "break-bone fever" for yellow fever.

Several lectures touched on epidemic diseases, and a curious, albeit interesting, lecture discussed Pennsylvania's climate and its effects on the health of its inhabitants.

Volumes 3 and 4 limited their discussions to the various epidemics that had plagued Philadelphia annually from 1793 onward—mostly yellow fever, but also measles and influenza. He also looked at a variety of illnesses that affected an abnormally high number of people, including cholera, dysentery, and "bowel complaints." He ended Volume 4 with a long, spirited "Defense of Blood-Letting . . . as a Remedy for Fevers and Certain Other Diseases." Calling objections to bloodletting "founded in error and fear," he insisted that the procedure "frequently strangles a fever . . . in its formative state . . . by removing . . . the remote cause of the fever." He went on to cite twenty-two other benefits of blood-letting, sustaining his argument with citations from Sydenham, who, Rush contended, cured "a putrid fever, which was epidemic and fatal in the year 1678, by copious bleeding."[24]

On May 11, 1801, Cobbett's insults and the humiliating attacks on his integrity by once-obsequious colleagues all but faded from fifty-five-year-old Benjamin Rush's mind when Julia Rush gave birth to William, their thirteenth child. With the arrival of their newborn son, the lethargy that had gripped Benjamin Rush vanished, replaced by a spasm of energy the doctor had not experienced since his student days. The patriot-physician suddenly leaped back into the current of the nation's political, scientific, and educational mainstream, reassuming his role as the nation's first and foremost humanitarian, dedicated to healing the nation's wounds wherever they threatened the nation's health.

Although he limited his medical practice to occasional private consultations, he renewed his work promoting abolition, expanding prison reform, promoting humane treatment of the insane, promoting and improving public education, advocating temperance, and improving the education and training of future doctors. He stepped up his teaching and writing and his correspondence with a small army of distinguished friends in leadership positions in every area of public life.

"Permit me to revive a friendship once very dear to me," he wrote to Secretary of State James Madison. Rush had first befriended him during the 1787 Constitutional Convention and the two became fast friends when Madison served in Congress in the temporary capital of Philadelphia. "The commerce of our country has suffered greatly by our absurd quarantine laws in the different states," he told Madison.

Under presidential orders to avoid nepotism, Secretary of State James Madison was unable to obtain a diplomatic posting for Richard Rush, the son of Benjamin Rush. (THE WHITE HOUSE HISTORICAL ASSOCIATION)

These laws, which admit the contagious nature of our American yellow fever, had produced a reaction in the governments of Europe which has rendered our commerce . . . extremely expensive and oppressive. The evils complained of abroad can only be remedied by removing them at home . . . by convincing our citizens that our fever is not contagious. . . . The benefits to commerce . . . and prosperity which the abolition of quarantine laws and a regard to cleanliness of our cities would produce are incalculable.[25]

Ironically, Rush had insisted a few years earlier that yellow fever was contagious and urged those who could afford to do so to flee Philadelphia. But he never stopped observing and taking careful notes, and, by

1800, his notes revealed so many households in which some, but not all, members had contracted the disease that he reached the inescapable conclusion that yellow fever was not contagious. After his colleague Philip Syng Physick came to the same conclusion, Rush believed their findings important enough to inform Madison of the implications for the nation's trade and commerce.

Later, in preparing a third edition of his four-volume *Medical Inquiries and Observations*, Rush added a new chapter in Volume 3: "Facts Intended to Prove the Yellow Fever Not to Be Contagious."[26] In it he conceded, "Many hundred instances have occurred this year which clearly demonstrate that it is not propagated by contagion."

Still unable to conceive of any insect involvement, however, he argued that yellow fever "can originate and spread only in an atmosphere contaminated by exhalations from putrid animal and vegetable matters."[27] In effect, he was still on target; as he had been in 1793, he correctly attributed the breeding grounds of mosquitoes as a key factor in the genesis of the disease, but he was unable to take the last critical step towards discovering the mosquito itself as the actual carrier and transmitter of the disease to humans.

His continuing work revising *Medical Inquiries and Observations* allowed him more time at home, where he doted over his wife and children as he had not been able to do for years. His third son, fifteen-year-old James Rush, had gained admission to his father's alma mater at Princeton in the fall of 1801, and after receiving the boy's first letter home, the proud father replied with great warmth—but could not suppress his compulsion to instruct:

My dear Son. Your letter diffused pleasure through all our family. I hope all your letters will be composed with the same regard to spelling, punctuation and grammar. In the use of capitals remember to use them only in the beginning of sentences and for the names of persons, cities, countries, and important words such as Religion, Revolution, Reformation, and the like. . . . Your Mama is so much dissatisfied with your brown coat that she has concluded not to send it to you. She will send you the cloth for another. . . . Keep your receipts carefully . . . and bring them home in the spring. . . . Remember, my dear son . . . you are very dear to me, and be assured no exertions on my part shall be wanting to promote your interest and happiness. . . . Your Mama and all the family join in love to you with your affectionate father.[28]

His second son, twenty-one-year-old Richard Rush, meanwhile, had long earlier completed his studies at Princeton. He had enrolled in 1794, when he was only fourteen. The youngest member of his class, he graduated in 1797 at seventeen and completed his law studies by 1800 at the age of nineteen. In 1801, Rush wrote to Secretary of State Madison, saying that Richard "has long felt a strong desire to visit Europe in the capacity of a private secretary to a foreign minister.

He has been regularly educated to the profession of the law. . . . His application to study has been unwearied. In addition to his attainments in the law, he has laid in a large stock of information in history and politics. . . . His principles and temper are alike republican. . . . His morals are pure and his manner amiable. In short, it is not possible for a son to be more dear to his parents. . . . Should an opportunity offer of gratifying my son's request, you will much oblige me by mentioning his name to [President] Mr. Jefferson.[29]

Three weeks later, Madison did as Rush had asked, but the President, fearing charges of nepotism in government, laid the letter aside and never spoke of it again. Undeterred by Jefferson's snub, however, young Rush went into private practice and quickly won acclaim as a successful trial lawyer.

In March of 1802, fifty-five-year-old Benjamin Rush acquired a new responsibility of sorts after a fire of unknown cause devoured all but the outer walls of Nassau Hall, the central building of the college at Princeton. Like Madison, Rush was one of the college's most prominent and visible alumni and an obvious candidate to lead fund-raising efforts. Over the next two years, Rush helped raise $40,000, and Princeton was able to reopen historic Nassau Hall in 1808.

Early 1802 also brought Rush a curious letter from his friend the President of the United States: "My health has always been so uniformly firm that I have for some years dreaded nothing so much as living too long,"

Thomas Jefferson wrote. "I think, however, that a flaw has appeared which ensures me against that. . . . I have said as much to no mortal breathing, and my florid health is calculated to keep my friends as well as foes quiet."[30]

Clearly the fifty-eight-year-old President trusted only his friend Rush with his fear of having contracted some sort of chronic illness—which he failed to specify. Rush knew of the President's deep distrust of doctors and that he usually refused any treatments by doctors in favor of letting nature take its course. So Rush waited a while before responding.

"Permit me, my dear and long respected friend, to request you to inform me of the seat and nature of that flaw," Rush finally wrote to the President. "Perhaps it is in the power of medicine to heal it or protract its fatal effects to a very distant day. Should my reading or experience be insufficient for that purpose, I will lay the history of your case before the most intelligent members of our profession in Philadelphia (without mentioning your name) and transmit to you our united opinions and advice."[31]

Realizing Rush could do little without knowing the identity of his "flaw," the President relented and, in his next letter, revealed his flaw as chronic diarrhea.

"I have great pleasure to tell you," Rush replied, "that complaints of the bowels such as yours have very generally yielded to medicine under my care." Rush went on to recommend small meals of bland foods—potatoes, biscuits, and boiled rice—with a bit of sherry or Madeira and water. He urged the President to keep warm and limit himself to gentle exercise.

> When your bowels are much excited, rest should be indulged. . . . Carefully avoid fatigue of body and mind from all its causes. Late hours and midnight studies and business should likewise be avoided. . . . To relieve the diarrhea when troublesome, laudanum [10 percent opium plus codeine and morphine] should be taken in small doses during the day and in larger doses at bedtime to prevent your being obliged to rise during the night.[32]

Unlike other Rush remedies such as bleeding, his advice for Jefferson's problem was not out of line with twenty-first-century remedies, depending on the severity of the intestinal malfunction. Jefferson followed

Rush's advice, and his problem did indeed disappear, prompting Rush to respond, "I was made very happy by learning . . . that your disease is less troublesome than formerly. As I know you have no faith in the principles of our science, I shall from time to time combat your prejudices (and your disease, should it continue) with facts."[33]

By then, Rush had embraced the revolutionary new procedure of vaccination to immunize patients against smallpox. Unlike inoculation, which infected subjects with diseased smallpox serum and sickened them for a week or more, vaccination* infected subjects with cowpox, a milder form of the disease that had almost no ill effects but nonetheless immunized them against smallpox. British physician Edward Jenner had discovered the process in 1796, and, by 1800, it had replaced inoculation in Europe. A colleague of Jenner sent samples of the vaccine to Harvard professor Benjamin Waterhouse, a physician who successfully introduced the procedure in New England. Waterhouse, in turn, sent reports of his work to Benjamin Rush and, because of the President's interest in scientific developments, Rush sent copies to Thomas Jefferson. Awed by Waterhouse's work, Jefferson ordered the vaccine and administered it to some 200 relatives and neighbors in the summer of 1800. His work proved so successful that he gained confidence in medicine and doctors, and, when he developed chronic diarrhea, he had consulted Rush.

Rush by then was also administering the new vaccine. Contrary to accusations by his professional opponents and scandal mongers like Cobbett, Rush was far from obstinate in his opposition to change and to new medicines and medical techniques. Indeed, he had leaped at the opportunity to apply Jenner's new approach, hailed it as "a new era . . . in the medical history of man." He delivered the first lecture on the subject at the University of Pennsylvania Medical School, and he notified the newspapers about the ease of its administration for both doctor and subject. "It requires no preparation in diet and medicine," he told his students and the press. "It may be performed with equal safety in all seasons . . . seldom confining a patient to his house or interrupting his business . . . does no injury . . . is not contagious . . . is never mortal."

---

*The word is derived from the Latin *vacca*—"cow."

Far from being the self-serving opportunist portrayed by Cobbett, Rush went on to predict that smallpox would be a word found only in books of medicine and that Jenner's name would be "extended to every part of the globe. His extensive and durable fame will be merited, for he has introduced into the world the means of saving millions and millions of lives."[34]

Rush sent a warm, gracious letter to Benjamin Waterhouse: "Accept my thanks for your friendly and instructing letter. Our whole city will, I hope, be benefited by it, as well as myself, for I have put the most important facts into the hands of a printer, and they will appear in a day or two in one of our daily papers. . . . I have adopted the discovery with as much zeal and confidence as you have done, and I look forward to the complete extinction of the smallpox by it. . . . Continue to diffuse the results of your inquiries and observations throughout our country."

Rush signed the letter, "From, dear sir, your friend and brother in the Republic of Medicine."[35]

Aware of the President's involvement with the vaccine, he wrote to Jefferson: "I am happy to . . . inform you that the vaccine is generally adopted in our city and that its success has hitherto equaled the best wishes of its most sanguine and zealous friends," and he signed it, "your sincere old friend."[36]

Jefferson responded by confiding in Rush about an expedition he was organizing for "about ten chosen woodsmen headed by Captain [Meriwether] Lewis, my secretary . . . to undertake the long desired object of exploring the Missouri [River] and whatever river that leads into the western [Pacific] ocean." Writing to Rush "in confidence," Jefferson called Lewis "brave, prudent, habituated to the woods" but "not regularly educated." Knowing the Lewis party would be traveling without a doctor, Jefferson asked Rush to train Lewis in emergency medical aid and basic health care and guide him in researching the native population he encountered. Rush agreed, and Jefferson sent Lewis to Philadelphia, where he studied with Rush for three months before leaving on his landmark expedition westward.[37]

Rush gave Lewis a list of subjects to explore during his trip, a list of medicines to take (including Rush's "Thunderbolts"), and ten tips "for the preservation of his health" and that of his men. These included fasting and rest "when you feel the least indisposition . . . lying down when fatigued . . . washing feet with spirit when chilled" and "always take a little raw spirits after being wet or much fatigued." He gave Lewis a list of ten questions to study about Indian diseases, four questions about their morals and four about their religion. He asked Lewis to identify "acute diseases" and remedies, the pulse rates of adults and children at various times of day, the age they married and length of time they suckled their infants, and their diet, cooking methods, times of eating, and methods of food preservation.

"What are their vices?" Rush asked Lewis, " . . . rates of suicide and murder?" He asked Lewis to identify "the principal objects of their worship," whether they practiced animal sacrifices, and how they disposed of the dead. Seeking to confirm a then-popular notion that American Indians had descended from the ten lost tribes of Israel, he asked Lewis to study "the affinity between their religious ceremonies and those of the Jews."[38] Although Lewis failed to discover any Indian ties to ancient Israel, he did manage to answer many of Rush's other questions, including their diet—bear, deer, ducks, "sammon [*sic*]" and "roots, which do not appear a suitable diet for us." Although Lewis subsequently suffered "pane [*sic*] in the bowels and stomach,"[39] his journals record his having used Rush's remedies without ever addressing Rush's questions about Indian customs and daily lives.

After Rush had helped Lewis prepare for his western journey, the President surprised his physician with a startling revelation: "In some of the delightful conversations with you . . . the Christian religion was sometimes our topic," Jefferson wrote to his friend, "and I promised you that one day or other I would give you my views of it.

> They are the result of a life of inquiry and reflection and very different from that anti-Christian system imputed to me by those who know nothing of my opinions. To the corruptions of Christianity I am indeed opposed; but not to the genuine precepts of Jesus himself. I am a Christian in the only sense he wished anyone to be: sincerely attached to his doctrines in preference to all others, ascribing to himself every human excellence and believing he never claimed any other.[40]

Jefferson told Rush that from the time the doctor had raised the question, he, the President, had thought long and hard about his beliefs—especially on the long journeys between Washington and Monticello. His meditations provoked his writing a "Syllabus of an Estimate of the Merit of the Doctrines of Jesus." (See Appendix D, p. 265.)

"This I now send you," he wrote to Rush, "and in confiding it to you, I know it will not be exposed to the malignant perversions of those who make every word from me a text for new misrepresentations and calumnies."

In one of the most extraordinary letters ever written by a sitting President on religion, Jefferson said he had refused to make his religious tenets public because he feared it would foster what he called an "inquisition over the rights of conscience.

> It behooves every man who values liberty of conscience for himself to resist invasions of it in the case of others. . . . It behooves him, too, in his own case, to give no example of concession betraying the common right of independent opinion by answering questions of faith, which the laws have left between God and himself.[41]

The "syllabus" that Jefferson sent with his letter shocked the devout doctor as he read its opening lines declaring the parentage of Jesus as "obscure, his condition poor, his education null." Although Jefferson conceded that "his endowments [were] great, his life correct and innocent," he noted that unlike the authors of the life of Socrates, "unlettered and ignorant men wrote the story of the life of Jesus and his doctrines" and did so from memory long after Jesus had died. The result, Jefferson argued, was that only fragments of "the most perfect and sublime doctrines . . . ever taught by man" were preserved, albeit "mutilated, misstated, and unintelligible."

Jefferson denied that Jesus was "a member of the Godhead," or in direct communication with it, saying it was "foreign" to his view. He nonetheless called "the system of Jesus . . . superior over all others . . . [by] inculcating universal philanthropy, not only to kindred and friends, to neighbors and countrymen, but to all mankind, gathering all into one family under the bonds of love, charity, peace, common wants and common aids."[42]

Rush was too devout a Christian not to be stunned by what he considered Jefferson's blasphemy. "I have read your creed with great attention," the doctor responded in chilly diplomatic language, "and was pleased to find you are by no means so heterodox as you have been supposed to be by your enemies.

> I do not think with you in your account of the character and mission of the Author of our Religion, and my opinions are the result of a long and patient investigation of that subject. You shall receive my creed shortly. In the meanwhile we will agree to disagree.

Rush ended his letter with a prayer that gently mocked Jefferson's beliefs: "May the Ruler of Nations direct and prosper you in all your duties and enterprises in the present difficult and awful posture of human affairs."[43]

The President's wasn't the only disturbing letter Rush received in early 1803. His nineteen-year-old daughter, Mary, who had gone to Canada to visit her sister Emily and her husband, had met a British army captain in Ottawa, fallen in love, and wanted her father's permission to marry. Her parents were not pleased, but not about to alienate their only surviving daughters by outright rejection of one of them.

What aging parents call the "empty-nest" syndrome today was far more devastating in colonial days and the early national period. The tiny communities in which parents raised their children seldom offered enough land or opportunity to support several generations of the same families. And, because of the nation's huge distances, the absence of public communication and transportation networks, and low literacy rates, many parents never again saw or heard a word from their children when the latter moved away to take advantage of opportunities on the frontier.

"My beloved Daughter," the shocked father replied, admitting he had experienced "uncommon emotions" after reading her letter and had been "at a loss" for a reply. Having tapped his connections across Britain and Europe, Rush conceded that all who knew the young officer "had spoken of him as a gentleman of great worth and of highly polished and attracting manners.

"Under all these circumstances," Rush wrote to Mary, "your parents unite in declaring our willingness to adopt him as a son from his character as a man."

Well . . . not quite.

The possessive father said he and Julia were "reconciled to your separation from us (although the surrender of your society so necessary to our comfort in the approaching evening of our lives would be extremely painful to us)." He also warned her that because "your father's [other] children are still young and uneducated," any dowry Rush might provide might prove too small "for a gentlemen . . . disposed by his habit and compelled by the rank of his connections to live beyond his means." Then Rush laid the crushing blow, pointing out that "however much Mr. M. may esteem and love you, he has offered his hand *without* the consent of or knowledge of his father, that it is possible he may have destined him to a more wealthy and advantageous alliance, and that his whole family may complain of your having interfered in their plans of domestic establishments."[44]

Rush had learned that Mary's "Mr. M." was, in fact, Captain Thomas Manners, who carried the same blood as the Duke of Rutland and bore ancestral ties to the House of York and the Plantagenet kings. Unlike his daughter, Rush had read literary tales describing the lust of young aristocrats and their conquests—and subsequent dismissals or desertions—of pretty little common girls.

Left unsaid in his letter was the young man's failure to present himself to his loved one's father—that is, Dr. Rush—for permission to ask for her hand.

Rush insisted that his daughter "form no engagement . . . until his father's approbation be obtained to the proposed connection of our respective families," and he ended his letter, "Adieu! My ever dear and beloved child."

The young man complied with some of the doctor's conditions, writing to ask for Mary's hand. Eight months later he married Mary Rush in Philadelphia, but returned to Canada with his bride and remained in the British army.

"We hear from them weekly." Rush told a childhood friend of his daughters. "They say they are happy. I am sure they deserve to be so. But the pang which attended the separation of our daughter from her parents is still felt; time we hope will reconcile us to it."[45]

By the end of 1803, fifty-seven-year-old Benjamin Rush declared he was "tired out and distressed with the unsuccessful issue of all my public labors for the benefit of my fellow citizens." In his view, the sweeping social reforms he had already initiated and achieved had not been sweeping enough. Having failed to transform American society into a Utopia, he decided to rein in his humanitarian efforts and "limit my studies and duties wholly to my profession." He nonetheless continued supporting a Quaker philanthropist who was trying to implement further reforms in the penal code and prison system. "I shall never think our penal code perfect," Rush explained, "till we deprive our laws of the power of taking away life for *any* crime. It is in my opinion murder to punish murder by death. It is an act of legal revenge."[46]

Rush, however, was aging and he willingly ceded many of his responsibilities in the penal reform movement and various other social reform movements. Although he accepted Benjamin Franklin's former role as president of the Pennsylvania Society for Promoting the Abolition of Slavery, he limited his participation to public appearances. Founder Anthony Benezet had died in 1784 when Pennsylvania abolished the slave trade by law (though not slavery), and the organization lost some momentum for several years. Rush helped the group form new goals helping free blacks find jobs and establishing free schools for blacks of all ages. Although he continued supporting such projects in speaking appearances, he subordinated them to the revision and publication of his medical articles and books.

"I am now devoting all my leisure hours to preparing a new edition of my medical works for the press," he wrote to his presidential friend in the White House, adding a note of rare contrition: "They will contain some corrections, particularly a retraction of my former belief in the contagion of yellow fever, and many additions suggested by the experience and observations of the last years of my life."[47]

In the spring of 1804, his oldest son, twenty-seven-year-old John Rush, and fourteen other young men became the first graduating class at the University of Pennsylvania Medical School. He entitled his graduating thesis *An Inaugural Essay on the Causes of Sudden Death and the Means of Preventing It* and opened it with a moving dedication to his father. After graduating, John added to his father's pride by winning appointment to the staff of the Philadelphia General Hospital. Several months later, however, the erratic young man crushed his father's hopes by quitting medicine and leaving for South Carolina where he rejoined the navy. Rush believed his son was on the brink of insanity and on his way to a slow death in a medieval dungeon for maniacs in the Deep South.

CHAPTER 12

Healing the Last Wound

T HE LETTER WAS unexpected but the handwriting and message were unmistakable:

"It seemeth unto me that you and I ought not to die without saying Goodby or bidding each other Adieu."

The language was pure John Adams.

After a hiatus of twelve years, the embittered former President of the United States had sent his old friend Rush a hilarious effort to renew what had been a warm friendship of more than a decade—a friendship punctuated by both their signatures on the most famous document in American history.

Forgotten and all but despised by the republican throng that filled the Congress and gorged itself at President Jefferson's banquet table, Adams asked his once-dearest friend, "Pray how do you do?

"How does that excellent Lady Mrs. R?

"Where is my surgeon?"

Then the anger began seeping out. He had long wanted to renew his correspondence with Rush, but had awaited the right opportunity. The runaway reelection of Thomas Jefferson in 1804 gave him that opportunity—especially after the press reported Jefferson adopting monarchic habits in the White House by hiring a French chef and spending upwards of $2,500 a year on imported wines.

227

"In good sooth, my old Friend," Adams continued his letter. "Let me put a few questions to your conscience, for I know you have one.

Is the present state of the Nation republican enough? Is virtue the principle of our Government? Is honor? Or is ambition and avarice, adulation, baseness, covetousness, the thirst of riches . . . the spirit of party and of faction the motive and the principle that governs? My family unite with me in presenting respects and assurance of old regard to you and yours.[1]

Adams's evident bitterness stemmed in part from the libels cast against him during his term as President and his losing presidential campaign of 1800. Opponents and friends alike—including Rush—had charged him with favoring monarchism over republican government, without, however, any evidence to support their charges. "My friend Dr. Rush will excuse me," Adams had written in his last, angry letter to Rush in April 1790, "if I caution him against a fraudulent use of the word Monarchy and Republick [sic!]. I am a mortal and irreconcilable enemy to Monarchy."[2]

At the time, Adams had the lead role in the Senate's comedic debate over terms of address for the President, and Rush had joined other critics of Adams for favoring a European-style address over the egalitarian simplicity of "Mr. President." Rush's career had peaked then. His practice was expanding exponentially, students stood in the rear of the university lecture halls to hear his every word, and his praises echoed across the American skies as the nation's greatest physician and humanitarian. Back-to-back yellow fever epidemics beginning in 1793, however, provoked the first criticisms Rush had ever suffered in his saintly career, with several respected physicians charging that Rush's bleed-and-purge remedies killed more patients than they cured.

Although he worked day and night for months treating hundreds upon hundreds of yellow-fever victims and usually earned nothing, the press attacked Rush as they would a cold-blooded killer and all but wiped out his practice by the time the epidemic ended. Rush grew as bitter at times as Adams had been after the latter's reelection defeat. Only the love of his wife, Julia, and his children and the fidelity of a core of patients he had saved and doctors he had mentored finally dispelled the gloom.

"My much respected and dear friend," he emoted as he replied to Adams's writing initiative. "I have not forgotten—I cannot forget you. You and your excellent Mrs. Adams often compose a subject of conversation by my fireside." Rush went on to bring Adams up to date on the evolution of the Rush family before turning to "the present state of the United States.

> My children are often witnesses to my contrition for my sacrifices and of my shame for my zeal in the cause of our country. Among the fatherly cautions I deliver to them are the dangers of public [service] and the sin of party spirit. I live like a stranger in my native state. My patients are my only acquaintances, my books my only companions, and the members of my family nearly my only friends. The odious opinions I have propagated respecting the domestic origin of our American pestilence have placed me *permanently* in the same situation in Philadelphia that your political opinions placed you for a while in 1775.[3]

Although Adams and Rush not only believed themselves victims of libel and abuse—and justifiably so—both patriots believed their political enemies had revised history. With little else of consequence to do in retirement, Adams had been writing his autobiography, but grew appalled at accounts of the Revolution he now read in the press.

"I read the public papers and documents, and I cannot and will not be indifferent to the condition and prospects of my country. I love the people of America," he wrote to Rush. "They have been, they may be, and they are deceived . . . by a dozen volumes of lying newspapers and pamphlets edited annually for some twenty, thirty, or forty years without contradictions and aggravated by as many more volumes of private letters at least as lying as the newspapers. . . . It is the duty of somebody to undeceive them."[4]

Adams had long earlier complained to Rush that the written history of the American Revolution would be "one continued lie. . . .

> The essence . . . will be that Dr. Franklin's electrical rod smote the Earth and out sprung General Washington—and thence forward these two

conducted all the *Policy, Negotiations, Legislatures and War* [Adams's ital-ics]. These underscored lines contain the whole fable, plot and catastro-phe. . . . But this, my friend, to be serious, is the fate of all nations. . . . No nation can adore more than one man at a time.[5]

The exchange of letters between Adams and Rush at the beginning of 1805 started what would be eight years of uninterrupted correspondence between the two Founding Fathers—a historic treasure that includes some one hundred letters from Adams to Rush and almost ninety known letters from Rush to Adams—about one letter a month from each man to the other at a time when the trip from Boston to Philadelphia took at least five days by coach—if all went well.

Although Rush and Adams would never meet face-to-face again, their letters brought them closer than any personal encounter could have. The last sight each had had of the other had been more than five years ear-lier, when Adams was still a robust sixty-five and Rush a vigorous fifty-four. By limiting future intercourse to letters, neither would ever grow a minute older in the mind of his friend—nor would their words reflect advancing age.

Their letters would not, of course, change the course of American his-tory, and both men knew so, but they hoped their letters would affect the way perspicacious, unbiased historians would record their stories.

The Rush-Adams letters exposed and discussed in depth the range of early American history and early nineteenth-century life, including ordi-nary chit-chat about their own family lives. "I have been made very happy by a visit from my two daughters [from Canada], with the husband of one of them and their four children," Rush wrote to Adams. "My daughter [Mary] Manners has refuted by her cheerful deportment all the gloomy fears I had entertained of her destiny in marriage. Her husband is every-thing the most indulgent parents would wish a husband to be for . . . a favorite daughter. She expects to sail with him to England in the course of the present year."[6]

A month later, Rush was far sadder as he wrote his friend: "My daugh-ters . . . left us last week and under distressing apprehension of being long, long separated from us."[7]

Adams tried to console his friend: "Parting with your daughters must have been a tender scene in your Family. . . . I have suffered these pangs so often that I know how to sympathize with every sufferer."[8]

Rush was more distraught than he let on, however. "This day," he wrote in his diary on July 2, "my two beloved daughters with their four children . . . left on their return to Canada. It was to us all a day of sorrow. One of them, *Mary*, we shall probably never see again."[9]

It was indeed the last time Rush would ever see his daughter Mary. Her husband, Captain Thomas Manners, was still in the British army and would serve in the War of 1812 against the United States, before moving to Britain with Mary and the children. They would never return to North America.

As usual, Rush plunged into his work to divert his mind from personal misfortune. In addition to refining and preparing a new edition of his book on *Diseases of the Mind*, Rush searched for ways to expand the benefits and reach of modern medicine. In 1807 he delivered a lecture that opened a new field of medicine in America—medical care of domestic animals. Having visited Paris as a medical student, he was well aware that the French had opened the world's first school of veterinary medicine in 1762—designed at the time to combat a cattle plague. Its subsequent efforts so improved the quality of animal life—and farmer revenues—that similar schools opened during the 1790s in England, Germany, Denmark, and Sweden.

When, by 1807, veterinary medicine had failed to gain a foothold in the United States, Rush—still the fervent humanitarian intent on making the world a better place—prepared a lecture that, for the first time in American history, cited the vast benefits of veterinary medicine to farmers and to the nation's agriculture. In a nation where 90 percent of the population lived on, worked, or owned farms, Rush's argument had far-reaching effects.

"We are bound to study the diseases of domestic animals and the remedies that are proper to cure them, by a principle of gratitude," Rush insisted as he began his lecture.

They live only for our benefit. They cost us nothing in wages or clothing. They require in exchange for their labor . . . nothing from us but food

and shelter, and these of the cheapest and coarsest kind. . . . This motive
to take care of their health and lives will appear more striking when we
consider the specific benefits we receive from each of them.

Later published as a widely read pamphlet, *On the Duty and Advan-*
tages of Studying the Diseases of Domestic Animals and the Remedies Proper
to Remove Them, his lecture went on to list the economic benefits of each
category of domestic animal—horses, mules, sheep, cattle, poultry, and
others. "The horse . . . ploughs our fields . . . drags home our harvests and
fruits . . . conveys them . . . to market." The horse fostered communication
in society and permitted friendships to flourish between neighbors living
too far from each other to visit on foot. Even the nation's democracy, he
added, relied on the horse for its existence. It was a radical new argument
never heard before in the Americas.

"In vain would country churches and courts be opened without the
strength of this noble animal," Rush explained. "Nor could the great system of representative government be supported in an agricultural country
unless he conveyed the elector to the place of suffrage. In maintaining the
freedom and independence of nations, the horse bears a distinguished
part."[10]

Rush went on to extol the benefits of other domestic animals. To the
"horned cattle," he said, "we are indebted the strength and patience of
the ox in the plough . . . [which] has added to the wealth of the farmer
in every age and every country." He said cows had "still greater demands
on our gratitude" for milk, cream, butter, and cheese. "A pustule on her
udder supplies a matter which defends the body against small pox forever.
Their tallow and oil supply candles and lamps whereby labor and study
are extended during part of the night. Their hair furnishes an ingredient
of the plaster in our houses. Their skins give us shoes and boots, protect
our feet, make coverings for our books, saddles, wagon seats; horns make
combs; bones, when dried and ground, are in medicines." In a climactic
flourish, Rush reminded farmers that sheep, goats, dogs, poultry, and all
other domestic animals leave droppings that "furnish us with perpetuat-
ing the fertility of ours lands."

Rush pointed out the emotional appeal of domestic animals. "They
lessen the solitude and silence of country life. They please us with their

gambols when young and delight us with their looks and gestures in mature life, every time they receive food or shelter from our hands."[11]

The Rush foray into animal husbandry earned him new recognition as the father of veterinary science in America and champion of humane treatment of animals.

As usual, John Adams fired several good-natured barbs at Rush: "I respect your Science and Humanity as a Veterinarian, but is there not a little 'disease of the mind' in your . . . enthusiasm for old horses. . . . Would not the experience of keeping old useless horses be more humanely employed in relieving prisoners, orphans, and widows?" Commenting on the manuscript of *Diseases of the Mind* that Rush had sent, Adams wrote, "Your book has made it very clear that we all labor under diseases of the mind. . . . I am almost afraid to read it all, lest I should see my own character in the mirror and see more symptoms of mental malady . . . I have read enough to make me tremble."[12]

Unfortunately, the Rush lecture on the care of animals failed to provoke action by American educators or other humanitarians. More than four decades would elapse before the University of Pennsylvania would open the nation's first school of veterinary medicine—in 1852—and six decades would pass before the founding of the American Association for the Prevention of Cruelty to Animals in 1866.

Just as Rush was earning new honors, he received word from his old nemesis Dr. William Shippen, the director-general of hospitals during the Revolutionary War, that he was dying. Of all the doctors in Philadelphia, Shippen now chose Rush to treat him.

"He was my enemy from the time of my settlement in Philadelphia in 1769 to the last year of his life," Rush noted in his diary. "He sent for me to attend him notwithstanding in his last illness, which I did with a sincere desire to prolong his life."[13] The Rush visit, however, came too late to save his old foe.

In 1810, the US Navy confirmed Rush's worst fears: John had been "relieved of duty in consequence of mental derangement" after killing a fellow officer in a duel and engaging in gunplay aboard ship before attempting suicide.

"My eldest son," Rush lamented to Jefferson, "was brought home to me . . . in a state of melancholy derangement induced by killing a brother naval officer. Ragged clothes, disheveled hair, long nails, and beard and a dirty skin, with a dejected countenance accompanied by constant sighing and an unwillingness to speak or even to answer a question, and an apparent insensibility to the strongest expressions of parental and fraternal affection." Rush said he had no choice but to commit him to a cell in the Philadelphia Hospital for the Insane, "where there is too much reason to believe he will end his days."[14] Rush told Jefferson he planned to establish a chair at Pennsylvania Hospital "to aid in the cure of madness," but it would be of no help to John Rush. As his distraught father predicted, he would remain in the hospital until his death in 1837.

Rush apologized to Jefferson for opening his letter with so long a story of woe. "Judge of the distress," he said by way of acknowledging his failure to respond to Jefferson's last letter. "For some time I was in a degree unfitted for study or business. . . . You are a father. . . . ," and he left the line unfinished.[15]

Because of his troubles with John, Rush had let a year slip by without writing to congratulate Jefferson on his retirement from the presidency and his "escape," in the spring of 1809, "from the high and dangerous appointment which your country (to use the words of Lord Chesterfield) inflicted upon you during the last eight years of your life. Methinks I see you renewing your acquaintance with your philosophical instruments and with the friends of your youth in your library."[16]

After writing to Jefferson, Rush's mood changed abruptly as he learned of his son James's graduation from University of Pennsylvania Medical School "with credit to himself and satisfaction to his father." Indeed, James would now sail to Scotland to supplement his medical education at Edinburgh Medical School—as his father had done. In sending the good news to John Adams, Rush came up with a scheme to heal the wounds of his two friends and, in turn, some of the nation's deepest political wounds—many inflicted by bitter political rivalries created by Jefferson and Adams.

The two patriarchs had first met in 1775 at the Continental Congress, where they bonded over their commitment to independence and drew closer a year later as they collaborated in writing the Declaration of Independence. In 1784, Congress appointed Jefferson to replace John

Adams as minister plenipotentiary to France, with Adams appointed to assume the same role in Britain. When Jefferson arrived in Paris with his daughter, both pined for family life after the death of his wife two years earlier and frequently went to dine with the Adams family. Following Paris customs, Jefferson enrolled his daughter in a convent school, and he compensated for her absence by bonding with John Quincy Adams, the teenage son of John and Abigail Adams, taking him to theaters, concerts, and museums and becoming an important figure in the young man's life. The two formed such close ties that John Adams quipped to Jefferson that John Quincy "appeared to me to be almost as much your boy as mine."[17] When the Adamses left for England, Jefferson confessed, "The departure of your family has left me in the dumps. My afternoons hang heavily on me."[18]

Twenty-five years later, however, geographic and political distances had separated the two former presidents, and much of the nation reflected their schism. When Adams the Federalist had become President, his support for strong central government authority so alienated his republican antifederalist vice president that Jefferson flirted with treason by proposing to the Kentucky state legislature that it annul federal laws it deemed unconstitutional.

Although Jefferson's presidential inauguration speech of 1801 spoke of bringing republicans and Federalists together, his sentiment proved to be nothing more than words, and, after eight years in the White House, Jefferson and Adams and their two political factions were as divided as ever. With no political figures of any consequence left to unite the nation or its nominal leaders—Franklin, Washington, and the others were gone—Rush believed he could use his close personal ties to both Adams and Jefferson to heal their personal and political wounds. As the elder statesmen of the two political factions, he reasoned, their reconciliation would influence the nation to follow suit, and he now set out to bring the two old friends—and the nation—together again.

He wrote to Adams of having dreamed of reading a page in a history book that began, "Among the most extraordinary events of this year [1809] was the renewal of the friendship and intercourse between Mr. John Adams and Mr. Jefferson. They met for the first time in the

Continental Congress of 1775. Their principles of liberty . . . being exactly the same, they . . . became personal as well as political friends."[19]

Rush told Adams the dream described the differences that had separated the two friends—the French Revolution and political rivalries in the United States—then told of their rapprochement after Jefferson's retirement from office in 1809, when Adams "addressed a short letter to congratulate him on his retirement and wish him well.

"The letter did great honor to Mr. Adams," Rush continued relating his dream. "It discovered a magnanimity known only to great minds" and provoked a cordial reply from Jefferson and the beginning of a correspondence of many years that reviewed their presidencies and became one of the nation's historic treasures.[20]

"A DREAM AGAIN!" Adams opened his sarcastic reply—in uppercase letters—referring to Rush's work on psychiatry. With his letter all but spewing smoke, he said he did not object to Rush dreaming . . .

" . . . but that is not history!

"There has never been the smallest interruption of the personal friendship between me and Mr. Jefferson that I know of," Adams protested disingenuously. "You should remember that Jefferson was but a boy to me. I was at least ten yours older than him in age and more than twenty years older than him in politics. I am bold to say that I was his preceptor in politics and taught him everything that is good and solid in his whole political conduct."[21]

Adams blamed his break with Jefferson on the Virginian's open patronage of "my most abandoned and unprincipled enemies. Fare them all well," he declared. With that, he rejected Rush's suggestion that he, Adams, effect a reconciliation with Jefferson. Rush did not bring it up again for eighteen months, when in writing Jefferson of his despair over the descent of his son John into insanity, his thoughts recalled the dream he had fabricated of a Jefferson-Adams reconciliation.

"Your and my old friend Mr. Adams now and then drops me a line," Rush tried sounding nonchalant. "His letters glow with the just opinions he held and defended in the patriotic years 1774, 1775, and 1776.

When I consider your early attachment to Mr. Adams and his to you; when I consider how much the liberties and independence of the United

States owe to the concert of your principles and labor . . . I have ardently wished a friendly and epistolary intercourse might be revived between you before you take a final leave of the common object of your affection. Such an intercourse will be . . . highly useful to the course of republicanism not only in the United States but all over the world. Posterity will revere the friendship of two ex-Presidents that were once opposed to each other. Human nature will be a gainer by it. I am sure an advance on your side will be a cordial to the heart of Mr. Adams.[22]

Jefferson replied with a long polemic that blamed Adams for the rupture of his friendship and the longtime enmity that followed. "The discontinuance of friendly correspondence," Jefferson protested like a schoolboy, "has not proceeded from me, nor from the want of sincere desire and of effort on my part to renew our intercourse."[23]

Like the lawyer that he was, Jefferson went on to build his case against Adams: as vice president, Jefferson charged, Adams had revealed his monarchic tendencies by extolling Julius Caesar as "the greatest man that ever lived." He (Adams) had believed "the thousand calumnies which the Federalists . . . daily invented against me [Jefferson]." And, of course, Adams had stood behind the notorious Alien and Sedition Acts of 1798 aborting First Amendment protections of free speech and a free press. Jefferson said he had tried to restore their friendship, but that Adams had rejected his offer, even after his wife, Abigail Adams, had tried to encourage renewal of their relationship.

Rush replied, saying, "I acquit you" of responsibility for the continuing rupture of ties to Adams, but he nonetheless reminded Jefferson again of how close they had once been. Rush said he lamented "the evils of a political life" that provoke "dissolution of friendships and the implacable hatreds which too often take their place."[24]

Neither Jefferson nor Adams, however, relented in their refusals to initiate a reconciliation. Knowing each as intimately as he did, however, Rush continued peppering his letters to Jefferson with citations of Adams's embrace of republicanism. At the same time, he focused attention in his letters to Adams on instances where members of the press or historians have omitted credit due to Adams in the founding of the Republic. As the celebrations of July 4, 1811, approached, Adams condemned what he called "a theatrical show" at the signing of the Declaration of Independence. "Jefferson ran away with all the stage effect of that: i.e., all the glory of it," said Adams. "Our citizens are . . . great masters of Theatrical Exhibitions of Politicks.

> Were there ever more striking Coups de Theatre than Mock Funerals?* . . . Washington understood this . . . he was the best Actor of Presidency we ever had. His address to the States when he left the Army; his solemn leave taken of Congress when he resigned his commission; his Farewell Address to the people when he resigned his presidency. These were all in a strain of Shakespearian and Garrickal excellence in dramatic exhibitions. We never instituted mock funerals for Warren . . . Hancock . . . Patrick Henry.[25]

"Mr. Adams continues to deplore the evils which impend our country," Rush wrote to Jefferson:

> The 4th of July has been celebrated in Philadelphia in the manner I expected. The military men . . . ran away with all the glory of the day. Scarcely a word was said of the solicitude and labors and fears and sorrows and sleepless nights of the men who projected, proposed, defended, and subscribed the Declaration of Independence. Do you recollect your memorable speech upon the day on which the vote was taken? Do you recollect the pensive and awful silence which pervaded the house when we were called up, one after another, to the table of the President of Congress to subscribe what was believed by many at that time to be our own death warrants?

And in a letter to Adams, Rush added an anecdote he hoped would provoke the New Englander to rethink his refusal to correspond with Jefferson, citing the reaction of a tourist at the statue of Franklin in

---

*Four days after George Washington's death in December 1899, his wife and close relatives buried George Washington on his Mount Vernon estate. Eight days later, Congress held a massive mock funeral, with an empty coffin, and, in the weeks that followed, communities across the nation followed suit.

Philadelphia: "But for that fellow," said the tourist, "we should never have had independence."[26]

As summer's end approached, Rush applied what he hoped would be the coup de grace in his effort to crush Adams's obstinacy: "The time cannot be very distant when you and I must both sleep with our fathers," Rush wrote, citing an "epistolary intercourse" with Jefferson as essential to emendation of accumulated historical inaccuracies about the Revolution and subsequent administrations that governed the new nation.

> The distinguished figure you made in life . . . will render your removal from the world an object of universal attention. Suppose you avail yourself while in health . . . by leaving behind you a posthumous address to the citizens of the United States . . . Your name and fame have always been dear to me. I wish you to survive yourself for ages in the veneration, esteem, and affection of your fellow citizens and to be useful to them even in the grave. None but those persons who knew you in the years 1774, 1775, and 1776 will ever know how great a debt the United States owe to your talents, knowledge, unbending firmness, and intrepid patriotism.[27]

Instead of a reply from John Adams, however, the next letter he received from Massachusetts was from the Adams daughter Nabby writing for advice. She had discovered a lump in her breast and Boston doctors advised a radical mastectomy. Rather than reply to Nabby, Rush wrote to her father to allow him to pass on the advice "gradually" and avoid "distress and alarm."

Advising against "all local applications and internal medicines," Rush said, "in 19 cases out of 20 in tumors of the breast . . . the remedy is the knife. . . . It shocks me to think of the consequences of procrastination."[28]

Knowing how frightened Nabby was about the surgery, Rush cited his experience two years earlier when Dr. Physick had removed a tumor from Rush's own neck. Anesthesia still lay decades in the future.* "I was

---

*Although the anesthetic effects of nitrous oxide had been demonstrated in 1800, surgeons did not begin to use anesthesia until 1842, when a Boston surgeon successfully demonstrated the use of ether.

surprised when the doctor's assistant told me the operation was finished."
On Rush's advice, Nabby consented to a mastectomy and survived.[29]

Shortly thereafter, Jefferson seemed ready to relent in the standoff with
John Adams, saying that two Jefferson neighbors had visited Adams in
Massachusetts the previous year and returned with a report that Adams
had denied having any animosity towards Jefferson. "I always loved Jefferson," Adams reportedly replied, "and I still love him."

With that, Jefferson wrote to Rush saying, "This is enough for me. I
only needed this knowledge to revive all the affections of the most cordial
moments of our lives . . . with a man possessing so many inestimable
qualities. Why should we be separated by mere differences of opinions in
politics, religion, philosophy or anything else? His opinions are as honestly formed as my own. I wish therefore . . . to express to Mr. Adams my
unchanged affection for him."[30]

Nabby's ordeal forced her father to face his own mortality and the real-
ities of the Rush warning that the two former presidents were approaching
the time when they would join their fathers.

"I wish you Sir many happy New Years," John Adams replied to
Thomas Jefferson on January 1, 1812, "and that you may enter the next
and many succeeding years with as animating prospects for the public as
those at present before us. I am Sir with a long and sincere esteem your
friend and servant, John Adams."[31]

Adams's letter delighted and, indeed, moved Jefferson. "A letter from
you calls up recollections very dear to my mind," he replied to Adams. "It
carries me back to the time when, beset with difficulties and dangers, we
were fellow laborers in the same cause, struggling for what is most valuable to man, his right of self-government.

> Laboring always at the same oar . . . we rode through the storm with
> heart and hand. . . . Still we did not expect to be without rubs and diffi-
> culties, and we have had them. . . . But whither is senile garrulity leading
> me? Into politics, of which I have taken final leave. . . . I have given up
> newspapers for Tacitus and Thucydides, for Newton and Euclid, and I
> find myself much happier. Sometimes indeed I look back to . . . our old
> friends and fellow laborers who have fallen before us. Of the signers of the

Declaration of Independence I see now living not more than half a dozen on your side of the Potomac and, on this side, myself alone. . . . I should have the pleasure of knowing that, in the race of life, you do not keep in its physical decline the same distance ahead of me which you have done in political honors and achievements. No circumstances have lessened the interest I feel in . . . yourself; none have suspended for one moment my sincere esteem for you; and I now salute you with unchanged affection and respect.[32]

Jefferson's long, detailed letter—nearly 1,000 words—moved Adams as much as his had obviously touched Jefferson, and he sat down to begin a letter that exceeded 1,500 words and began, "Sitting at my fireside . . . my servant brought me a bundle of letters . . . one of the letters struck my eye. . . . Is that not Mr. Jefferson's hand? . . . How is it possible a letter can come from Mr. Jefferson to me in seven or eight days? I had no expectation of an answer. . . . This history would not be worth recording but for the . . . fact, very pleasing to me, that the communication between us is much easier and may be more frequent than I had ever believed or suspected to be possible. . . .

Your life and mine for almost half a century have been nearly all of a piece. . . . The Union is still to me an object of as much anxiety as ever Independence was. To this I have sacrificed my popularity. . . . I walk every fair day . . . ride now and then . . . but I have a . . . palsy . . . which makes my hands tremble. . . . I have the start of you in age by at least ten years, but you are advanced to the rank of a great grandfather before me. . . . I cordially reciprocate your professions of esteem and respect.[33]

And so began an exchange of more than 150 letters over fourteen years from 1812 to their deaths in 1826, between two patriarchs who had signed their nation's Declaration of Independence, then led their new nation during twelve of its first twenty years of existence. Cited by historians as one of the most historically significant exchanges of letters in American history, they touched on every aspect of American history before and after the nation's founding. They discussed national and international affairs, the American and French Revolutions and other historical events, their own administrations and the backgrounds of their decisions—some of which changed the course of history. They assessed other political leaders of their generation, of course, and they veered into ancient history, discussing political leaders and philosophers of ancient Greece and Rome.

"So many subjects crowd upon me that I know not with which to begin," Adams admitted to Jefferson in one letter.[34] And of course, both men were aging human beings, fathers, grandfathers, and, in Jefferson's case, a great grandfather, who confided their hopes, fears, loves, hatreds, and aches, both physical and emotional. After Jefferson responded to Adams's letter with "the assurances of my sincere friendship,"[35] Adams replied in kind with "assurances of friendship and respect," and, later, "I am still as I ever have been and ever shall be with great esteem and regards, your friend and servant."[36] Jefferson, in turn, assured Adams, "That you may live in health and happiness is the sincere prayer of yours affectionately. . . ."[37]

Rush was ecstatic; he had healed one of the nation's great political wounds. "Few of the acts of my life have given me more pleasure," he wrote to Jefferson, "than to hear of a frequent exchange of letters between you and Mr. Adams."[38] To Adams he wrote, "I rejoice in the correspondence which has taken place between you and your old friend Mr. Jefferson. I consider you and him as the North and South Poles of the American Revolution. Some talked, some wrote, and some fought to promote and establish it, but you and Mr. Jefferson *thought* for us all." Rush told Adams he believed all the "political, moral, and intellectual achievements" of the Continental Congress in 1775 and 1776 were "the products of the opinions, speeches, and conversations of Adams and Jefferson."[39]

Rush had other reasons to rejoice. Political events of greater import to the nation had left the acrimony over his bleed-and-purge treatments in the archives of the nation's newspapers. In the meantime, the worlds of science and of medicine had rediscovered the far-reaching contributions he had made to humanity. In 1805, the University of Pennsylvania Medical School appointed him dean; his *Diseases of the Mind* had won international acclaim; the King of Prussia awarded him a gold medal, the Czar of Russia a diamond ring, the king of Spain "royal thanks." Literary and philosophical societies showered him with certificates of achievement.

The Three Patriarchs, reunited in old age: the two former presidents, John Adam left, and Thomas Jefferson, right, and their mutual friend and physician, Benjamin Rush, M.D., center.

"My lectures, the hospital, and my private practice have occupied every moment of my time," he crowed to John Adams. My class amounts to 300, 260 of whom are students of medicine. The rest are graduates in medicine, clergymen, and private gentlemen."[40]

But there were more reasons to rejoice still to come. In August 1809, his son Richard, a respected lawyer by then, married a doctor's daughter in Maryland. Rush assured her "that I should consider [her] not as an adopted but as my own child."[41] Shortly thereafter, Richard Rush won appointment as attorney general of Pennsylvania, while his wife gave birth to their first child, a boy whom they named after his grandfather Benjamin.

In July 1812, Rush went to visit a patient nine miles out of town and took his youngest child, the ebullient eleven-year-old William, who was home from school for the summer vacation. "I was within three or four miles of the farm upon which I was born," Rush related to John Adams, "where my ancestors for several generations had lived and died." He took William to visit the farm, where the owners "received me kindly" and let the two explore at will. Rush took William into the room where Rush "drew my first breath and made my first unwelcome noise in the world." He repeated for William the tales of his ancestors he had often related to his older children: how the earliest Rush settlers had cleared the land of wolves, bears, and snakes; how the next generation had reared livestock and plowed the earth; and how a third generation had used reapers, mowers, threshers to turn the fields into the most productive on earth.

And at all times, in every generation—Rush drew his son closer to look into the boy's eyes—the family had sustained itself with prayer. "All of my family were pious people."[42]

On their way back to Philadelphia, Rush stopped at "a small family graveyard in which were buried three and part of four successive generations . . . descended from Captain John Rush, who with six sons and three daughters had followed William Penn to Pennsylvania in 1683." Rush found a gravestone marked

IN MEMORY OF JAMES RUSH
WHO DEPARTED THIS LIFE
MARCH 16, 1727, AGED 48 YEARS.

and inscribed below

I'VE TRIED THE STRENGTH OF DEATH,
AND HERE LIE UNDER GROUND,
BUT I SHALL RISE ABOVE THE SKIES,
WHEN THE LAST TRUMP SHALL SOUND.

"This James was my grandfather," Rush told Adams, "My son the physician was named after him." Rush ended his letter paraphrasing Alexander Pope, telling Adams, "There are seldom more than two or three persons in the world who are interested in anything a man says of himself. . . . I have flattered myself that you are one of those two or three persons to whom the simple narrative . . . in this letter will not be unacceptable from, my dear and much respected friend, yours very affectionately, [signed] Benjn: Rush."[43]

Only a few days before Rush visited his ancestral home, Congress had declared war on England at the behest of President James Madison, but, from the first, American forces embarrassed themselves badly. US troops had invaded Canada on three fronts that stretched from Detroit in the west to Lake Champlain in upstate New York. Although one force managed to burn public buildings in a surprise raid on York [now Toronto], the capital of Upper Canada [now Ontario], it quickly retreated back to the United States after British troops counterattacked.

Undermining the American military effort was the refusal of New York and the New England states to participate in the war. All traded extensively with Britain and claimed that the terms of troop enlistments in their state militias did not permit crossing state lines. With New England unaffected by fighting, a huge smuggling trade developed, driving prices up uncontrollably as merchants in Massachusetts, Rhode Island, and Connecticut openly defied the American central government and traded illicitly with England and her colonies, paying whatever prices smugglers demanded.

Both Rush and Adams were appalled, with Rush citing a sermon of his uncle Samuel Finley, the schoolmaster-preacher, based on words from Proverbs: "Madness is in their hearts while they live."[44]

Adams called the war an "imbecility. . . . Disgrace after disgrace. Disaster on the heels of disaster. If Canada must be invaded," he raged to Rush, "not a foot should have been set on that shore till we had a decided superiority of naval force upon all the [Great] Lakes. Trails of field artillery and of heavy cannon and mortars. . . . Powder in abundance."[45]

As the war dragged on, the demand for doctors increased and spurred Benjamin Rush to embark on a new crusade in January 1813, when he determined to reform American medical education. "In Edinburgh," he wrote to the trustees of the University of Pennsylvania, "an attendance upon medical lectures for three winters is required before a student can offer himself as a candidate for a degree in medicine.

> The lectures . . . each season continue six months so that a student spends eighteen months in the whole course of his medical education. The lectures on our university continue but four months in each season, so that a student spends but eight months . . . to qualify for a degree. This immense difference . . . cannot surely be defended by a supposed superiority of intellect in the American student nor by less value of human life in the United States.[46]

When the trustees failed to respond, Rush persisted: "The number and subjects of our lectures have been increased," he explained to trustees, "and the insufficiency of two years' instruction was evinced last year by the rejection of six of the applicants for degrees." Calling a two-year medical school education inadequate and "a danger to life," Rush urged adding a third year to medical school and requiring students to study physics, midwifery, and a course on diseases of women and children before granting them an M.D. He also urged the trustees to add botany to the list, saying it was required at the University of Edinburgh Medical School. "Most of our medicines are obtained from the objects of that science. . . . A physician cannot be completely educated who is not . . . acquainted with it." He said all the medical schools in Europe and in Boston and New York had added botanical gardens "to facilitate the study of it."[47]

Rush would never see the outcome of his last crusade. In the days following his appeal to the trustees, he developed a persistent cough that eroded his strength, even sending the indefatigable doctor to bed for an occasional day of rest.

On April 10, 1813, he penned a letter to John Adams asserting that "my time is short and the night of imbecility of mind or of death is fast approaching."[48]

Four days later, he left his bed to try to resume his practice, but felt a chill while visiting a patient and returned home. He developed a fever during the night and awakened the next morning with pains in his side—indicative of pneumonia. True to form, Rush insisted that a bleeder come and draw ten ounces—a procedure that left him still weaker. Unsure whether he suffered from typhus, tuberculosis, or pneumonia, he called for his friend and disciple Dr. Physick, who tried extracting more blood. Only three viscous ounces oozed out, and Rush grew worse.

That afternoon, April 19, 1813, Physick drew the last drop of blood from the arm of Benjamin Rush, M.D., and, after sixty-seven years, the life of America's great humanitarian came to an end.

Post Mortem

"A NOTHER OF OUR friends of seventy-six is gone, my dear Sir," Thomas Jefferson lamented to his friend John Adams. "And a better man than Rush could not have left us; more benevolent, more learned, of finer genius, or more honest. We too must go, and that ere long. I believe we are under half a dozen at present; I mean the signers of the Declaration. I am the only one south of the Potomac."[1]

Too grief-stricken to respond at length, Adams could only pen a few words in reply: "I lament with you the loss of Rush. I know of no character living or dead who has done more real good in America."[2]

A few days later, when he had recovered his emotions somewhat, Adams wrote to Vice President Elbridge Gerry, a long-standing friend from Massachusetts who had also signed the Declaration of Independence: "As a man of science, Letters, Taste, Sense, Philosophy, Patriotism, Religion, Morality, Merit, Usefulness, taken all together, Rush has not left his equal in America, nor that I know in the world. In him is taken, and in a manner most sudden and totally unexpected, a main prop of my life."[3] Next to members of his immediate family, Adams admitted, Rush had become the most important person in his life and their "epistolary intercourse" had been the most important activity in his life.

John Adams and Thomas Jefferson continued their dialogue for thirteen more years, into the spring of 1826, when tremors in their hands and arms made writing more difficult and forced them to keep their letters short. "I am ever your friend," Adams signed off to Jefferson, while Jefferson wrote of the decline in his health, "but not my friendship and respect for you."[4] Both men died on July 4 of that year, the fiftieth anniversary of the Declaration of Independence that they would sign with their mutual friend Dr. Benjamin Rush and fifty-three other Founding Fathers. Jefferson was eighty-two when he died, and Adams, who died five hours later, was ninety.

Benjamin Rush lies beside his beloved Julia in Christ Church Burial Ground in Philadelphia, near his mother and father and his friends Benjamin Franklin and Dr. Philip Syng Physick. His gravestone bears an inscription from Matthew:

> WELL DONE GOOD AND FAITHFUL SERVANT.
> ENTER THOU INTO THE JOY OF THE LORD.

Julia Rush, who lies beside him, survived her husband by more than three decades, dying in 1848 at Sydenham, the Rush country home. When Benjamin Rush died, they had been married thirty-seven years.

Of their surviving children, those girls not already married when Rush died subsequently found husbands and led happy, uneventful lives as wives and mothers. Of the surviving men and boys, John, as noted, spent the rest of his life in an institution for the insane.

Richard Rush emerged as the most distinguished of the Rush sons. After serving as Pennsylvania attorney general, he assumed the same role in the federal government in 1814 under President Madison. In 1817, President Monroe appointed him acting secretary of state before naming him minister to Great Britain, a post he held from 1817 to 1825. Monroe's successor, President John Quincy Adams, appointed Rush secretary of treasury in 1825, a position he held for four years before becoming President Adams's running mate in the latter's unsuccessful effort to win reelection in 1828. After leaving government, Richard Rush practiced law for nearly twenty years before a brief reentry into government service as minister to France from 1847 to 1851.

James Rush, M.D., meanwhile, quit medicine after his father's death, turning instead to medical research and writing, while Samuel Rush, the second-youngest Rush boy, became an attorney in Philadelphia and held several positions in local government. William Rush, only twelve when his father died, graduated from the University of Pennsylvania six years later, then went to medical school, earned his M.D., and joined the medical staff of the Philadelphia Hospital, which his father helped found.

In 1837, a prominent American surgeon honored Benjamin Rush by obtaining a charter in Chicago to found a medical school he named the Rush Medical College. The college grew into today's Rush University, one of the nation's premier institutions in the fields of medicine and science. It includes the Rush University Medical Center, Rush College of Nursing, the College of Health Sciences at Rush University, the Graduate College at Rush University, and, of course, Rush Medical College.

APPENDIX A

SELECTED WRITINGS OF BENJAMIN RUSH BY TOPIC

Almost one hundred published works of Benjamin Rush, M.D., exist today, of which those with the greatest historic import are listed here. Their scope demonstrates Dr. Rush's self-description as "an enthusiastic lifelong student of everything under the sun." To understand the range of his involvement in humanitarian projects to improve the life and liberties of Americans, the books and pamphlets are classified by topic. Because he often incorporated many of his lectures and articles into books, writings listed individually can also be found as chapters in works such as the four-volume *Medical Inquiries and Observations* (Appendix B), the subsequent fifth volume, *Medical Inquiries and Observations upon the Diseases of the Mind* (Appendix B), and *Essays: Literary, Moral, and Philosophical* (Appendix C).

ABBREVIATIONS

AM *American Museum*
FG *Federal Gazette*
IG *Independent Gazetteer*
MIO *Medical Inquiries and Observations*
PG *Pennsylvania Gazette*
PJ *Pennsylvania Journal*
PMM *Philadelphia Medical Museum*
PP *Pennsylvania Packet*
T-APS *Transactions of the American Philosophical Society*

ABOLITION

An Address to the Inhabitants of the British Settlements in America upon Slave-Keeping (Philadelphia: John Dunlop, 1773).

AGRICULTURE/ECONOMICS

An Account for the Sugar Maple-Tree of the United States, and of the Methods of Obtaining Sugar from It, Together with Observations upon the Advantages, Both Public and Private, of This Sugar (Philadelphia: R. Aitken & Son, 1792).

An Account of the Mangel Wurzel, or Root of Scarcity, a New Vegetable [yellow field beet for cattle] (Philadelphia: *Columbian Magazine*, 1788).

Advice to American Farmers About to Settle in New Countries [meaning, new US states or territories] (AM, 1789).

A Comparison Between the Prospects of Advantage in the Unsettled and Unimproved Parts of Pennsylvania and in the New Countries at Niagara, Kentucky (AM, 1789).

An Open Letter to the Philadelphia Society for Promoting Agriculture and Rural Affairs (PG, 1786).

Information to Europeans Who Are Disposed to Migrate to the United States (Philadelphia: Carey, Stewart, & Co., 1790).

Thoughts on Paper Money (PG, 1786).

ANTHROPOLOGY

An Inquiry into the Natural History of Medicine among the Indians in North-America, and a Comparative View of Their Diseases and Remedies, with Those of Civilized Nations (Philadelphia: Joseph Cruikshank, 1774).

Observations Intended to Favour a Supposition That the Black Color of the Negroes Is Derived from Leprosy (T-APS, 1799).

EDUCATION

The Application of the Principles of Natural Philosophy and Chemistry to Domestic and Culinary Purposes (Philadelphia: Andrew Brown, 1787).

A Defense of the Use of the Bible as a School Book (AM, 1791).

Of the Mode of Education Proper in a Republic (*Gentleman's Magazine*, 1786).

A Plan for the Establishment of Public Schools and the Diffusion of Knowledge in Pennsylvania; To Which Are Added Thoughts upon the Mode of Education, Proper in a Republic (Philadelphia: Thomas Dobson, 1786).

A Plan of a Federal University (FG, 1788).

Thoughts upon Female Education, Accommodated to the Present State of Society, Manners, and Government in the United States of America (Philadelphia: Prichard and Hall, 1787).

Thoughts upon the Amusements and Punishments Which Are Proper for Schools (Philadelphia: *Columbian Magazine*, 1790).

Thoughts upon the Mode of Education Proper in a Republic (1786).

To the Citizens of Pennsylvania of German Birth and Extraction: Proposal of a German College (PG, 1785). [Founding of Franklin College]

To the Citizens of Philadelphia (IG, 1787). [Call for free, tax-supported public schools]

GERIATRICS

An Account of the Causes and Indications of Longevity and of the State of the Body and Mind in Old Age, with Observations upon Its Diseases and Their Remedies (MIO, 1:233).

GOVERNMENT/POLITICAL AFFAIRS

An Account of the Progress, Population, Agriculture, Manners and Government in Pennsylvania (*Essays*, 213).

Considerations upon the Present Test-Law of Pennsylvania (Philadelphia: Huff and Sellers, 1784).

Division of the People of America with Respect to Their Political Characters (PP, 1777).

Observations upon the Present Government of Pennsylvania (Philadelphia: Styner and Cist, 1777).

On American Whigs (PG, 1782).

On Public Credit as the Means of Obtaining a Navy (PG, 1782).

Plan of a Peace Office for the United States (*Essays*, 1793).

The Subject of an American Navy (PG, 1782).

Three Letters to the Public (Philadelphia: Bradford, 1783). [Discusses union, civil and military powers, public debt]

To the Rulers and People of America (PG, 1782).

HYGIENE AND HEALTH

An Enquiry into the Relation of Tastes and Ailments to Each Other and into the Influence of This Relation upon Health and Pleasure (AM, 1789).

On Exercise (PP, 1772).

On Intemperance in Eating (PG, 1772).

Sermons to the Rich and Studious on Temperance and Exercise (Litchfield, CT: T. Collier, 1791).

MEDICAL ETHICS

Observations on the Duties of a Physician and the Methods of Improving Medicine (Philadelphia: Prichard & Hall, 1789.)

MEDICINE AND MEDICAL PRACTICE

Account of a New Bitter Prepared from the Bark of the Root of the Liriodendron Tulipifera [tulip tree] (T-APS, 1793).

Account of a Supposed Case of Internal Dropsy of the Brain, Successfully Treated by Mercury (T-APS, 1793).

Account of a Tetanus from the Extraction of Two Teeth, Successfully Treated by the Use of Wine and Mercury (T-APS, 1793).

An Account of Several Cases of General Diseases Cured by the Extraction of Decayed and Diseased Teeth (*The Medical Repository*,1809).

An Account of the Bilious Remitting Yellow Fever as It Appeared in the City of Philadelphia in the Year 1793 (Philadelphia: Thomas Dobson, 1794).

An Account of the Climate of Pennsylvania and Its Influence upon the Human Body (AM, 1789).

An Account of the Diseases Peculiar to the Negroes in the West-Indies, and Which Are Produced by Their Slavery (AM, 1788).

An Account of the Efficacy of Sugar of Lead [lead acetate] *in Curing Epilepsy* (PMM, 1804).

An Account of the Late Dr. Hugh Martin's Cancer Powder, with Brief Observations on Cancers (T-APS, 1786).

An Account of the Salutary Effects of a Salivation and also of Tonic Remedies in Pulmonary Consumption (*The Medical Repository*, 1802).

An Account of the Salutary Effects of Blood-letting in Curing the Disease Brought on by Taking Excessive Quantities of Opium (*The Medical Repository*, 1802).

An Account of the Successful Use of Opium, Cordial Drinks, and Animal Food in Two Cases of Pulmonary Consumption (PMM, 1806).

An Account of the Usefulness of Wort [malt] *in Some Ill-Conditioned Ulcers* (MIO, 1771, 4:367–370).

Case of a Curvature of the Spine (T-APS, 1793).

A Case of Variolous Pustules, Occurring from Inoculation After Having Previously Had the Small-Pox (PHM, 1811).

Directions for Recovering Persons, Who Are Supposed to Be Dead from Drowning. Also for Preventing and Curing the Disorders Produced . . . by the Action of Noxious Vapors, Lightning, and Excessive Heat and Cold upon the Human Body (Philadelphia: Joseph Jones, 1789).

Directions for the Use of Mineral Water and Cold Bath (Philadelphia: Melchior Steiner, 1786).

An Enquiry into the Cause of the Increase of the Bilious and Intermitting Fevers in Pennsylvania, with Hints for Preventing Them (T-APS, 1786).

An Enquiry into the Methods of Preventing the Painful and Fatal Effects of Cold upon the Human Body (Philadelphia: *Columbian Magazine*, 1787).

Free Thoughts upon the Cause and Cure of the Pulmonary Consumption (AM, 1789).

An Inquiry into the Functions of the Spleen, Liver, Pancreas, and Thyroid Gland (Philadelphia: [publisher omitted], 1806).

An Inquiry into the Use of the Thymus Gland (PMM, 1811).

An Inquiry into the Various Sources of the Usual Forms of Summer and Autumnal Diseases in the United States and the Means of Preventing Them to Which Are Added Facts Intended to Prove the Yellow Fever Not to Be Contagious (Philadelphia: J. Conrad & Co., 1805).

Medical Inquiries and Observations, 4 vols. (Philadelphia: J. Conrad & Co., 1805, 2nd ed.) See Appendix B.

Observations on the Cymanche Trachialis [croup] (MIO, 1789).

Observations upon the Origin of the Malignant Bilious, or Yellow Fever in Philadelphia and upon the Means of Preventing It (Philadelphia: Thomas Dobson, 1799).

Pathological and Practical Remarks upon Certain Morbid Affections of the Liver (PMM, 1811).

Remarks upon the Hydrophobia (*Eclectic Repertory*, 1813).

Six Introductory Lectures to Courses of Lectures upon the Institutes and Practice of Medicine, Delivered in the University of Pennsylvania (Philadelphia: John Conrad & Co., 1801). [See below, *Sixteen Introductory Lectures . . .*]

Sixteen Introductory Lectures to Courses of Lectures upon the Institutes and Practice of Medicine (Philadelphia: Bradford and Inskeep, 1811).

> On the Necessary Connection between Observation and Reasoning in Medicine.
> On the Character of Dr. Sydenham.
> On the Causes of Diseases.
> On the Influence of Physical Causes in Promoting the Strength and Activity of the Intellectual Faculties of Man.
> On the Vices and Virtues of Physicians.
> On the Causes Which Have Retarded the Progress of Medicine and on the Means of Promoting Its Certainty and Greater Usefulness.
> On the Education Proper to Qualify a Young Man for the Study of Medicine.
> On the Construction and Management of Hospitals.
> On the Pains and Pleasures of a Medical Life.
> On the Means of Acquiring Business and the Causes Which Prevent the Acquisition and Occasion the Loss of It in the Profession of Medicine.
> On the Utility of Knowledge of the Faculties and Operations of the Human Mind to a Physician.
> On the Opinions and Modes of Practice of Hippocrates.

On the Duty and Advantages of Studying the Diseases of Domestic Animals and the Remedies Proper to Remove Them.

On the Duties of Patients to Their Physicians.

On the Means of Acquiring Knowledge.

On the Study of Medical Jurisprudence.

Two Lectures upon the Pleasures of the Senses and of the Mind, with an Inquiry into Their Proximate Cause.

A Syllabus of a Course of Lectures on the Institutes of Medicine (Philadelphia: Thomas Bradford, 1795).

On the Necessary Connection between Observation and Reasoning in Medicine (Includes Syllabus of a Course of Lectures upon Physiology, Pathology, Therapeutics, and the Practice of Medicine).

On the Character of Dr. Sydenham.

On the Causes of Death in Diseases That Are Not Incurable.

On the Influence of Physical Causes in Promoting the Strength and Activity of the Intellectual Faculties of Man.

Of the Vices and Virtues of Physicians.

On the Causes Which Have Retarded the Progress of Medicine and on the Means of Promoting Its Certainty and Greater Usefulness.

A Syllabus of a Course of Lectures on the Institutes of Medicine (Philadelphia: Thomas Bradford, 1798). [See preceding entry]

MILITARY AFFAIRS

Directions for Preserving the Health of Soldiers Addressed to the Officers of the Army (Philadelphia: John Dunlop, 1778).

MISCELLANEOUS

Directions for Conducting a Newspaper in Such a Manner as to Make It Innocent, Useful, and Entertaining (FG, 1988).

Essays: Literary, Moral & Philosophical (Philadelphia: Thomas & Samuel Bradford, 1798). [See Appendix B]

Information to Europeans Who Are Disposed to Migrate to the United States (Philadelphia: Carey, Stewart, & Co., 1790).

MORALITY

The Benefits of Charity: A Dream (Philadelphia: *Columbian Magazine*, 1787).

An Interpretation of the Sacred Scriptures in the Ancient Eastern Manner . . . with a Philosophical and Medical Commentary (Edinburgh: J. Dickson, 1797).

OBSTETRICS

On the Means of Lessening the Pains and Dangers of Child-Bearing and of Preventing the Consequent Diseases (*The Medical Repository*, 1803).

PEDIATRICS

A Dissertation on the Spasmodic Asthma of Children (London: T. Cadell, 1770).

PENAL REFORM

Considerations on the Injustice and Impolicy of Punishing Murder by Death (Philadelphia: Mathew Carey, 1792).
An Enquiry into the Effects of Public Punishments upon Criminals and upon Society (Philadelphia: Joseph James, 1787).
An Enquiry into the Justice and Policy of Punishing Murder by Death (AM, 1788).

PERSONAL

Autobiography (1798).
Commonplace Book (1789–1813).
De Coctione Ciborum in Ventriculo [Latin: "Digestion of Food in the Stomach," Rush Dissertation for M.D.] (1765).
Travels Through Life (1800).

PSYCHIATRY

History of a Case of Mania Successfully Treated in a Series of Letters Between Dr. John Spence and Dr. Benjamin Rush (PMM, 1808).
Medical Inquiries and Observations, upon the Diseases of the Mind (Philadelphia: Kimber & Richardson, 1812). [The first psychiatry text]
Observations on the Tranquilizer (PMM, 1810).
On the Different Species of Mania (Philadelphia: *Columbian Magazine*, 1786).
On the Different Species of Phobia (Philadelphia: *Columbian Magazine*, 1786).

PUBLIC HEALTH

Experiments and Observations on the Mineral Waters of Philadelphia, Abington, and Bristol in the Province of Pennsylvania (Philadelphia: James Humphreys, Jr., 1773).
The New Method of Inoculating for the Small Pox (Philadelphia: Charles Cist, 1781).

*Proofs of the Origin of the Yellow Fever in Philadelphia in 1797, from Domestic Exhala-
tion and from the Foul Air of the* [ship] *Snow Navigation from Marseilles and from
the Ship Huldah from Hamburgh* (Philadelphia: Thomas & Samuel F. Bradford,
1798).

SCIENCE

An Account of the Manufactury of Salt-Petre (Philadelphia: W. and T. Bradford, 1775).
Experiments with the Manufacture of Nitre from Tobacco (PP,1774).
The Process of Making Salt-Petre (PJ, 1776).
Syllabus of a Course of Lectures on Chemistry (Philadelphia: R. Aitken, 1770.) [First
chemistry text by an American]

TEMPERANCE

*The Drunkard's Emblem, or an Enquiry into the Effects of Ardent Spirits upon the Hu-
man Body and Mind, with an Account of the Means of Preventing and the Remedies
for Curing Them* (Philadelphia: Amos Henkel and Co., 1804).
*An Enquiry into the Effects of Spirituous Liquors upon the Human Body and Their
Influence upon the Happiness of Society* (Philadelphia: Thomas Bradford, 1784).
Sermons to Gentlemen upon Temperance and Exercise (Philadelphia: John Dunlop, 1772).
Sermons to the Rich and Studious, on Temperance and Exercise (London: Edward and
Charles Dilly, 1772).

TOBACCO

*Observations upon the Influence of the Habitual Use of Tobacco upon Health, Morals,
and Property* in *Essays: Literary, Moral, and Philosophical* (Philadelphia: Thomas
and William Bradford, 1806).

VETERINARY MEDICINE

*On the Duty and Advantages of Studying the Diseases of Domestic Animals and the Rem-
edies Proper to Remove Them* (1811).
Three Lectures upon Animal Life (Philadelphia: Thomas Dobson, 1799).

BENJAMIN RUSH, M.D. AS EDITOR

The Works of Thomas Sydenham, M.D., Benjamin Rush, M.D., ed. (Philadelphia:
Dobson, 1809).
Sir John Pringle, *Observation on the Diseases of the Army*, Benjamin Rush, ed. (Phila-
delphia: Edward Earle, 1810).

APPENDIX B

MEDICAL INQUIRIES AND OBSERVATIONS BY BENJAMIN RUSH

Rush published the first edition of this four-volume work in 1796, subsequently adding new material in later editions to incorporate advances and discoveries in American medicine. The fourth, most complete but last, edition did not appear in print until 1815, two years after his death. It is this edition whose contents are cited below.

VOLUME I

An Inquiry into the Cause of Animal Life.

An Inquiry into the Natural History of Medicine among the Indians of North America, and a Comparative View of Their Diseases and Remedies with Those of Civilized Nations.

An Inquiry into the Influence of Physical Causes upon the Moral Faculty.

An Account of the Influence of the Military and Political Events of the American Revolution upon the Human Body.

An Inquiry into the Relation of Tastes and Aliments to Each Other and into the Influence of This Relation upon Health and Pleasure.

The Result of Observations Made upon the Diseases Which Occurred in the Military Hospitals of the United States During the Revolutionary War Between Great Britain and the United States.

An Inquiry into the Effects of Ardent Spirits upon the Human Body and Mind, with an Account of the Means of Preventing and the Remedies for Curing Them.

Observations upon the Tetanus.

An Account of the Disease Occasioned by Drinking Cold Water in Warm Weather and of the Means of Curing It.

An Account of the Cure of Several Diseases by the Extraction of Decayed Teeth.

Observations upon Worms, and upon Anthelmintic [worm-killing] Medicines.

An Account of the External Use of Arsenic in the Cure of Cancers.

An Inquiry into the Cause and Cure of Sore Legs.

An Account of the State of the Body and Mind in Old Age, with Observations on Its Diseases and Remedies.

Observations on the Duties of a Physician and the Methods of Improving Medicine, Accommodated to the Present State of Society and Manners in the United States.

VOLUME 2

An Account of the Climate of Pennsylvania, and Its Influence on the Human Body.

An Account of the Efficacy of Common Salt in the Cure of Haemoptysis [spitting blood].

Thoughts upon the Cause and Cure of Pulmonary Consumption.

Observations upon the Cause and Cure of Dropsies.

An Inquiry into the Cause and Cure of the Internal Dropsy of the Brain.

Observations upon the Cause and Cure of the Gout.

Observations upon the Cause and Cure of Hydrophobia.

An Inquiry into the Cause and Cure of the Cholera Infantum.

Observations upon the Cynanche Trachealis [croup].

An Account of the Bilious Remitting Fever, as It Appeared in Philadelphia in the Summer and Autumn of 1780.

An Account of the Scarlatina Anginosa, as it appeared in Philadelphia, in the Years 1783 and 1784.

An Account of the Measles, as They Appeared in Philadelphia in the Spring of 1789.

An Account of the Influenza, as It Appeared in Philadelphia in the Autumn of 1789, in the Spring of 1790, and in the Winter of 1791.

VOLUME 3

Outlines of the Phenomena of Fever.

An Account of the Bilious Yellow Fever, as It Appeared in Philadelphia in 1793.

An Account of the Bilious Yellow Fever, as It Appeared in Philadelphia in 1794.

An Account of Sporadic Cases of Bilious Yellow Fever as They Appeared in Philadelphia in 1795 and 1796.

VOLUME 4

An Account of the Bilious Remitting and Intermitting Yellow Fever, as It Appeared in Philadelphia in 1797.

An Account of the Bilious Yellow Fever, as It Appeared in Philadelphia in the Year 1798.

An Account of the Bilious Yellow Fever, as It Appeared in Philadelphia in the Year 1799.

An Account of Sporadic Cases of Yellow Fever, as They Appeared in Philadelphia in the Year 1800.

An Account of Sporadic Cases of Yellow Fever, as They Appeared in Philadelphia in the Year 1801.

An Account of the Measles, as They Appeared in Philadelphia in the Year 1801.

An Account of the Bilious Yellow Fever, as It Appeared in Philadelphia in the Year 1802.

An Account of the Bilious Yellow Fever, as It Appeared in Philadelphia in the Year 1803.

An Account of Sporadic Cases of Yellow Fever, as They Appeared in Philadelphia in 1804.

An Account of the Bilious Yellow Fever, as It Appeared in Philadelphia in the Year 1805.

An Account of the Diseases of 1806, 1807, 1808, and 1809.

An Inquiry into the Various Sources of the Usual Forms of Summer and Autumnal Diseases in the United States and the Means of Preventing Them.

Facts, Intended to Prove the Yellow Fever Not to Be Contagious.

A Defense of Bloodletting, as a Remedy for Certain Diseases.

An Inquiry into the Comparative State of Medicine in Philadelphia Between the Years 1760 and 1766, and the Year 1809.

ARTICLES FROM THE FIRST EDITION THAT WERE OMITTED IN THE FOURTH EDITION

Additional Observations upon the Scarlatina Anginosa.

An Account of the Effects of Blisters and Bleeding in the Case of the Obstinate Intermitting Fever.

Additional Observations upon the Tetanus and Hydrophobia.

The New Method of Inoculating for the Small Pox. [British physician Edward Jenner, M.D., invented vaccination in 1798, rendering inoculation obsolete by 1815.]

VOLUME 5

Medical Inquiries and Observations Upon the Diseases of the Mind.
[The world's first English-language work on psychiatry.]

Of the Faculties and Operations of the Mind, and on the Proximate Cause of Intellectual Derangement.

Of Its Remote, Exciting and Predisposing Causes.

Of Partial Intellectual Derangement, and Particularly of Hypochondriosis, or Tristimania; Of the Remedies for Hypochondriosis or Tristimania.

Of Amenomania, Or Partial Intellectual Derangement, Accompanied with Pleasure, or Not Accompanied with Distress.

Of General Intellectual Derangement; Of the Symptoms of Mania; Of the Different Forms of Mania; Of the Influence of the Moon on Mania.

Of the Remedies for Mania.

Of Manicula [a milder form of mania].

Of Manalgia [possibly, a form of catatonia]; Of the Remedies for Manalgia; Of the Means of Improving the Condition of Mad People; Signs of Favorable and Unfavorable Issue of All the Forms of Intellectual Derangement; Usual Modes of Death from Them.

Of Demence, or Disassociation.

Of Derangement in the Will.

Of Derangement in the Principle of Faith, or the Believing Faculty.

Of the Derangement of the Memory; Of the Remedies for It.

Of Fatuity.

Of Dreaming, Incubus, or Night Mare, and Somnambulism.

Of Illusions.

Of Reverie, or Absence of Mind.

Of Derangement of the Passions; Of Love; Of Grief; Of Fear; Of Anger; Of the Morbid Effects of Envy, Malice, and Hatred; Of the Torpor of the Passions.

Of the Morbid State of the Sexual Appetite.

Of the Derangement in the Moral Faculties.

APPENDIX C

ESSAYS: LITERARY, MORAL & PHILOSOPHICAL*

Contents

---

*Philadelphia: Thomas and William Bradford, 1806.

A Plan of a Peace Office for the United States.

Information to Europeans Who Are Disposed to Migrate to the United States of America.

An Account of the Progress of Population, Agriculture, Manners, and Government in Pennsylvania.

An Account of the Manners of the German Inhabitants of Pennsylvania.

Thoughts on *Common Sense.*

An Account of the Vices Peculiar to the Indians of North America.

Observations upon the Influence of the Habitual Use of Tobacco upon the Health, Morals, and Property.

An Account of the Sugar Maple Tree of the United States.

An Account of the Life and Death of Edward Drinker, Who Died on the 17th of November, 1782, in the 103rd Year of His Age.

Remarkable Circumstances in the Constitution and Life of Ann Woods, an Old Woman of 96 Years of Age.

Biographical Anecdotes of Benjamin Lay.

Biographical Anecdotes of Anthony Benezet.

Paradise of Negro Slaves—A Dream.

An Inquiry into the Causes of Premature Deaths.

Eulogium upon Dr. William Cullen.

Eulogium upon David Rittenhouse.

APPENDIX D

THOMAS JEFFERSON'S SYLLABUS
OF AN ESTIMATE OF THE MERIT OF THE DOCTRINES
OF JESUS, COMPARED WITH THOSE OF OTHERS*

In a comparative view of the Ethics of the enlightened nations of antiquity, of the Jews and of Jesus, no notice should be taken of the corruptions of reason among the ancients, to wit, the idolatry and superstition of the vulgar, nor of the corruptions of Christianity by the learned among its professors.

Let a just view be taken of the moral principles inculcated by the most esteemed of the sects of ancient philosophy or of their individuals; particularly Pythagoras, Socrates, Epicurus, Cicero, Epictetus, Seneca, Marcus Antoninus.

I. **Philosophers.**

1. Their precepts related chiefly to ourselves, and the government of those passions which, unrestrained, would disturb our tranquility of mind. In this branch of philosophy they were really great.

2. In developing our duties to others, they were short and defective. They embraced, indeed, the circles of kindred and friends, and inculcated patriotism, or the love of our country in the aggregate, as a primary obligation: towards our neighbors and countrymen they taught justice, but scarcely viewed them as within the circle of

---

*Confidential Document President Jefferson Shared with Benjamin Rush, M.D.

benevolence. Still less have they inculcated peace, charity and love to our fellow men, or embraced with benevolence the whole family of mankind.

II. Jews.

1. Their system was Deism; that is, the belief in one only God. But their ideas of him and of his attributes were degrading and injurious.

2. Their Ethics were not only imperfect, but often irreconcilable with the sound dictates of reason and morality, as they respect intercourse with those around us; and repulsive and anti-social, as respecting other nations. They needed reformation, therefore, in an eminent degree.

III. Jesus.

In this state of things among the Jews, Jesus appeared. His parentage was obscure; his condition poor; his education null; his natural endowments great; his life correct and innocent: he was meek, benevolent, patient, firm, disinterested, and of the sublimest eloquence.

The disadvantages under which his doctrines appear are remarkable.

1. Like Socrates and Epictetus, he wrote nothing himself.

2. But he had not, like them, a Xenophon or an Arrian to write for him. I name not Plato, who only used the name of Socrates to cover the whimsies of his own brain. On the contrary, all the learned of his country, entrenched in its power and riches, were opposed to him, lest his labors should undermine their advantages; and the committing to writing his life and doctrines fell on unlettered and ignorant men, who wrote, too, from memory, and not till long after the transactions had passed.

3. According to the ordinary fate of those who attempt to enlighten and reform mankind, he fell an early victim to the jealousy and combination of the altar and the throne, at about thirty-three years of age, his reason having not yet attained the *maximum* of its energy, nor the course of his preaching, which was but of three years at most, presented occasions for developing a complete system of morals.

4. Hence the doctrines he really delivered were defective as a whole, and fragments only of what he did deliver have come to us mutilated, misstated, and often unintelligible.

5. They have been still more disfigured by the corruptions of schismatizing followers, who have found an interest in sophisticating and perverting the simple doctrines he taught, by engrafting on them the mysticisms of a Grecian sophist, frittering them into subtleties, and obscuring them with jargon, until they have caused good men to reject the whole in disgust, and to view Jesus himself as an impostor.

Notwithstanding these disadvantages, a system of morals is presented to us which, if filled up in the style and spirit of the rich fragments he left us, would be the most perfect and sublime that has ever been taught by man.

The question of his being a member of the godhead, or in direct communication with it, claimed for him by some of his followers and denied by others, is foreign to the present view, which is merely an estimate of the intrinsic merits of his doctrines.

1. He corrected the Deism of the Jews, confirming them in their belief of one only God, and giving them juster notions of His attributes and government.

2. His moral doctrines, relating to kindred and friends were more pure and perfect than those of the most correct of the philosophers, and greatly more so than those of the Jews; and they went far beyond both in inculcating universal philanthropy, not only to kindred and friends, to neighbors and countrymen, but to all mankind, gathering all into one family under the bonds of love, charity, peace, common wants and common aids. A development of this head will evince the peculiar superiority of the system of Jesus over all others.

3. The precepts of philosophy, and of the Hebrew code, laid hold of actions only. He pushed his scrutinies into the heart of man; erected his tribunal in the region of his thoughts, and purified the waters at the fountain head.

4. He taught, emphatically, the doctrines of a future state, which was either doubted or disbelieved by the Jews, and wielded it with efficacy as an important incentive, supplementary to the other motives to moral conduct.

[Jefferson's note:] To explain, I will exhibit the heads of Seneca's and Cicero's philosophical works, the most extensive of any we have received from the ancients. Of ten heads in Seneca, seven relate to ourselves, viz. *de ira, consolatio, de tranquilitate, de constantia sapientis, de otio sapientis, de vita beata, de brevitate vitae*; two relate to others, *de clementia, de beneficiis*; and one relates to the government of the world, *de providentia*. Of eleven tracts of Cicero, five respect ourselves, viz. *de finibus, Tusculana, academica, paradoxa, de Senectute*; one, *de officiis*, relates partly to ourselves, partly to others; one, *de amicitia*, relates to others; and four are on different subjects, to wit, *de natura deorum, de divinatione, de fato*, and *sommium*.

NOTES

PROLOGUE

1. Thomas Jefferson to John Adams, May 27, 1813, John Adams and Thomas Jefferson, *The Adams-Jefferson Letters, The Complete Correspondence between Thomas Jefferson & Abigail & John Adams*, Lester J. Cappon, ed. (Chapel Hill: University of North Carolina Press, 1959), 323–325. [Henceforth, *A–J Letters*]

2. John Adams to Elbridge Gerry, April 26, 1813, Founders Online.

CHAPTER 1: THE MAKING OF A PHYSICIAN

1. Benjamin Rush, *The Autobiography of Benjamin Rush: His "Travels Through Life," Together with his Commonplace Book for 1789–1813* (Philadelphia: American Philosophical Society, 1948), 24. [Henceforth, *Autobiography*]

2. BR to John Adams, August 8, 1812, *Letters of Benjamin Rush* (Philadelphia: American Philosophical Society, 1951, 2 vols., L. H. Butterfield, ed.), 2:1156–1159. [Henceforth, *Letters*]

3. BR to John Adams, July 13, 1812, *Letters*, 2:1150–1153.

4. *Autobiography*, 33.

5. Ibid., 29–30.

6. Ibid., 36.

7. Ibid., 38.

8. *Pennsylvania Gazette*, November 11, 1762.

9. BR to Ebenezer Hazard, November 8, 1765, *Letters*, 1:18–19.

10. BR to Benjamin Franklin, October 22, 1766, ibid., 1:27.

11. BR to [?], December 29, 1766, ibid., 1:31–32.

12. Ibid., 1:42–43.

13. *Autobiography*, 43.

14. Ibid., 47.

15. Ibid., 49.

16. Ibid., 46.

17. BR to John Adams, July 13, 1812, *Letters*, 2:1150–1153.

18. BR to John Witherspoon, April 23, 1767, *Letters*, 1:136–138; *Autobiography*, 50–51.

19. *Autobiography*, 59.

20. BR to James Abercrombie, April 22, 1793, *Letters*, 2:632–635.

21. *Autobiography*, 60.

22. Ibid., 61.

23. BR to Catherine Macaulay, January 18, 1769, *Letters*, 1:69–72.

24. *Autobiography*, 61.

25. BR to Catherine Macaulay, January 18, 1769, *Letters*, 1:69–72.

26. *Autobiography*, 61–62.

27. BR to [?], January 19, 1769, *Letters*, 1:72.

28. BR to Ebenezer Hazard, October 22, 1768, Ibid., 1:67–69.

29. Ibid., 1:66.

30. David Freeman Hawke, *Benjamin Rush: Revolutionary Gadfly* (Indianapolis: Bobbs-Merrill, 1971), 79. Unpublished Benjamin Rush manuscript, *French Journal: Account of a Trip to Paris*, J. Pierpont Morgan Library, New York, NY; Nathan G. Goodman, *Benjamin Rush, Physician and Citizen* (Philadelphia: University of Pennsylvania Press, 1934), 22.

31. *Autobiography*, 69–70.

32. Jean-Jacques Rousseau, *The Basic Political Writings: On the Social Contract*, translated and edited by Donald A. Cress (Indianapolis, IN: Hackett Publishing Company, 1987), 141.

33. *Autobiography*, 73–74.

34. Ibid., 74.

35. Ibid., 69.

36. David Hume, *A Treatise of Human Nature: Being an Attempt to Introduce the Experimental Method of Reasoning into Moral Subjects*, 3 vols. (London: John Noon, 1738), 3:14–20.

37. *Autobiography*, 117.

CHAPTER 2: THE MAKING OF A PATRIOT

1. "A Treatise of the Eternal Predestination of God," by John Calvin, 1532.

2. *Autobiography*, 84.

3. Thomas G. Morton, *History of the Pennsylvania Hospital, 1751–1895* (Philadelphia: Times Printing House, 1895), 451.

4. BR, *Medical Inquiries and Observations* (Philadelphia: Thomas Dobson, 1789), 55–91, esp.65. [First of two volumes, with second volume published in

1793. Rush added a third volume in 1794, detailing the yellow fever epidemic of 1793, a fourth in 1796, and a fifth, *Medical Inquiries and Observations upon the Diseases of the Mind*, in 1812.]

5. Published in Philadelphia by printer John Sparhawk in 1773.

6. BR to Barbeu-Dubourg, April 29, 1773, *Letters*, 1:76–78.

7. *Autobiography*, 83.

8. Goodman, *Benjamin Rush*, 275; Benjamin Rush's "Moral and Physical Thermometer," *The Columbian Magazine*, January 1789, as displayed in BR *Letters*, 1: opposite p. 512.

9. James Thomas Flexner, *Doctors on Horseback: Pioneers of American Medicine* (New York: Viking Press, 1937), 92.

10. Dagobert D. Runes, ed., *The Selected Writings of Benjamin Rush* (New York: Philosophical Library, 1947), 363.

11. Miguel de Cervantes, *El Ingenioso Hidalgo Don Quixote de la Mancha* (Madrid: Francisco de Robles, Part 1:1605; Part 2: 1615).

12. Benjamin Rush, "Observations upon the Influence of the Habitual use of Tobacco upon Health, Morals, and Property of Mankind," *Essays: Literary, Moral and Philosophical* (Philadelphia: Thomas and William Bradford, 1806), 261–270.

13. *Pennsylvania Journal*, October 20, 1773.

14. George Washington, *The Diaries of George Washington*, 6 vols., Donald Jackson and Dorothy Twohig, eds. (Charlottesville: University Press of Virginia, 1976–1979), June 3, 1744.

15. *Autobiography*, 110.

16. John Adams, *Diary and Autobiography of John Adams*, 4 vols., L. H. Butterfield, ed. (Boston: Massachusetts Historical Society, 1961), 2:182.

17. Plato, *The Republic*, translated by G. M. A. Grube (Indianapolis, IN: Hackett Publishing, 1992), 150. [Original written between 380–360 B.C.]

18. BR to Thomas Jefferson, October 6, 1800, *Letters*, 1:824–827.

19. *Autobiography*, 110–112.

20. Ibid., 113–114.

21. William Wirt Henry, *Patrick Henry: Life, Correspondence and Speeches*, 3 vols. (New York: Charles Scribner's Sons, 1891), 1:262–268.

22. Benjamin Rush to Thomas Rustin, October 29, 1775, *Letters*, 1:91–94.

23. *Autobiography*, 112.

24. Ibid., 112–113.

25. BR to Owen Biddle, December 26, 1775, *Letters*, 1:94.

26. BR to Lady Jane Wishart Belsches, April 21, 1784, *Letters*, 1:325–329.

27. *Autobiography*, 116.

28. BR to Thomas Hogg, September 16, 1783, L. H. Butterfield, "Further Letters of Benjamin Rush," *Pennsylvania Magazine of History and Biography*, vol. 78, no. 1, January 1954.

29. *Autobiography*, 114–115.

30. George Washington to Lieutenant Colonel Joseph Reed, April 1, 1776, *The Papers of George Washington, Revolutionary War Series*, vol. 4, W. W. Abbott, ed. (Charlottesville: University of Virginia Press, 1984–[multivolume, in progress]), 9–13.

31. BR to Mrs. Rush, June 1, 1776, *Letters*, 1:101–102.

32. BR to Mrs. Rush, May 27, 29, and June 1, 1776, ibid., 1:96–103.

33. Resolution at the Continental Congress, June 7, 1776, Worthington C. Ford et al., eds., *Journals of the Continental Congress, 1774–1789* (Washington, DC, 1904–1937), Folio 26, No. 7.

34. Benjamin Rush to John Adams, July 20, 1811, *Letters*, 2:1089–1091.

35. John Sanderson, *Biography of the Signers to the Declaration of Independence* (Philadelphia: Thomas, Cowperthwait & Company, 1820–1827), 722.

36. BR to Barbeu-Dubourg, September 16, 1776, *Letters*, 1:110–112.

37. *Journals of the Continental Congress, 1774–1789*, 6:1081.

38. *Autobiography*, 116–117.

39. BR to Richard Henry Lee, December 20, 1776, Richard H. Lee, *Memoir of the Life of Richard Henry Lee and Correspondence*, 2 vols. (Philadelphia: H. C. Carey and I. Lea, 1825), 2:159–160.

40. Ibid.

CHAPTER 3: BROKEN BY A CANNON BALL

1. Colonel Joseph Reed to George Washington, December 22, 1776, *Papers of George Washington, Revolutionary War Series*, 7:414–417.

2. George Washington to Colonel Joseph Reed, December 23, 1776, ibid., 7:423–424.

3. *Autobiography*, 128.

4. Ibid.

5. Ibid., 128–129.

6. BR to Richard Henry Lee, January 7, 1777, *Letters*, 1:125–127.

7. Carl Binger, M.D., *Revolutionary Doctor: Benjamin Rush, 1746–1813.* (New York: W. W. Norton, 1966), 121.

8. Benjamin Rush, M.D., *Directions for Preserving the Health of Soldiers, Addressed to the Officers of the Army* (first published in the *Pennsylvania Packet* No. 284 by order of the Board of War, September 5, 1777; republished in pamphlet form: Lancaster, PA, John Dunlop, 1778), 12.

9. Ibid.

10. See *Letters*, 1:145–147.

11. *Autobiography*, 131–132.

12. BR to John Adams, October 1, 1777, *Letters*, 1:154–158.

13. Ibid.

14. BR to John Adams, October 31, 1777, ibid., 163–166.

15. John Adams to BR, February 8, 1778, *Old Family Letters: Copied from the Originals for Alexander Biddle* (Philadelphia: J. B. Lippincott Company, 1892), 10–12. [Alexander Biddle was married to Julia Williams Rush, Benjamin Rush's granddaughter and daughter of Samuel Rush, the twelfth of Benjamin Rush's thirteen children.]

16. *Autobiography*,133.

17. BR to George Washington, December 26, 1777, *Letters*, 1:180–182.

18. Ibid.

19. Thomas Conway to Horatio Gates, January 4, 1778, Robert Douthat Meade, *Patrick Henry, Practical Revolutionary* (Philadelphia: J. B. Lippincott, 1969), 138–140.

20. George Washington to BR, January 12, 1778, *Papers of George Washington, Revolutionary War Series*, 13:210.

21. BR *Notes on Continental Congress*, cited in *Letters*, 2:1198.

22. "Historical Notes of Dr. Benjamin Rush, 1777," *Pennsylvania Magazine of History and Biography*, vol. 27, no. 2 (1903).

23. John Adams to BR, February 8, 1778, *Old Family Letters*, 10–12.

24. BR to John Adams, October 13, 1777, *Letters*, 1:158–159.

25. BR to Patrick Henry, January 12, 1778, ibid., 1:182–185.

26. Ibid.

27. BR to John Adams, January 22, 1778, ibid., 1:190–192.

28. John Adams to BR, November 4, 1779, *Old Family Letters*, 17–19.

29. Julia Rush to BR, October 10, 1793, American Philosophical Society Library, manuscripts. [Henceforth, APS]

30. Patrick Henry to George Washington, February 20, 1778, *Papers of George Washington, Revolutionary War Series*, 13:609.

31. George Washington to Patrick Henry, March 27, 1778, ibid., 14:328–329.

32. George Washington to Patrick Henry, March 28, 1778, ibid., 14:335–337.

33. Ibid., 14:336–337.

34. Patrick Henry to George Washington, March 29, 1777, ibid., 9:12–13.

35. Patrick Henry to Richard Henry Lee, April 7, 1778, Henry, *Patrick Henry*, 2:559–560.

36. *Autobiography*, 133.

CHAPTER 4: "THE REVOLUTION IS NOT OVER!"

1. BR to Mrs. Rush, January 15, 1778, *Letters*, 1:185–188.

2. *Pennsylvania Packet*, November 25, 1780; 2:1204–1205.

3. BR to John Adams, February 8, 1778, *Letters*, 1:199–200.

4. BR to William Shippen, November 18, 1780, published in *Pennsylvania Packet* (Philadelphia), November 21, 1780, *Letters*, 1:256–260.

5. Ibid.

6. BR to George Washington, February 25, 1778, ibid., 1:200–204.

7. George Washington to John Augustine Washington, July 4, 1778, *Papers of George Washington, Revolutionary War Series*, 16:25–26.

8. *Autobiography*, 138.

9. Ibid., 160.

10. BR to Jeremy Belknap, October 13, 1789, *Letters*, 1:526–527.

11. Benjamin Rush, *An Enquiry into the Effects of Public Punishments upon Criminal and upon Society*, read to the Society for Promoting Political Enquiries, March 9, 1787, *Essays*, 136–163.

12. "To the Citizens of Philadelphia: A Plan for Free Schools, *The Independent Gazetteer* (Philadelphia), March 28, 1787, *Letters*, 1:412–415.

13. *Thoughts upon Female Education*, delivered to the Board of Visitors, Young Ladies' Academy, Philadelphia, 1787, reprinted in *Columbian Magazine*, May 1790, 188–293.

14. *Autobiography*, 242.

15. Benjamin Rush, "A Plan for Establishing Public Schools in Pennsylvania and for Conducting Education Agreeable in a Republican Form of Government: Addressed to the Legislature and Citizens of Pennsylvania, in the Year 1786," *Essays*, 1–6.

16. Benjamin Rush, "Plan of a Federal University," *American Museum* 4, July 1888, 442–444. [*The American Museum* was a monthly magazine published from January 1787 to December 1972. It contained original works as well as reprints of significant documents of the time such as Thomas Paine's *Common Sense* and the proposed *Constitution of the United States*. Besides Benjamin Rush, contributors included John Adams, Benjamin Franklin, Alexander Hamilton, Thomas Jefferson, James Madison, and George Washington, all of whom also subscribed to the magazine.]

17. "On the Defects of the Confederation," 1787, Runes, *The Selected Writings of Benjamin Rush*, 36–31.

18. BR to Nathanael Greene, October 30, 1781, *Letters*, 1:266.

19. "Duties of a Physician: A Closing Lecture to Medical Students," 1789, Runes, *The Selected Writings of Benjamin Rush*, 308–321.

20. Harriet W. Warner, *Autobiography of Charles Caldwell* (Philadelphia: Lippincott, Grambo, and Company, 1855), 116, 119; David Ramsay, *Eulogium upon Benjamin Rush* (Philadelphia: Medical Society of South Carolina, 1813), 128.

21. BR, "Observations on the Duties of a Physician and the Methods of Improving Medicine, Accommodated to the Present State of Society and Manners in the United States," lecture to the University of Pennsylvania, February 7, 1789, *Medical Inquiries and Observations*, 1:251–264.

22. BR to Timothy Pickering, November 19, 1808, in Goodman, *Benjamin Rush*, 151, citing Timothy Pickering Papers, XLIII, 208, at the Massachusetts Historic Society, Boston.

23. BR to Thomas Smith, March 14, 1793, *Letters*, 2:631–632.

24. BR, "Duties of a Physician," Runes, *The Selected Writings of Benjamin Rush*, 308–321.

25. Ibid., 313.

26. Ramsay, *Eulogium upon Benjamin Rush*, 119–121.

27. BR to Walter Stone, January 30, 1791, *Letters*, 1:576–577.

28. BR, *Medical Inquiries and Observations*, 1:331–333.

29. BR to Horatio Gates, July 27, 1803, *Letters*, 2: 870–872.

30. Thomas Jefferson to Dr. Caspar Wistar, June 21, 1807, describing his "Unlearned Views of Medicine," Jefferson Letters, *Thomas Jefferson Writings* (New York: Literary Classics of the United States, 1984), 1181–1185.

31. Benjamin Rush, M.D., *Medical Inquiries and Observations upon the Diseases of the Mind* (Philadelphia: Grigg and Elliot, 1835, 5th ed.), 298–303.

32. Thomas Jefferson to Dr. Caspar Wistar, June 21, 1807, *Thomas Jefferson Writings*, 1181–1185.

33. *Pennsylvania Packet*, July 3, 1779, *Letters*, 1:229–237.

34. Henry Knox to George Washington, January 31, 1785, *The Papers of George Washington, Confederation Series, January 1784–September 1788*, 6 vols., W. W. Abbott and Dorothy Twohig, eds. (Charlottesville: University Press of Virginia), 2:201–306.

Chapter 5: My Friends in Jails

1. George Washington Circular to the States, *The Writings of George Washington, from the Original Manuscript Sources, 1745–1799*, 39 vols., John C. Fitzpatrick, ed. (Washington, DC: US Government Printing Office, 1931–1944), 26:483–496.

2. George Washington to John Jay, May 18, 1786, *Papers of George Washington, Confederation Series*, 4:55–56.

3. James Madison, *Notes of Debates in the Federal Convention of 1787, Reported by James Madison* (New York: W. W. Norton, 1987), 7. [Hereafter, *Notes*]

4. *Autobiography*, July 25, 1791, 202.

5. BR to Mrs. Rush, August 12, 1791, *Letters*, 1:602–603.

6. *Autobiography*, 228–229; BR to Mrs. Rush, August 22, 1793, *Letters*, 2:639–640.

7. BR to Mrs. Rush, August 22, 1787, *Letters*, 1: 436–437.

8. BR, "An Enquiry into the Effects of Public Punishment upon Criminals and upon Society," March 9, 1787, *Essays*, 136–163.

9. BR to Richard Price, June 2, 1787, *Letters*, 1:384–385.

10. BR to John Coakley Lettsom, September 28, 1787, ibid., 1:441–445.

11. Benjamin Rush, M.D., "A Plan of a Peace-Office for the United States," *Essays*, 183–188.

12. BR to John Coakley Lettsom, September 28, 1787, *Letters*, 1:441–445.

13. Madison, *Notes*, 651.

14. *Documentary History of the Ratification of the Constitution*, Merrill Jensen, ed. (Madison: State Historical Society of Wisconsin, 1976–[in progress, multivolume]), 9: 929–931.

15. George Washington to David Humphries, October 19, 1787, *Papers of George Washington, Confederation Series*, 5:365–366.

16. *Documentary History of the Ratification of the Constitution*, 2:346.

17. Ibid., 2:447–448.

18. Ibid., 2:458.

19. Ibid., 2:547–548.

20. Ibid., 2:553.

21. *Autobiography*, 161.

22. Ibid., 162.

23. Hawke, *Benjamin Rush*, 361; *Autobiography*, 246.

24. BR to John Adams, July 2, 1788, *Letters*, 1:468–469.

25. Ibid.

26. BR to ?, July 9, 1788, "Observations on the Federal Procession in Philadelphia, ibid., 1:470–477.

27. "A Letter from a Gentleman in This City to His Friend in a Neighboring State, *American Museum* 4, July 1788, 75–78.

28. John Adams to Abigail Adams, December 19, 1793, Massachusetts Historical Society, *The Adams Papers: Adams Family Correspondence* (Cambridge, MA: The Belknap Press of Harvard University Press, 2009–[multivolume, in progress]), 9:476–477.

29. BR to John Adams, June 4, 1789, *Letters*, 1:513–515.

30. John Adams to BR, May 17, 1789, *Old Family Letters*, 33–36.

31. John Adams to BR, July 24, 1789, Charlene Bangs Bickford and Kenneth R. Bowling, *Birth of the Nation: The First Federal Congress, 1789–1791* (Lanham, MD: Madison House Publishers, 1989), 28.

32. BR to John Adams, June 4, 1789, *Letters*, 1:513–515.

33. John Adams to BR, June 9, 1789, *Old Family Letters*, 36–40.

34. Fitzpatrick, *Writings of George Washington*, 30:359–366.

35. John Adams to BR, July 5, 1789, *Old Family Letters*, 41–43.

36. BR to Elisha Hall, July 6, 1789, *Letters*, 1:518–520.

37. BR to Mrs. Rush, August 16, 1787, *Letters*, 1:435–436.

38. Julia Rush to BR, July 19, 1783, APS.

39. BR to Mrs. Rush, June 27, 1787, *Letters*, 1:429–432.

40. Benjamin Rush, *Sixteen Introductory Lectures . . . Upon the Institutes of and Practice of Medicine* (Philadelphia: Bradford and Innskeep, 1811), 171–172.

CHAPTER 6: MURDER BY WAR

1. BR to John Coakley Lettsom, September 28, 1787, *Letters*, 1:441–445.
2. BR to John Redman Coxe, October 5, 1795, ibid., 2:762–763.
3. BR to Jeremy Belknap, May 6, 1788, ibid., 1:460–461.
4. Benjamin Rush, *An Inquiry into the Effects of Spirituous Liquors on the Human Body and the Mind* (Boston: Thomas and Andrews, 1790).
5. Ibid.
6. *A Defense of the Use of the Bible as a School Book*, in *Essays*, 93–113; see also BR to Reverend Jeremy Belknap, April 5, 1791, *Letters*, 1:578–580.
7. BR to John Howard, October 14, 1789, *Letters*, 527–528.
8. BR to James Madison, February 27, 1790, ibid., 538–542.
9. *Autobiography*, 182–183.
10. Ibid.
11. BR, "Information to Europeans Who Are Disposed to Migrate to the United States of America," *Essays*, 189–212, first published in *American Museum* 6, May 1790, from a letter to unnamed addressee, April 16, 1790.
12. Abigail Adams to Her Sister [Mary Cranch], December 12, 1790, *New Letters of Abigail Adams, 1788–1801* (Boston: Houghton Mifflin, 1947), 65, 69.
13. Edmund Burke, *The Annual Register, or a View of the History, Politics, and Literature for the Year 1787* (London: J. Dodsley, 1789), 375–376.
14. Thomas Jefferson to Richard Price, January 8, 1789, in Dumas Malone, *Jefferson and the Rights of Man* (Boston: Little, Brown, 1951), 214.
15. Jean Tulard, Jean-François Fayard, and Alfred Fierro, *Histoire et Dictionnaire de la Révolution Française, 1789–1799* (Paris: Robert Laffont, 1998), 349.
16. Thomas Jefferson to William Short, January 3, 1793, *Thomas Jefferson Writings*, 1003–1006.
17. Abigail Adams to Mary Smith Cranch, March 20, 1792, *The Adams Papers*, 9:271–273.
18. Thomas Jefferson to William Stephens Smith, November 13, 1787, Library of Congress.
19. BR to John Coakley Lettsom, April 26, 1793, *Letters*, 2:635–636.
20. Ibid.
21. BR to James Madison, February 27, 1790, *Letters*, 1: 538–542.
22. John Adams to Abigail Adams, January 1, 1797, *My Dearest Friend: Letters of Abigail and John Adams*, Margaret A. Hogan and C. James Taylor, eds. (Cambridge, MA: The Belknap Press of Harvard University Press, 2007), 422–424.
23. Douglas Southall Freeman, *George Washington: A Biography*, 7 vols., completed by John Alexander Carroll and Mary Ashworth (New York: Charles Scribner's Sons, 1948–1957), 7:36.
24. Archives des Affaires Étrangères, Ministère des Affaires Étrangères, Quai d'Orsay, Paris, vol. 38, Dossier *Correspondence Consulaire: Genet*; Frederick A.

Schminke, *Genet: The Origins of His Mission to America* (Toulouse: Imprimerie Toulousaine Lion et Fils, 1939), 31.

25. Meade Minnigerode, *Jefferson—Friend of France* (New York: G. P. Putnam & Sons, 1928), 207.

26. Archives des Affaires Étrangères: *Genet.*

27. John Adams to Thomas Jefferson, June 30, 1813, *A–J Letters*, 346–347.

28. Minnigerode, *Jefferson—Friend of France*, 184.

29. BR to John Nicholson, August 12, 1793, *Letters*, 2:636–637.

Chapter 7: The Hundred Days of Doom

1. John Adams to Thomas Jefferson, June 30, 1813, *A–J Letters*, 346.

2. Thomas Jefferson to James Madison, September 1, 1793, *The Papers of James Madison, Congressional Series*, William T. Hutchinson et al., eds., vol. 15 (Charlottesville: University Press of Virginia, 1985), 88–91.

3. BR to Mrs. Rush, August 21, 1793, *Letters*, 2:637–639.

4. Ibid., August 25, 1793, *Letters*, 2:640–642.

5. Ibid., August 27, 1793, *Letters*, 2:643.

6. Ibid., August 29, 1793, *Letters*, 2:644–645.

7. Ibid. [Rush's citation: the cry of Jabez to the God of Israel in 1 Chronicles 4:9, King James Bible.]

8. Julia Rush to BR, September 24, 1793, APS.

9. BR to Mrs. Rush October 27, 1793, *Letters*, 2:727–728.

10. Ibid., August 26, 1793, *Letters*, 2: 642–643.

11. Mathew Carey, *A Short Account of the Malignant Fever of 1793* (Philadelphia: Clark and Raser, 1793), 7.

12. Ibid., 8.

13. Ibid.

14. Ibid., 10.

15. Ibid., 16.

16. Ibid., 8.

17. BR to Mrs. Rush, September 1, 1793, *Letters*, 2:646–647.

18. Julia Rush to BR, October 14, 1793, APS.

19. BR to Mrs. Rush, September 1, 1793, *Letters*, 2:646–647.

20. John Mitchell, "Account of the Yellow Fever in Virginia in 1741," *The Philadelphia Medical Museum*, 1:1–20, 1805; "Account of the Yellow Fever Which Prevailed in Virginia in the Years, 1737, 1741, and 1742, *American Medical and Philosophical Register*, 1814. [Some readers of Mitchell's work assert he may have confused hepatitis and yellow fever.]

21. BR, *An Account of the Bilious Remitting Yellow Fever, as It Appeared in the City of Philadelphia in the Year 1793* (Philadelphia: Thomas Dobson, 1794), 201–202.

22. Ibid., 203–204.

CHAPTER 8: "YOU CANNOT DIE NOW, DOCTOR!"

1. Goodman, *Benjamin Rush*, 180–181, citing Rush Correspondence, vol. 38: 12, 50, 55.

2. Julia Rush to BR, October 14, 1793, APS.

3. BR, *An Account of the Bilious Remitting Yellow Fever*, 206.

4. Henry Knox to George Washington, September 18, 1793, *The Papers of George Washington, Presidential Series*, multivolume, in progress, Theodore J. Crackel, editor-in-chief (Charlottesville: University of Virginia Press), 14:112–114.

5. Henry Knox to George Washington, September 24, 1793, ibid., 14:129–131.

6. (Philadelphia) *Federal Gazette*, September 17, 1793.

7. Sir Geoffrey Keynes, M.D., *Blood Transfusion* (London: Oxford Medical Publications, 1922), 1.

8. Alexander Hamilton to College of Physicians, September 11, *The Papers of Alexander Hamilton*, 27 vols., Harold C. Syrett et al., eds. (New York: Columbia University Press, 1961–1987), 15:331–332.

9. BR to Mrs. Rush, September 15, 1793, *Letters*, 2:664–665.

10. BR to Mrs. Rush, September 6, 1793, ibid., 2:653–655.

11. Julia Rush to BR, October 29, 1793, APS.

12. BR to Mrs. Rush, September 13, 1793, *Letters*, 2:663–664.

13. BR, *An Account of the Bilious Remitting Yellow Fever*, 346.

14. Jim Murphy, *An American Plague: The True and Terrifying Story of the Yellow Fever Epidemic of 1793* (New York: Clarion Books, 2003), 65.

15. BR, "To His Fellow Citizens: Treatment for Yellow Fever," (Philadelphia) *Federal Gazette*, September 12, 1793, in *Letters*, 2:660–661.

16. BR, "To the College of Physicians: Use of the Lancet in Yellow Fever," (Philadelphia) *Federal Gazette*, September 12, 1793, in *Letters*, 2:661–662.

17. Julia Rush to BR, October 10, 1793, APS.

18. BR to Mrs. Rush, September 5, 1793, *Letters*, 2:650–652.

19. BR, *Sixteen Introductory Lectures*, 266.

20. James Blundell, M.D., "Experiments on the Transfusion of Blood by the Syringe," *Proceedings of the Royal Society of Medicine*, Medico-Chirurgical Transactions, London, February 3, 1818, page 56.

21. Abigail Zuger, M.D., "Treatment for Medical Whiplash: Health Care's Ever-Changing Advice Can Frustrate Doctors and Patients Alike," *New York Times*, November 3, 2015, p. D3; Dr. Vinayak K. Prasad and Dr. Adam S. Cifu, *Ending Medical Reversal: Improving Outcomes, Saving Lives* (Baltimore: Johns Hopkins University Press, 2015), 245 ff.

22. BR to Mrs. Rush, August 25, 1793, *Letters*, 2:640–642.

23. BR to Mrs. Rush, September 1, 1793, ibid., 2:646–647.

24. Julia Rush to BR, October 1, 1793, APS.

25. BR to Rachel Ruth Montgomery [another BR sister], October 29, 1793, *Letters*, 2:730–731.

Chapter 9: Bleed, Bleed, Bleed

1. BR to Mrs. Rush, September 16, 1793, *Letters*, 2:664–665.

2. BR to Mrs. Rush, September 18, 1793, ibid., 2:668–671.

3. Elizabeth Drinker, *The Diary of Elizabeth Drinker*, 3 vols., Elaine Forman Crane, ed. (Boston: Northeastern University Press, 1991), 516.

4. BR to Mrs. Rush, September 21, 1793, *Letters 2*, 672–674.

5. BR to James Pemberton, November 8, 1793, Goodman, *Benjamin Rush*, 195 [unverified].

6. Drinker, *Diary*, 1: 514.

7. BR to Mrs. Rush, September 26, 1793, *Letters*, 2:683–684.

8. BR, *An Account of the Bilious Remitting Yellow Fever*, 344.

9. Drinker, *Diary*, 1:517.

10. Ibid., 523.

11. (Philadelphia) *Federal Gazette*, November 1, 1793.

12. Drinker, *Diary*, 524, 526, 527.

13. Ibid.

14. John Adams to Abigail Adams, December 1, 1793, Massachusetts Historical Society, Adams Family Papers. An Electronic Archive [online], Correspondence between John and Abigail Adams.

15. John Adams to Abigail Adams, February 23, 1794, cited in Alexander DeConde, *Entangling Alliance* (Durham, NC: Duke University Press, 1958), 398.

16. Minnigerode, *Jefferson—Friend of France*, 362.

17. BR to Mrs. Rush, November 7, 1793, *Letters*, 2:740–742.

18. Thomas Sydenham, M.D., *The Works of Thomas Sydenham, M.D., on Acute and Chronic Diseases: With Their Histories and Modes of Cure* (London: G.G.J. & J. Robinson, W. Otridge, S. Hayes, and E. Newbery, 1788).

19. BR to Mrs. Rush, November 4 and November 7, 1793, *Letters*, 2:740–742.

20. BR to Mrs. Rush, November 12, 1793, ibid., 2:745–746.

21. BR to Mrs. Rush, November 7, 1793, ibid., 2:740–742.

22. *Autobiography*, 238.

23. Ibid., 230.

24. BR to the Philadelphia Committee of Health, September 13, 1794, *Letters*, 2:749.

25. BR to John Redman Coxe, September 19, 1794, ibid., 2:750–751.

26. BR to John Redman Coxe, November 4, 1794, ibid., 2:751–753.

27. *Autobiography*, 236–237.

28. Ibid.

29. BR to the President of the Pennsylvania Abolition Society, *Letters*, 2:754–756. [Undated, but editor L. H. Butterfield estimates the date "at the end of 1794."]

30. Alexander Hosack, Jr., M.D., *History of the Yellow Fever as It Appeared in the City of New York in 1795* (Philadelphia: Thomas Dobson, 1797), 16–18.

31. BR to John Redman Coxe, May 5, 1795, *Letters*, 2:759–760.

32. BR to Ashton Alexander, M.D., December 21, 1795, ibid., 2:766–767; BR to John Redman Coxe, January 16, 1796, ibid., 2:769.

33. BR to Ashton Alexander, M.D., December 21, 1795, ibid., 2:766–767.

34. Sir William Ostler, *The Principles and Practice of Medicine* (New York: D. Appleton and Company, 1893), 129.

35. BR to Mrs. Rush, November 4, 1793, *Letters*, 2:739–740.

36. BR to Mrs. Rush, November 11, 1793, ibid., 2:744–745.

CHAPTER 10: FATHER OF PSYCHIATRY

1. BR to the Managers of Pennsylvania Hospital, December 26, 1812, *Letters*, 2:1172–1173.

2. BR to John Redman Coxe, January 16, 1796, ibid., 2:769–771.

3. Benjamin Rush, M.D., *Medical Inquiries and Observations upon the Diseases of the Mind* (Philadelphia: Kimber & Richardson, 1812), 7.

4. Rush, *Diseases of the Mind*, 15–16.

5. Ibid., 77–78.

6. Ibid., 104.

7. Ibid., 257–259.

8. Ibid., 28–30.

9. Ibid., 38–39.

10. Ibid., 31.

11. BR to John Redman Coxe, M.D., September 5, 1810, *Letters*, 2:1058–1060.

12. *Sixteen Introductory Lectures on the Institutes and Practice of Medicine*, delivered at the University of Pennsylvania by Benjamin Rush, 1811.

13. BR to John Adams, November 4, 1812, *Letters*, 2:1164–1166.

14. John Adams to BR, November 19, 1812, *Old Family Letters*, 317–321.

15. BR to Thomas Jefferson, January 4, 1797, *Letters*, 2:784–785.

16. John Adams to Elbridge Gerry, May 3, 1797, Adams Family Papers, Massachusetts Historical Society, reel 117.

17. BR to James Currie, July 26, 1796, *Letters*, 2:779–780.

18. Richard Folwell, *Short History of the Yellow Fever That Broke Out in the City of Philadelphia in July, 1797, with a List of the Dead; of the Donations for the Relief of the Poor, and a Variety of Other Interesting Particulars* (Philadelphia: Richard Folwell, 1797), 3.

19. Ibid., 7–9.

20. Ibid., 26.

21. BR to John R. B. Rodgers, M.D., September 25, 1797, *Letters*, 2:790–792.

22. Samuel Hodgdon to Timothy Pickering, August 17, 1797, ibid., 2:791n–792n.

23. Benjamin Rush, *A Memorial Containing Travels Through Life, or Sundry Incidents in the Life of Dr. Benjamin Rush*, Louis Alexander Biddle, ed. (Philadelphia: Made at the Sign of the Ivy Leaf, 1905 [written in 1800]), 73.

24. John Adams to Secretary of Treasury Oliver Wolcott, Jr., September 15, 1797, Founders Online, National Archives (http://founders.archives.gov /documents/Adams/99-02-02-2135), from *The Adams Papers*, Massachusetts Historical Society.

25. BR to Mrs. Rush, August 26, 1798, *Letters*, 2:803–804.

26. *Autobiography*, 238–239.

27. Winthrop Neilson and Frances Fullerton Neilson, *Verdict for the Doctor: The Case of Benjamin Rush* (New York: Hastings House, 1958), 131–132.

28. BR to Mrs. Rush, September 28, 1798, *Letters*, 808–810.

29. Benjamin Rush, "An Account of the Bilious Yellow Fever as It Appeared in Philadelphia in the year 1798," *Medical Inquiries and Observations*, 4:50–51.

30. BR to Mrs. Rush, September 28, 1798, *Letters*, 2:808–810.

31. *Columbian Centinel* [undated], ibid., 2:1214.

32. Neilson and Neilson, *Verdict*, 146.

33. *Porcupine's Works*, 12 vols. (London, 1799–1801 [self-published]), 7:254.

34. Ibid., 7:234.

35. Neilson and Neilson, *Verdict*, 135.

36. *Letters*, 2:818, footnote 5.

37. BR to Brockholst Livingston, March 5, 1800, ibid., 2:816–818.

38. Ibid., 2:818, n. 5.

39. Neilson and Neilson, *Verdict*, 134.

40. Ibid., 139.

41. *Porcupine's Gazette*, in Neilson and Neilson, *Verdict*, 143.

42. Neilson and Neilson, *Verdict*, 21.

43. Benjamin Rush, *A Report of an Action for Libel Brought by Dr. Benjamin Rush Against William Cobbett, in the Supreme Court of Pennsylvania, December Term, 1799, For Certain Defamatory Publications in a Newspaper, Entitled Porcupine's Gazette, of Which the Said William Cobbett Was Editor*, taken in shorthand by T[homas] Carpenter [court reporter] (Philadelphia: W. W. Woodward, 1800).

Chapter 11: On the Causes of Death

1. Rush, *A Report of an Action for Libel Brought by Dr. Benjamin Rush Against William Cobbett*.

2. Ibid.

3. Peter Porcupine, *Porcupine's Gazette*, January 1800, pp. 148–150.

4. Ibid., February 15, 1800.

5. Peter Porcupine, *American Rush-Light*, February 15, 1800, *Porcupine's Works*, 11:211–251.

6. BR to Thomas Jefferson, March 12, 1801, *Letters*, 2:831–833.

7. Thomas Jefferson to BR, September 13, 1800. Founders Online.

8. BR to Thomas Jefferson, August 22, 1800, *Letters*, 2:819–822.

9. Thomas Jefferson to BR, September 23, 1800, Founders Online.

10. Aaron Burr to Sen. Samuel Smith, December 16, 1800, *Political Correspondence and Public Papers of Aaron Burr*, Mary-Jo Kline, ed. (Princeton, NJ: Princeton University Press, 1984), 1:471.

11. Ibid.

12. *Autobiography*, 251.

13. BR to Thomas Jefferson, October 6, 1800, *Letters*, 2:824–827.

14. Ibid.

15. Benjamin Rush, *Six Introductory Lectures to Courses of Lectures upon the Institutes and Practice of Medicine, Delivered in the University of Pennsylvania* (Philadelphia: John Conrad & Co., 1801), Lecture 3.

16. Ibid.

17. BR, *Medical Inquiries and Observations*, 4:122–178.

18. Ibid., 3:16–37.

19. Ibid., 1:351.

20. Ibid., 3:163–218.

21. Ibid., 3:426–446.

22. BR, "An Account of the State of the Body and Mind in Old Age," *Medical Inquiries and Observations*, 1:293–321.

23. BR, *Medical Inquiries and Observations*, 2:123.

24. Ibid., 4:173–177.

25. BR to James Madison, June 23, 1801, *Letters*, 2:835–836.

26. BR, *Medical Inquiries and Observations*, 3:142.

27. BR to John Coakley Lettson, May 13, 1804, *Letters*, 2:880–881.

28. BR to James Rush, November 23, 1801, ibid., 2:839–840.

29. BR to James Madison, December 5, 1801, ibid., 2:841–842.

30. Thomas Jefferson to BR, December 20, 1801, Founders Online.

31. BR to Thomas Jefferson, March 12, 1802, *Letters*, 2:847–848.

32. Ibid. Thomas Jefferson to BR, December 20, 1801, Founders Online.

33. BR to Thomas Jefferson, May 5, 1803, *Letters*, 2:863–865.

34. BR to Benjamin Waterhouse, February 9, 1802, ibid., 2:844–846.

35. Ibid.

36. BR to Thomas Jefferson, March 12, 1803, *Letters*, 2:847–848.

37. Thomas Jefferson to BR, February 28, 1803, Founders Online.

38. "Questions to Merryweather [*sic*] Lewis before he went up the Missouri," May 17, 1803, *Autobiography*, 265.

39. *The Journals of the Lewis and Clark Expedition* Online, September 26, 28, October 6, 1805.

40. Thomas Jefferson to BR, May 21, 1803, Founders Online.

41. Ibid.

42. Thomas Jefferson, *Syllabus of an Estimate of the Merit of the Doctrines of Jesus Compared with Those of Others*, Washington, April 21, 1803, enclosed with letter to Benjamin Rush. *The Letters of Thomas Jefferson, 1743–1826* (Electronic Textcenter of University of Virginia).

43. BR to Thomas Jefferson, May 5, 1803, *Letters*, 2:863–864.

44. BR to Mary Rush, April 1, 1803, APS.

45. BR to John Syng Dorsey [nephew of Philip Syng Physick], May 23, 1804, *Letters*, 2:882–884.

46. BR to Thomas Eddy [a Quaker philanthropist], October 19, 1803, ibid., 2:874–876.

47. BR to Thomas Jefferson, August 29, 1804, ibid., 2:886–887.

CHAPTER 12: HEALING THE LAST WOUND

1. John Adams to BR, February 6, 1805, *Old Family Letters: Copied from the Originals for Alexander Biddle* (Philadelphia: Press of J. B. Lippincott Company, 1892), 61–63.

2. John Adams to BR, April 18, 1790, *Old Family Letters*, 58–61.

3. BR to John Adams, February 19, 1805, *Letters*, 2:890–892.

4. John Adams to BR, February 27, 1805, *Old Family Letters*, 63–65.

5. John Adams to BR, April 4, 1790, *Letters*, 2:1207.

6. BR to John Adams, June 9, 1807, *Letters*, 2:948.

7. BR to John Adams, July 9, 1807, ibid., 2:949–952.

8. John Adams to BR, September 1, 1807, *Old Family Letters*, 161–167.

9. *Autobiography*, 271.

10. BR, *On the Duty and Advantages of Studying the Diseases of Domestic Animals and the Remedies Proper to Remove Them* (Philadelphia: Jane Aitken, 1808).

11. Ibid.

12. John Adams to BR, January 15, 1812, *Old Family Letters*, 291–294.

13. *Autobiography*, 323.

14. BR to Thomas Jefferson, January 2, 1811, *Letters*, 2:1073–1076.

15. Ibid.

16. BR to Thomas Jefferson, May 3, 1809, *Letters*, 2:1003–1004.

17. John Adams to Thomas Jefferson, January 22, 1825, John Adams and Charles Francis Adams, *The Works of John Adams. Second President of the United States: With a Life of the Author*, 10 vols. (Boston: Little, Brown, 1856), 10:414.

18. Thomas Jefferson to John Adams, May 25, 1785, *A–J Letters*, 22–23.

19. BR to John Adams, October 17, 1809, *Letters*, 2:976–980.

20. Ibid.

21. John Adams to BR, October 25, 1809, *The Spur of Fame: Dialogues of John Adams and Benjamin Rush, 1805–1813*, John A Schutz and Douglass Adair, eds. (Indianapolis: Liberty Fund, 1966), 172–173.

22. BR to Thomas Jefferson, January 2, 1811, *Letters*, 2:1073–1076.

23. Thomas Jefferson to BR, January 16, 1811, Founders Online.

24. BR to Thomas Jefferson, February 1, 1811, *Letters*, 2:1078–1081.

25. John Adams to BR, June 21, 1811, *Old Family Letters*, 283–288.

26. BR to John Adams, July 20, 1811, *Letters*, 2:1089–1091.

27. BR to John Adams, August 10, 1811, ibid., 2:1095–1097.

28. BR to John Adams, September 20, 1811, ibid., 2:1104–1106.

29. Ibid.

30. BR to John Adams, December 16, 1811, *Letters*, 2:1110–1111, with Rush citing Thomas Jefferson letter to Benjamin Rush, dated December 5, 1811.

31. John Adams to Thomas Jefferson, January 1, 1812, *A–J Letters*, 290.

32. Thomas Jefferson to John Adams, ibid., 290–292.

33. John Adams to Thomas Jefferson, February 3, 1812, ibid., 293–296.

34. John Adams to Thomas Jefferson, July 9, 1813, ibid., 350.

35. Thomas Jefferson to John Adams, January 23, 1812, ibid., 292–293.

36. John Adams to Thomas Jefferson, May 1, 1812, ibid., 300–301.

37. Thomas Jefferson to John Adams, June 11, 1812, ibid., 305–308.

38. BR to Thomas Jefferson, February 11, 1812, *Letters*, 2:1118–1119.

39. BR to John Adams, February 17, 1812, ibid., 2:1126–1127.

40. BR to John Adams, December 5, 1809, ibid., 2:1026–1027.

41. *Autobiography*, 286.

42. BR to John Adams, July 13, 1812, *Letters*, 2:1150–1153.

43. Ibid.

44. BR to John Adams, August 8, 1812, *Letters*, 1156–1159.

45. John Adams to BR, September 4, 1812, *Spur of Fame*, 266–268.

46. BR to the Trustees of the University of Pennsylvania, March 1, 1813, *Letters*, 2:1179–1181.

47. Ibid., 1184–1185.

48. BR to John Adams, April 10, 1913, ibid., 1191–1192.

Post Mortem

1. Thomas Jefferson to John Adams, May 27, 1813, *A–J Letters*, 323–325.

2. John Adams to Thomas Jefferson, June 11, 1813, ibid., 328–329.

3. John Adams to Elbridge Gerry, April 26, 1813, Founders Online.

4. John Adams to Thomas Jefferson, January 14, 1826; Thomas Jefferson to John Adams, March 25, 1826, *A–J Letters*, 613, 614.

SELECTED BIBLIOGRAPHY

Adams, Abigail. *New Letters of Abigail Adams, 1788–1801* (Boston: Houghton Mifflin, 1947).

Adams, Abigail, and John Adams. *My Dearest Friend: Letters of Abigail and John Adams*, Margaret A. Hogan and C. James Taylor, eds. (Cambridge, MA: The Belknap Press of Harvard University Press, 2007).

Adams, John. *Diary and Autobiography of John Adams*, 4 vols., L. H. Butterfield, ed. (Boston: Massachusetts Historical Society, 1961).

———. *Old Family Letters: Copied from the Originals for Alexander Biddle* (Philadelphia: J. B. Lippincott Company, 1892).

Adams, John, and Charles Francis Adams. *The Works of John Adams. Second President of the United States: With a Life of the Author*, 10 vols. (Boston: Little, Brown, 1856).

Adams, John, and Thomas Jefferson. *The Adams-Jefferson Letters, The Complete Correspondence between Thomas Jefferson & Abigail & John Adams*, Lester J. Cappon, ed. (Chapel Hill: University of North Carolina Press, 1959).

Adams, John, and Benjamin Rush. *The Spur of Fame: The Dialogues of John Adams and Benjamin Rush, 1805–1813*, John A Schutz and Douglass Adair, eds. (Indianapolis: The Liberty Fund, 1966).

The Adams Papers: Adams Family Correspondence (Cambridge, MA: The Belknap Press of Harvard University Press, 2009–[multivolume, in progress]).

Bickford, Charlene Bangs, and Kenneth R. Bowling. *Birth of the Nation: The First Federal Congress, 1789–1791* (Lanham, MD: Madison House Publishers, 1989).

Binger, Carl, M.D. *Revolutionary Doctor: Benjamin Rush, 1746–1813* (New York: W. W. Norton, 1966).

Burke, Edmund. *The Annual Register, or a View of the History, Politics, and Literature for the Year 1787* (London: J. Dodsley, 1789).

Carey, Mathew. *A Short Account of the Malignant Fever of 1793* (Philadelphia: Clark and Raser, 1793).

Cervantes, Miguel de. *El Ingenioso Hidalgo Don Quixote de la Mancha* (Madrid: Francisco de Robles, 1605).

Cobbett, William [Peter Porcupine, pseud.]. *Porcupine's Works*, 12 vols. (London: 1799–1801 [self-published]).

de Morande, Charles Théveneau. *Le Gazetier cuirassé ou Anecdotes scandaleuses de la Cour de France* and *Mémoires secrets d'une femme publique* (Paris: Publiés à cent lieues de la Bastille sous l'enseigne de la liberté, 1772).

DeConde, Alexander. *Entangling Alliance* (Durham, NC: Duke University Press, 1958).

Documentary History of the Ratification of the Constitution, Merrill Jensen, ed. (Madison: State Historical Society of Wisconsin,1976–[in progress, multivolume]).

Drinker, Elizabeth. *The Diary of Elizabeth Drinker*, 3 vols., Elaine Forman Crane, ed. (Boston: Northeastern University Press, 1991).

Flexner, James Thomas. *Doctors on Horseback: Pioneers of American Medicine* (New York: Viking Press, 1937).

Folwell, Richard. *Short History of the Yellow Fever That Broke Out in the City of Philadelphia in July, 1797, with a List of the Dead; of the Donations for the Relief of the Poor; and a Variety of Other Interesting Particulars* (Philadelphia: Richard Folwell, 1797).

Ford, Worthington C., et al., eds. *Journals of the Continental Congress, 1774–1789* (Washington, DC, 1904–1937).

Freeman, Douglas Southall. *George Washington: A Biography*, 7 vols., completed by John Alexander Carroll and Mary Ashworth (New York: Charles Scribner's Sons, 1948–1957).

Good, Harry G. *Benjamin Rush and His Services to American Education* (Berne, IN: Witness Press, 1918 [A thesis presented to the faculty of the graduate school of the University of Pennsylvania in partial fulfillment of the requirements for the degree of doctor of philosophy in education].

Goodman, Nathan G. *Benjamin Rush, Physician and Citizen* (Philadelphia: University of Pennsylvania Press, 1934).

Hamilton, Alexander. *The Papers of Alexander Hamilton*, 27 vols., Harold C. Syrett et al., eds. (New York: Columbia University Press, 1961–1987).

Hawke, David Freeman. *Benjamin Rush: Revolutionary Gadfly* (Indianapolis: Bobbs-Merrill, 1971).

Henry, William Wirt. *Patrick Henry: Life, Correspondence and Speeches*, 3 vols. (New York: Charles Scribner's Sons, 1891).

Hume, David. *The History of England* [certain volumes entitled *The History of Great Britain*], 6 vols. (London: The London Printing and Publishing Company, 1754).

———. *A Treatise of Human Nature: Being an Attempt to Introduce the Experimental Method of Reasoning into Moral Subjects*, 3 vols. (London: John Noon, 1738).

Jefferson, Thomas. *Thomas Jefferson Writings* (New York: Literary Classics of the United States, 1984).

———. *The Writings of Thomas Jefferson,* 10 vols., Paul Leicester Ford, ed. (New York: G. P. Putnam's Sons, 1892–1899).

Journals of the Continental Congress, 1774–1789, 34 vols., Worthington C. Ford et al., eds. (Washington, DC, 1904–1937).

Keynes, [Sir] Geoffrey, M.D. *Blood Transfusion* (London: Oxford Medical Publications, 1922).

Lee, Richard H. *Memoir of the Life of Richard Henry Lee and Correspondence,* 2 vols. (Philadelphia: H. C. Carey and I. Lea, 1825).

Lewis, Meriwether, and William Clark. *The Journals of Lewis and Clark Expedition* (The Journals of Lewis and Clark Expedition Online).

Madison, James. *Notes of Debates in the Federal Convention of 1787, Reported by James Madison* (New York: W. W. Norton, 1987).

———. *The Papers of James Madison,* vol. 15, William T. Hutchinson et al., eds., (Charlottesville, VA: University Press of Virginia, 1985).

Malone, Dumas. *Jefferson and the Rights of Man* (Boston: Little, Brown, 1951).

Meade, Robert Douthat. *Patrick Henry, Practical Revolutionary* (Philadelphia: J. B. Lippincott, 1969).

Minnigerode, Meade. *Jefferson—Friend of France* (New York: G. P. Putnam & Sons, 1928).

Morton, Thomas G. *History of the Pennsylvania Hospital, 1751–1895* (Philadelphia: Times Printing House, 1895).

Murphy, Jim. *An American Plague: The True and Terrifying Story of the Yellow Fever Epidemic of 1793* (New York: Clarion Books, 2003).

Neilson, Winthrop, and Frances Fullerton Neilson. *Verdict for the Doctor: The Case of Benjamin Rush* (New York: Hastings House, 1958).

Ostler, Sir William. *The Principles and Practice of Medicine* (New York: D. Appleton and Company, 1893).

Plato. *The Republic,* translated by G. M. A. Grube (Indianapolis, IN: Hackett Publishing, 1992) [believed to have been written between 380 and 360 B.C.].

Porcupine, Peter [William Cobbett], *Porcupine's Works,* 12 vols. (London: 1799–1801 [self-published]).

Powell, J. M. *Bring Out Your Dead: The Great Plague of Yellow Fever in Philadelphia in 1793* (Philadelphia: University of Pennsylvania Press, 1949).

Prasad, Dr. Vinayak K., and Dr. Adam S. Cifu. *Ending Medical Reversal: Improving Outcomes, Saving Lives* (Baltimore: Johns Hopkins University Press, 2015).

Rousseau, Jean-Jacques. *The Basic Political Writings: On the Social Contract,* translated and edited by Donald A. Cress (Indianapolis, IN: Hackett Publishing Company, 1987).

Rush, Benjamin. *An Account of the Bilious Remitting Yellow Fever, as It Appeared in the City of Philadelphia in the Year 1793* (Philadelphia: Thomas Dobson, 1794).

———. *The Autobiography of Benjamin Rush: His Travels Through Life Together with His Commonplace Book for 1789–1813* (Philadelphia: American Philosophical Society, 1948).

———. *A Bibliographic Guide*, compiled by Claire G. Fox, Gordon L. Miller, and Jacquelyn C. Miller (Westport, CT: Greenwood Press, 1996).

———. *Essays: Literary, Moral, and Philosophical* (Philadelphia: Thomas and William Bradford, 1806).

———. *An Inquiry into the Effects of Spirituous Liquors on the Human Body and the Mind* (Boston: Thomas and Andrews, 1790).

———. *Letters of Benjamin Rush*, 2 vols., L. H. Butterfield, ed. (Philadelphia: American Philosophical Society, 1951).

———. *Medical Inquiries and Observations*, 4 vols. (Philadelphia: Thomas Dobson, 1796).

———. *Medical Inquiries and Observations upon the Diseases of the Mind* (Philadelphia: Kimber & Richardson, 1812).

———. *A Memorial Containing Travels Through Life or Sundry Incidents in the Life of Dr. Benjamin Rush*, Louis Alexander Biddle, ed. (Philadelphia: Made at the Sign of the Ivy Leaf, 1905 [written in 1800]).

———. *Report of an Action for Libel Brought by Dr. Benjamin Rush Against William Cobbett in the Supreme Court of Pennsylvania, December Term, 1799, for Certain Defamatory Publications in a Newspaper Entitled Porcupine's Gazette, of Which Said William Cobbett Was Editor*, taken in shorthand by T[homas] Carpenter [court reporter] (Philadelphia: W. W. Woodward, 1800).

———. *The Selected Writings of Benjamin Rush*, Dagobert D. Runes, ed. (New York: Philosophical Library, 1947).

———. *Sixteen Introductory Lectures to Courses of Lectures upon the Institutes and Practice of Medicine* (Philadelphia: Bradford and Innskeep, 1811). [See also Appendix A, pages 251–259.]

Sanderson, John. *Biography of the Signers to the Declaration of Independence* (Philadelphia: Thomas, Cowperthwait & Company, 1820–1827).

Schminke, Frederick A. *Genet: The Origins of His Mission to America* (Toulouse: Imprimerie Toulousaine Lion et Fils, 1939).

Schutz, John A., and Douglas Adair. *The Spur of Fame: Dialogues of John Adams and Benjamin Rush, 1805–1813* (Indianapolis: Liberty Fund, 1966).

Sydenham, Thomas, M.D. *The Works of Thomas Sydenham, M.D., on Acute and Chronic Diseases: With Their Histories and Modes of Cure* (London: G.G.J. & J. Robinson, W. Otridge, S. Hayes, and E. Newbery, 1788).

Tulard, Jean, Jean-François Fayard, and Alfred Fierro. *Histoire et Dictionnaire de la Révolution Française, 1789–1799* (Paris: Robert Laffont, 1998).

Unger, Harlow Giles. *Improbable Patriot: The Secret History of Monsieur de Beaumarchais, the French Playwright Who Saved the American Revolution* (Hanover, NH: University Press of New England, 2011).

————. *John Marshall: The Chief Justice Who Saved the Nation* (Boston: Da Capo Press, 2014).

Warner, Harriet W. *Autobiography of Charles Caldwell* (Philadelphia: Lippincott, Grambo, and Company, 1855).

Washington, George. *The Diaries of George Washington*, 6 vols., (Donald Jackson and Dorothy Twohig, eds., Charlottesville: University Press of Virginia, 1976–1979).

————. *The Papers of George Washington, Confederation Series, January 1784–September 1788*, 6 vols., W. W. Abbott and Dorothy Twohig, eds. (Charlottesville: University Press of Virginia).

————. *The Papers of George Washington, Presidential Series*, multivolume, in progress, Theodore J. Crackel, editor-in-chief (Charlottesville: University of Virginia Press).

————. *The Papers of George Washington, Revolutionary War Series, June 1775–April 1778*, W. W. Abbott, Dorothy Twohig, and Philander D, Chase, eds. (Charlottesville: University of Virginia Press, 1984–[multivolume, in progress].

————. *The Writings of George Washington, from the Original Manuscript Sources, 1745–1799*, 39 vols., John C. Fitzpatrick, ed., (Washington, DC: US Government Printing Office, 1931–1944).

Periodicals

American Museum
American Rush-Light
Columbian Centinel
Columbian Magazine
Federal Gazette
Independent Gazetteer (Philadelphia)
New York Times
Pennsylvania Gazette
Pennsylvania Journal
Pennsylvania Magazine of History and Biography
Pennsylvania Packet (Philadelphia)
Porcupine's Gazette

Archives

Adams Family Papers, Massachusetts Historical Society
American Philosophical Society
Founders Online, National Archives (http://founders.archives.gov/document)
The Journals of the Lewis and Clark Expedition, Online
Rush Correspondence, 43 vols., Library Company of Philadelphia

INDEX